Understanding Movements in Modern Thought
Series Editor: Jack Reynolds

This series provides short, accessible and lively introductions to the major schools, movements and traditions in philosophy and the history of ideas since the beginning of the Enlightenment. All books in the series are written for undergraduates meeting the subject for the first time.

Published

Understanding Existentialism
Jack Reynolds

Understanding Poststructuralism
James Williams

Understanding Virtue Ethics
Stan van Hooft

Forthcoming titles include

Understanding Empiricism
Robert Meyers

Understanding Ethics
Tim Chappell

Understanding Feminism
Peta Bowden and Jane Mummery

Understanding German Idealism
Will Dudley

Understanding Hegelianism
Robert Sinnerbrink

Understanding Hermeneutics
Lawrence Schmidt

Understanding Naturalism
Jack Ritchie

Understanding Phenomenology
David Cerbone

Understanding Rationalism
Charlie Heunemann

Understanding Utilitarianism
Tim Mulgan

understanding **existentialism**

Jack Reynolds

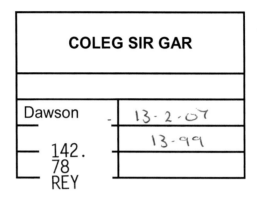

© Jack Reynolds, 2006

First published in 2006 by Acumen

Acumen Publishing Limited
15a Lewins Yard
East Street
Chesham
Bucks HP5 1HQ
www.acumenpublishing.co.uk

ISBN 1-84465-042-1   (hardcover)
ISBN 1-84465-043-X   (paperback)

British Library Cataloguing-in-Publication Data
A catalogue record for this book is available from the British Library.

Designed and typeset by Kate Williams, Swansea.
Printed and bound in Malta by Gutenberg Press.

Contents

Acknowledgements

Above all, for this book I am indebted to my parents, Laurel and Angus. I have been remiss enough to have never thanked them in such an author's note before, and I hope that they have been aware of their ongoing importance to my life and work. More academically, Marion Tapper and Penny Deutscher have been vital to this book. Having been involved in their courses on existentialism over a period of several years, and in many different capacities, they were instrumental in fostering my enjoyment and appreciation of existentialism. Without doubt there are aspects of this book that are indebted to their teachings, although as always the faults remain mine alone. Bernadette Pierce also gave me some of my first opportunities to discuss existentialism in a public forum and for that, as well as her intellectual encouragement, I am grateful.

More recently, I would like to acknowledge and thank the following people who have read drafts of this book and whose suggestions have contributed to its improvement, both in terms of content and stylistically: Kim Atkins, Craig Barrie, David Cerbone, Stan van Hooft, Jonathan Roffe, Tessa Saunders, Robert Sinnerbrink, Ashley Woodward and the anonymous Acumen referees. Somewhat more idiosyncratically, I should also like to thank Ryan and May Johnston, Pein and Anh Lee, Andrew McUtchen, Steve Orr and Joanne Shiells. All of you have helped and inspired me in many different ways. On an institutional level, I am indebted to the University of Tasmania and my colleagues there. Without their support, and particularly that of my Heads of School, Robyn Ferrell and Jeff Malpas, this book might have taken much longer.

On the publishing front, I must also thank Ohio University Press for allowing me to use and reconfigure a few pages of my exegesis of Merleau-Ponty from my monograph *Merleau-Ponty and Derrida: Intertwining Embodiment and Alterity* (2004). Finally, thanks are due to Tristan Palmer, Steven Gerrard and Kate Williams at Acumen, who have been of great help, both with this book and the series of which it is a part.

Jack Reynolds

Abbreviations

BN   J.-P. Sartre, *Being and Nothingness: An Essay on Phenomenological Ontology* (1994 [1943])

BT   M. Heidegger, *Being and Time* (2004 [1927])

BW   M. Heidegger, *Basic Writings* (1996)

EA   S. de Beauvoir, *The Ethics of Ambiguity* (1976 [1947])

EH   J.-P. Sartre, *Existentialism is a Humanism* (2001 [1946])

M   R. Descartes, *Meditations on First Philosophy* (1986 [1641])

MS   A. Camus, *The Myth of Sisyphus* (1942)

OT   M. Foucault, *The Order of Things* (1970)

PC   S. de Beauvoir, *Pyrrhus et Cinéas* (2005 [1943])

PP   M. Merleau-Ponty, *Phenomenology of Perception* (1996 [1945])

PrP   M. Merleau-Ponty, *The Primacy of Perception* (1964)

S   M. Merleau-Ponty, *Signs* (1964)

SB   M. Merleau-Ponty, *The Structure of Behaviour* (1965 [1938])

SIT   J.-P. Sartre, *Situations* (1965)

SNS   M. Merleau-Ponty, *Sense and Non-Sense* (1964)

SS   S. de Beauvoir, *The Second Sex* (1972 [1949])

VI   M. Merleau-Ponty, *The Visible and the Invisible* (1968 [1964])

one

Existentialism and its heritage

Existentialism, perhaps to an extent unprecedented in the history of philosophy, has managed to capture the attention of the general public. Estimates of the number of people at Jean-Paul Sartre's funeral in 1980 vary from 50,000 to 100,000, and this was well after his cultural and intellectual heyday. Simone de Beauvoir's famous treatise on the situation of women, *The Second Sex*, has been one of the most widely read non-fiction books of the twentieth century. Existential plays and novels – in particular Sartre's *Nausea* and Albert Camus's *The Outsider* – have been read voraciously and critically acclaimed. Sartre and his more academically inclined colleague Maurice Merleau-Ponty were the co-editors of the influential magazine *Les Temps modernes*, which considered all things philosophical, political and aesthetic, providing an intellectual point of reference for much of France. Without quite the same mainstream accessibility, or the literary bent (notwithstanding his preoccupation with poetry), Martin Heidegger has been enormously influential on generations of philosophers, as well as people working in cognitive science and artificial intelligence, and his work has helped to spawn at least two very significant contemporary philosophical movements: hermeneutics and deconstruction.

There are obviously many reasons for this primarily philosophical phenomenon capturing the attention of the public in the way that existentialism did, not least the Second World War and the German occupation of France, which intensified existential concerns with freedom, responsibility and death. The literary manifestations of existentialism also allowed a greater proportion of people to possess at least a tentative grasp of what it meant and certainly a greater grasp than might have been attained through the sometimes obscure philosophy of Heidegger, Sartre, Merleau-Ponty and de Beauvoir. These four philosophers will be the main focus of this book, and this means that chronologically we will be concerned with the post-Heideggerians, or what we might term the atheistic existentialists, although it will soon become clear that atheism is not a necessary component of existential thought. This book could alternatively be called "Understanding Existential Phenomenology" because all of these philosophers are significantly indebted to the phenomenological project, even if they also contest the "pure" phenomenology of Edmund Husserl. But without digressing unduly in justifications of the thinkers to be considered here, this book will focus on these roughly contemporaneous philosophers because of the conviction that it is the exchange of ideas between them that reveals existentialism in both its most sophisticated and also its most diverse forms.

Many of the important philosophical ancestors to these philosophers will be briefly discussed in this introduction, including the nineteenth-century philosophers Søren Kierkegaard and Friedrich Nietzsche, as well as the early-twentieth-century thinkers Husserl, Karl Jaspers and Gabriel Marcel. Some of the main themes that have preoccupied these early existential thinkers will be introduced (recognizing that their responses to such themes has not been unified and consensual), particularly in relation to the aspects of their work that have also been taken up by subsequent incarnations of existentialism. Proceeding in this way allows this introduction to serve as primer for much of what will follow in the heart of this book, and some of the fundamental existential themes to be dealt with include:

- freedom;
- death, finitude and mortality;
- phenomenological experiences and "moods", such as anguish (or anxiety), nausea and boredom;
- an emphasis on authenticity and responsibility as well as the tacit denigration of their opposites (inauthenticity and bad faith);
- a suggestion that human individuality tends to be obscured and denied by the common social mores of the crowd, and, arguably, a pessimism about human relations *per se* (owing to the influence of Hegel's master–slave dialectic on Sartre and de Beauvoir);
- a rejection of any external determination of morality or value, including certain conceptions of God and the emphasis on rationality and progress that were foregrounded during the Enlightenment.

Of course, these formulations are approximate and await more nuanced handling in the main body of the book, which will compare and contrast the "existential phenomenologists" on these six themes, with the intention of exploring their many areas of disagreement and discord while nevertheless revealing the shared areas of concern that give existentialism its integrity as a discernible moment in the history of philosophy.

One difficulty with such a project is that the term "existentialism" was not initially used by any of these philosophers, and it does not appear in any of the canonical texts of the tradition: neither in Sartre's *Being and Nothingness* nor in Heidegger's *Being and Time*. In fact, the term was initially coined by Marcel, describing Sartre and others, and it only came to be accepted by Sartre and de Beauvoir a couple of years later in 1945. Merleau-Ponty never accepted the label wholeheartedly, whereas Heidegger vehemently rejected it. It is hence difficult to argue that existentialism represents a single, unified philosophical movement, although Sartre's famous comment that "existence precedes essence" is perhaps a good starting-point, even if this dictum has also been used by many other philosophers – such as Ayn Rand – for decidedly different purposes. We might summarize Sartre's comment as suggesting that human existence is notable for the fact that we are always ahead of ourselves, and "on the way", with various projects, intentions and aspirations for the future. Rather than our identity being determined by our biological or social status, existentialism insists that our identity must be continually created, and there is a resultant emphasis on our freedom or, in the preferred philosophical vocabulary of the existentialists, our transcendence.

In various different ways this insistence is common to all existential theorists, but what will become more obvious as this book progresses is that there are many other shared areas of concern between these existential theorists in relation to the above six points, and there is certainly clear interactions between them. Sartre famously draws on Heidegger, usually quite uncritically, whereas Heidegger very critically responds to Sartre in places. Merleau-Ponty often writes in direct response to Sartre, even if his criticisms of Sartre are subtler than those of, say, Heidegger. In her work, de Beauvoir responds to and develops the work of both Merleau-Ponty and Sartre, while also offering an account of the phenomenological experience of the look that preceded and influenced Sartre's more famous account of it. However, before beginning to analyse the position of these theorists in any detail, some important historical influences on these twentieth-century thinkers need to be considered.

Some key early existential thinkers and themes

Kierkegaard and religion

Existentialism is most frequently traced backed to the Danish Christian philosopher Søren Kierkegaard (1813–55), and not without good reason. In texts such as *Either/Or* (1843), *Philosophical Fragments* (1844) and *Concluding Unscientific Postscript* (1846), Kierkegaard challenges the Enlightenment emphasis on rationality, as well as the rampant systematization of Hegelian dialectics. Whereas Merleau-Ponty argues that the early work of Hegel, such as *The Phenomenology of Spirit*, could be described as a forerunner of existentialism (SNS: 66), Kierkegaard holds the opposite position. For him, the later Hegelian insistence that the movement of history follows a logical and dialectical necessity (this idea was later appropriated and transformed by Karl Marx) obscures the significance of individual existence. In contrast to this kind of account, Kierkegaard instead espouses a highly subjective account of meaning, which rejects doctrinaire and orthodox Christianity that seeks to preach the truth to the people.

The son of a minister, Kierkegaard holds that believing in God will always involve an individual choice, and an individual "leap of faith", and he goes so far as to argue that true religious faith is antithetical to the demands of public organizations such as the church. As he eloquently suggests, the Christian tradition requires that the believer "dance on the point of the paradox" that God, through Christ, walked among men. According to him, this paradox (that the infinite could become finite), and indeed the experience of God *per se*, cannot be resolved through conceptual thought or institutionalized religion, because the reality that we subjectively experience in faith is incapable of rational synthesis (against Hegel). In other words, for Kierkegaard, what is involved in a life of faith cannot be refuted, or for that matter validated, by conventional logic. It is not the doctrine of Christianity but the example of Christ that is all important, in that it highlights that the resolution of the religious paradox – and the tensions and contradictions of all existence – can only be accomplished through a radical leap of faith in which the individual makes that paradox meaningful through a lived commitment to a course of action. While the philosophy of religion has traditionally sought to reconcile faith and reason, Kierkegaard takes the opposite path and insists on their incompatibility; that is, on an absolute discontinuity between the human and the divine. Kierkegaard's *Fear and Trembling*, for example, dramatically highlights the incommensurability of these orders through an analysis of the biblical story of Abraham's decision to sacrifice Isaac and the "madness" that it entails from the perspective of the human order.

Of course, it needs to be recognized that, at least on a superficial understanding of the post-Heideggerian existentialists, existentialism might seem to deny the possibility of faith: something that, in his own way, Kierkegaard very much held on to. After all, Sartre and most of his French compatriots were atheists, even if Merleau-Ponty was a Catholic for some time. However, it is worth pointing out that even Sartre suggests that the declaration of atheism is not a necessary component of existential thought. This is because existentialism is not, or at least is not intended to be, metaphysics. It is not a metaphysical attempt to explain and categorize what is the world and what is the beyond, and it hence does not seek to prove or disprove God. While ontological, cosmological and teleological attempts to prove the existence of God may be seen to miss the point, it should be noted that, for Kierkegaard, God is simply the unknown and he hence avoids the trap that he thinks afflicts much theology: presuming that rational discourse can make the religious experience comprehensible.

As well as Kierkegaard, existentialism has spawned several other religious figures including the Protestant Karl Jaspers and the Catholic Gabriel Marcel, both of whom are considered below. Within the theological tradition proper, Rudolph Bultmann and Paul Tillich have been productively associated with existential concerns. If faith involves nothing more than believing in something without proof, then this is very much necessary to existential thought, for which there are no external facts or values that dictate our action although we are nevertheless confronted with the necessity of acting and choosing. Without the guidance of universal rules of morality, human nature or a knowable God who has issued certain indisputable commandments (and various theologies can agree with that), we must endow the world with meaning and it is only we who can do this. We must make this leap of faith: create the meaning in which we seek to live. Every act, then, which is not compromised by a form of what Sartre calls "bad faith", can be seen as a type of faith: as a commitment to act in the face of "nothingness" and not pretend that things are compelled or necessitated, whether it be socioculturally or biologically.

Importantly, Kierkegaard was also one of the first to highlight the philosophical significance of experiences like despair and dread, both of which are forerunners of Heideggerian "*Angst*" and Sartrean anguish. For Kierkegaard, an individual choice, or act of self-determination, is inevitably accompanied by an experience of dread, in which we realize that rational calculation will never be sufficient to provide the answers to the religious paradox, or to other issues of major existential significance in our lives (such as whether or not Kierkegaard should leave his bride to be, Regina), much less to motivate us to adopt any particular course of action on the basis of that deliberation. Interestingly, the contemporary French philosopher Jacques Derrida draws on Kierkegaard's account of the decision and we will examine his position in Chapter 7. For the moment it is enough to ascertain that from Kierkegaard's perspective reflection involves a withdrawal into uncertainty, and as such is almost inevitably accompanied by despair.

It is worth emphasizing, however, that Kierkegaard's "subjectivism" – and indeed any subjectivism or individualism that might be ascribed to existentialism more generally – cannot be equated with the liberal emphasis on free choice that pervades contemporary capitalist culture and arguably does not take seriously the kinds of consequences that radical freedom of choice entails on both a personal and a moral level. For Kierkegaard, we need to live and endure *with*, and not against, the tension of a belief – that is, in despair – and not dogmatically and happily resolve a paradoxical belief into either a final objective truth or a flippant consumerist whim.

Kierkegaard's work is also preoccupied with something that concerns more recent existential thought: the distinction between an authentic and an inauthentic life. For him it is the inauthentic life that dominates. Most people flee from this despair and anguish of decision-making into inauthentic modes of existence: the aesthetic and the ethical, in the terms of his book *Either/Or*.

KEY POINT *Kierkegaard's three life stages*
- The *aesthetic stage* embraces the sensuous moment, pleasure and beauty, but is said to be trivial.
- The *ethical stage* tries to legitimate absolute moral standards based on societal mores, or rationality, but is said to be merely transitory.
- The *religious stage* involves the person on their own, divested of their reliance on social customs, and without the self-assuredness and dogmatism of the ethical stage.

A transition from one stage to the next stage again requires a leap, or a radical change in direction; it cannot be accomplished incrementally through rational development, block upon block. Kierkegaard insists that the root of any genuine morality that is not mere convention lies in the third religious stage: the individual on their own. It does not lie in "herd morality", in which the individual merely believes what others believe, nor in establishing some external guarantor of value, whether it be God, wealth, power or even rationality. Kierkegaard's insistence that morality resides more in the character and attitudes of the person who is acting (a kind of "virtue ethics", to use the contemporary parlance), rather than in whether or not a certain action maximizes the overall happiness of a society (utilitarianism), or respects each singular person as an "end in themselves" (Kantian ethics), is one of the enduring insights of existentialism generally.

Although some important questions remain about whether or not too much of a preoccupation with the individual as the foundation of morality can in fact preclude the ethical, it needs to be noted that as well as this pessimism about other people that underpins Kierkegaard's writings, a definite pessimism about the prospect of death also pervades his work. Many members of Kierkegaard's family died of various illnesses before they were 30, and he was convinced that the family curse would also get him (he managed to reach 42). As a consequence, his life was lived in the shadow of this approaching death. *Ad hominem* arguments aside – that is, arguments that evaluate the person, rather than the idea – this feeling of impending death that Kierkegaard describes has been given a sustained philosophical analysis by Heidegger, as we will shortly see.

Nietzsche, ressentiment *and the death of God*

Whereas Kierkegaard turns to the "inner" rather than the "outer", this is not the case for the famous German philosopher Friedrich Nietzsche (1844–1900). Presaging some aspects of Merleau-Ponty's phenomenology of embodiment, Nietzsche affirms the importance of the body and of what is ostensibly "outer". Moreover, while Kierkegaard reinvented a version of both God and Christianity, Nietzsche repeats Ludwig Feuerbach's declaration that God is dead and castigates Christianity for encouraging a form of what he calls "slave morality". Whereas Kierkegaard casts himself as a latter-day version of Socrates, Nietzsche denounces Socrates as also exhibiting this kind of slave morality, or what, from the individual in question's perspective, he terms *ressentiment*. This French term, which is not suitably translated in the English "resentment", basically suggests that both culturally and philosophically the Western tradition has tacitly perpetuated an attitude of disgust for life.

According to Nietzsche's quasi-historical genealogy in *On the Genealogy of Morals* (1887), this started when the Christian slaves turned inwards, and posited a soul – an interior mental reserve – as a last resort in order to allow them to escape from, and eventually turn the tables on their more powerful Greco-Roman oppressors, who were clearly in control in the physical realm. Whereas these "nobles" proclaimed, metaphorically, their own greatness before denigrating those lesser (what Nietzsche calls the "good–bad morality of masters"), the Christians first of all denigrated their oppressors as evil and only secondarily affirmed themselves as good by contrast (what Nietzsche calls the "good–evil morality of slaves"). The former is affirmative: the latter is negative and tends towards bitterness, because so much time and energy is invested in denigrating those who have control. Nietzsche wants to reject this latter tendency and instead valorize life, although he is not naive enough, at least after *The Birth of Tragedy* (1872), to believe that any simple return to the Greeks and master morality is possible (his notorious notion of the *Ubermensch*, or overman, is not reducible to master morality).

Importantly, Nietzsche also focuses on the problems of his age, particularly as they were manifest in Germany and Europe, and he is not very concerned with traditional academic disputes. Rather, he is concerned with morals and values. Claiming that no one before him, philosopher or otherwise, had seen that morality was a problem, in that morality always serves immoral ends, he calls for a revaluation of all values and asserts that there is no final arbiter of value outside the experience of satisfaction. But unlike utilitarianism, which takes this insight to one extreme, Nietzsche does not simply want to maximize pleasure for the greatest number of people, or of sentient beings, for several reasons. First, he sees suffering and cruelty as necessary to creativity and what might be termed a higher level of satisfaction, and, secondly, he is an elitist of sorts, whose concern is more with exalting certain individuals to great acts of creativity than emancipating the masses. This is no doubt overly schematic, but Nietzsche clearly encourages individuals to move beyond the pretensions of their age.

One tool that he uses to try and achieve this is his famous thought of the *eternal return of the same*. Although Nietzsche argues for some different and not always compatible interpretations of the eternal return, according to the account offered in *The Gay Science* (1887) the idea of the eternal return poses a single but complicated question that can be schematized as follows: what if a malevolent genie informs you that whatever mode of action you choose now, it will recur indefinitely as you have once experienced it? Nietzsche intends this thought experiment to function as a test designed to intensify experience, and to ensure that we choose to do something that we are prepared to affirm over and over again. For any mode of action, we should act as *if* that particular action were to recur indefinitely, and Nietzsche's imperative would be something like: act in such a manner that you could never say "it just happened", but rather "I willed it thus". It is an exaltation to genuinely experience the moment. Would you act according to slave morality, or the dictates of the masses, if you knew that a particular action would be repeated indefinitely? Most people are inclined to agree that they probably would not, and hence you can see how such a thought experiment has existential import in encouraging "authentic" behaviour, even though Nietzsche does not use this term.

Equally famously, in *The Gay Science* Nietzsche has a madman declare that God is dead. This comment is not meant to be a simple thesis, however, and nor does it constitute a sustained argument against theology. Rather, it is a reflection that although belief in God has dissipated in European culture, the morals of Judeo-Christian culture remain dominant, yet without their foundation and support. While this carries Dostoyevskian implications that given the death of God surely everything is permissible, Nietzsche is more interested in the way in which it reveals that morality is a problem, not something preordained by God.

Other ideas of significance regarding Nietzsche's relationship to existentialism are his ongoing battles with and against nihilism (the view that there is no justification for values), as well as his perspectivist rejection of any absolute moral standard, which is clearly very influential on both Camus and Sartre. At the same time, however, his tendency to deny that we act freely and his curious version of biological naturalism places him at a distance from existentialism – which has long been associated with arguments for freedom and also with a humanism of sorts – and he is an enigmatic figure in the history of philosophy, not easily reducible to any school or movement. His other main texts include *Beyond Good and Evil* (1886) and *Thus Spoke Zarathustra* (1883–85), and he has been very influential on key theorists associated with postmodernism and poststructuralism, such as Foucault, Derrida, Deleuze and Lyotard.

Jaspers, existenz *and "limit situations"*

The German philosopher Karl Jaspers (1883–1969) sought to combine the best insights of both Nietzsche and Kierkegaard while also extending their thought to the question of the relationship between philosophy and science. Unlike Kierkegaard and Nietzsche he was a professional academic philosopher, but like them there are many aspects of his account that call into question traditional philosophy and its construction of universal systems, metaphysics and moralities. He emphasizes the importance of individual authenticity against such systems and in the process poses pointed questions to the entire project of philosophy, at least if philosophy is conceived of as erecting universal systems.

At the same time, Jaspers nevertheless also seeks to describe and enumerate three aspects of being: being-there, being-one-self and being-in-itself. For our purposes, being-one-self, or the reflective thinker's transcendence, is important. He holds that this mode of being, which involves a movement beyond and a dislocation from day-to-day affairs, is inevitably accompanied by the experience of anguish, much as Kierkegaard also held. Moreover, being-one-self is radically disjunct from what he calls being-there: the objectively determined empirical world. This disjunction cannot ever be simply overcome, but these three orders of being nevertheless limit, break and interpenetrate one another.

Jaspers also thematizes the notion of *existenz*, which can be summarized as the idea that there is no fixed or essential self; the self is instead only its possibilities and what it might become. This notion of the self not being fixed, but being primarily about a future orientation, was directly influential on the work of his compatriot, Heidegger, and indirectly on Sartre, de Beauvoir and Merleau-Ponty. In fact, it is arguably still a dominant feature of contemporary French thought and this will be examined in Chapter 7.

Importantly, Jaspers argues that the condition of *existenz*, the revelation of the lack of any essential self, is best revealed in what he terms "limit situations", which include death, suffering, guilt and, like Kierkegaard, the uncertainty of decisions. This conviction that certain moods and feelings can disclose philosophical truths about the structure of the world also plays a large role in the work of Heidegger and Sartre, but for Jaspers suffering, guilt, and uncertainty occur when there is a conflict between the contingent situation and the need to choose absolutely: in other words, between the situation which in and of itself has no inherent meaning and human aspirations, which seek to impose such a meaning. As we will see shortly, this is quite closely related to Camus's theory of the absurd, but the important point, for Jaspers, is that in limit situations the conflict between these orders becomes starkest. In some respects, Jaspers is more clearly an existential thinker than his German compatriot Heidegger because his work is an invitation to experience, as well as a description of it; it is not an ontological description of Being in the way that Heidegger's work is, as we will soon see.

Like Kierkegaard and Nietzsche, Jaspers rails against any provision of external and objective substitutes for personal decisions, such as party, wealth, state or the mediocrity of the herd. His ethics are again primarily negative in their criticisms of other positions and, as will become apparent throughout this book, no existentialist will be what Kierkegaard and Derrida call a "knight of good conscience", preaching prescriptive moral truths to all and sundry.

Husserl and phenomenology

All of the thinkers to be considered in the main body of this book were to varying degrees influenced by Edmund Husserl (1859–1938) and the method of phenomenology – roughly, the sustained attempt to describe experiences without theoretical speculations – that he founded, or at least was the first to explicitly thematize. Heidegger, for example, was Husserl's assistant for some years and eventually replaced him at the University of Freiburg. He also took phenomenology in a radical new direction. Although in *Being and Time* he carefully avoided using Husserlian terms – such as consciousness, the transcendental ego, the natural attitude, the phenomenological reduction, and the *epochē* – and although he had also come to consider Husserl's project as idealist, he comments in his introduction to this work that "the following would not have been possible if the ground had not been prepared by Edmund Husserl, with whose *Logical Investigations* phenomenology first emerged". Although Heidegger elsewhere extends the origins of phenomenology back to the Greeks, his indebtedness to Husserl is clear, despite employing idioms vastly different from those of his teacher and predecessor.

Similarly, the French existentialists were among the first serious interpreters of Husserl in France. Merleau-Ponty and Sartre's divergent interpretations of Husserl revealed to each other the richness and depth of his work. As Sartre observed in his moving eulogy for Merleau-Ponty entitled "Merleau-Ponty vivant": "Alone, each of us was too easily persuaded of having understood the idea of phenomenology. Together, we were, for each other, the incarnation of its ambiguity" (SIT: 159). Along with Emmanuel Levinas, who translated some of Husserl's main texts into French, they were the major players in making phenomenology so dominant in France either side of the Second World War. Furthermore, Sartre and Merleau-Ponty both considered themselves "Husserlians", although they gave different characterizations of the two main tools of the phenomenological method (see below). What unifies Sartre and Merleau-Ponty's work is their shared effort to make Husserlian phenomenology a little less abstract, and this is also the case with Heidegger, who emphasizes the ontological significance of "moods" such as boredom and anxiety. Roughly speaking, these three thinkers, and perhaps also de Beauvoir, although her allegiances to phenomenology are less clear, can be characterized as propounding a version of existential phenomenology. Of course, the fact that these very different philosophers consider themselves phenomenologists calls into question exactly what the term "phenomenology" refers to and it is hence important to clarify phenomenology's two main tools.

KEY POINT *The two components of the phenomenological method*
1. The negative move consists in suspending judgement on anything that might prevent us attending to the "things themselves" (the famous *epochē*, or suspension of the "natural attitude" that assumes, for example, that there is an outside world).
2. The positive move involves a "return" to the specific mode of appearing of the phenomenon and requiring some kind of search for essences (technically called an *eidetic reduction*).

Probably the most important concept to understand in this tradition is what is termed the *phenomenological reduction* (point 1 above). Phenomenology is often characterized as a "return to the things themselves", or to phenomena as they are experienced *before* the "natural attitude". In the so-called "natural attitude", we assume that there is an outside world and that other people exist. Husserlian phenomenology wants us to abandon these and other presuppositions, and see if such insights are actually given to us in the purity of experience. This problem then will be one regarding how we can actually know that other people exist, for example, based solely on attending to our own experience. Without yet answering this question, philosophy has often constructed theories and then returned to experience to see if those theories are true. Phenomenology, however, wants to begin with the experiences themselves, and, secondly, to perform an *eidetic reduction* to see if those experiences have any essential or necessary conditions (point 2 above). In Sartre's work, this is apparent in his consistent use of examples, which appear almost literary in character, but from which he deduces certain essential and necessary conditions: usually that we are free. His use of eidetic analysis also involves attempts to characterize the essence of bad faith, as well as to look at one emotion and deduce the essence of all other emotions from that.

Two things are worth noting about phenomenology before we go any further. First, phenomenology is not simply a form of introspective subjectivism because it involves a search for essences, or exemplifications, and hence retains a generalizing tendency. In fact, Husserl famously goes so far as to proclaim the opposite – that phenomenology is a rigorous science – although he insisted that it is a science of consciousness rather than of empirical things. This is not surprising given that in Husserl's hands phenomenology began as a critique of both naturalism (which is roughly the idea that everything belongs to the world of nature and can be studied by the methods appropriate to studying that world) and the valorization of science and the scientific method. Phenomenologists tend to argue that the study of consciousness must actually be very different from the study of nature. Indeed, phenomenology does not proceed from the collection of large amounts of data and generalize a theory beyond the data (the scientific method of induction). Rather, it aims to look at particular examples without theoretical presuppositions (such as the phenomenon of love, of two hands touching each other, etc.), before then discerning what is essential to these experiences, as well as their conditions of possibility.

This technique of argument is employed by all of these phenomenologists, although it needs to be noted that for Heidegger, Sartre and Merleau-Ponty "pure" phenomenology, or a complete bracketing away of the outside world, is impossible. We can attend to experience in order to discern essential conditions, but any kind of sustained bracketing away – or epochal reduction in Husserl's terms – is impossible, as we are necessarily what Heidegger calls beings-in-the-world, inextricable from our social situation. For them, in order to understand "concrete" human life we need to pay more attention to our essential historicity without abstracting from this by privileging rational reflection, as the above three thinkers accuse Husserl of in different ways.

Finally, it needs to be noted that from Husserl the existentialists also gained an understanding of the importance of intentionality (even if Heidegger abandoned the vocabulary in favour of emphasizing what he called a "comportment towards"): that conscious acts are directed toward objects and awareness of objects is always mediated by social meanings. For Merleau-Ponty, for example, Husserl's notion of the lifeworld (*Lebenswelt*) was very important in this regard. Although Husserl's rich and challenging work cannot be adequately summarized here, the extent of the existentialists' debts to Husserl and phenomenology will become more apparent as this book progresses.

Marcel and the body

The Catholic thinker Gabriel Marcel (1889–1973) provided a more optimistic account of the world, and our relationship to others, than Sartre, Kierkegaard and the other major existentialists. At the same time, he shares in their rejection of an exclusively technical view of the world. In fact, at the risk of generalization it might be suggested that all existentialists have some kind of critique of "scientism", if not of science. Following in the footsteps of Husserl's denigration of naturalism, it is generally felt by existential thinkers that although scientific endeavours are invaluable, they are not the primary way of relating to things, let alone to the world. The scientism of our culture has made the mistake of thinking that the scientific way of comprehending things and the world is our sole access to truth but, as we will see in detail in the work of Heidegger and Merleau-Ponty, good arguments can be marshalled to suggest that the scientific way of knowing is in fact secondary to the more practical aspects of our instrumental relationship to the world. Existential thinkers insist that misconstruing this order of priority has ethical consequences as much as epistemological ones.

But to return to Marcel, his importance to existentialism consists largely in his reintroduction of the question of the body. In the 1920s he declared "I am my body", and while this may seem to be a fairly banal observation, in the context of the tradition that had preceded him (with the exception of Nietzsche) it was an important affirmation. Historically, much of the Western philosophical tradition has downplayed the significance of our bodies. Our bodies, it has been argued, are capable of misleading us, and are certainly not as reliable as abstract thought; think of Plato and Descartes in this respect, who are merely the most obvious figures in this tradition. Although the issue of the body in Heidegger's work is complicated, it is safe to say that all twentieth-century existential thinkers emphasize the significance of our lived and embodied experience and the importance of our perceptual relation to the world, even if they disagree with one another about precisely what kind of relation this is.

This emphasis on embodied experience has also involved an emphasis on sexuality. Even before de Beauvoir wrote her monumental study of women, *The Second Sex*, in 1949, both Sartre and Merleau-Ponty had written a number of works on sexuality. Although there are reasons for considering their accounts either sexist (in the case of Sartre) or presuming a gender-neutral subject that is unrepresentative of the specificities of female sexuality (in the case of Merleau-Ponty), they did concern themselves with such matters in a manner unknown to the tradition, at least since the Greeks, and Marcel was a key precursor to this line of investigation.

Camus and the absurd

The work of the French novelist, playwright and philosopher Albert Camus (1913–60), is not often taught in courses on existentialism these days, and that is a cause for some regret. At the same time there are good reasons for such an omission. Camus was not an academic philosopher, and to some extent he was on the periphery of the exchange of ideas in France that revolved around the figures of Husserl, Hegel and Heidegger, and he always denied being an existentialist, despite inevitably being associated with the term. Camus describes his work as more a "sensitivity" to, rather than a philosophy of, existence. Moreover, unlike some of his compatriots, Camus is almost self-explanatory to read and the need for an exegetical discussion of his work is not as pressing. However, it remains the case that in the literary and political realm he was a pivotal player in French existentialism and extracts from *The Myth of Sisyphus* (1942), his first substantial non-fiction philosophical book, are very suitable to introduce existentialism, not least because of the accessibility of his expression when compared to the vocabularies of Heidegger and Sartre.

Rather than focus on questions pertaining to freedom, or our lack thereof, in *The Myth of Sisyphus* Camus's emphasis is on the absurd nature of existence, and how to deal with it and go on living. The character referred to in the title, Sisyphus, is a man from Greek mythology who was condemned to roll a boulder ceaselessly up a hill despite being aware that it would inevitably roll back down again. For Camus, this type of behaviour is typical of the human condition and he employs the concept of *the absurd* to describe this situation. The boredom associated with Sisyphus's repetition is fleshed out phenomenologically by Heidegger, but it is the resolution of this absurdity that Camus's book is essentially about, and he suggests that despite being burdened by that boulder, he can nevertheless imagine Sisyphus happy. Camus defines the absurd as follows: "This world in itself is not reasonable, that is all that can be said. But *what is absurd is the confrontation of the irrational and the wild longing for clarity whose call echoes in the human heart*" (MS: 26, emphasis added). He also goes on to offer a further clarification of what is at stake in a philosophy of the absurd:

> Man stands face to face with the irrational. He feels within him his longing for reason and happiness. The absurd is born of this confrontation between the human need and the unreasonable silence of the world. This must not be forgotten because the

whole consequence of a life can depend upon it. The irrational, the human nostalgia, and the absurd that is born of their encounter – these are the three characters in the drama …

(MS: 31–2)

In other words, Camus refers to the absurd as the gap between what human beings hope for in life and what they actually find. Individuals seek order, harmony and even perfection, yet can find no evidence that such things exist. In *The Myth of Sisyphus*, Camus seeks to rectify this, basically by encouraging individuals to give up their desire for a reasonable and coherent order to the world. It is the human urge for reason in an unreasonable world that is responsible for the absurdity of the human condition, and he suggests that the unceasing quest for reason, foregrounded in the Enlightenment, has alienated humanity from itself. Camus places more importance on the practical and aesthetic functions of reason, rather than the "pure reason" of metaphysics, which seeks to know the ultimate reality, what really exists and what makes that existence possible. In that sense he is at a distance from some of the other existentialists considered in this book, who do pose such questions, and are systematic philosophers, albeit in new ways.

For this reason a chapter has not been devoted to his thought, but if we agree with Camus about the irreconcilability of the human desire for order and intelligibility and the world that resists such a desire, the important question becomes one of how to go on living in such a world and indeed whether we can admit any truth without lying and without bringing in a hope that is fundamentally lacking from the human condition. To commit suicide or not? Camus begins *The Myth of Sisyphus* by claiming that this is the only truly serious philosophical question. Although this may seem to be a rather extreme position to hold, it does raise an important and enduring issue for existential literature and philosophy: how to authentically go on living given the absurdity, or the contingency, or the "thrownness" (these terms will be introduced shortly) of the human condition. Moreover, in reminding us of the importance of the question of suicide, Camus rejects the elaborate and obtuse system-building engaged in by some philosophers, as well as the detailed analytical work engaged in by others. The most important questions are those that pertain to the meaning of life, or its lack.

The Outsider
In his early theoretical and fictional work, Camus exhibits an insistent individualism that rails against simply doing what others do and

believing what others believe. This is most dramatically and powerfully illustrated in his famous novella *The Outsider* (1942), where the main character, Meursault, refuses to seek justification for his actions and is deliberately juxtaposed against numerous other individuals who are seeking such external justification for their behaviour. There are religious figures, juridical figures and the people of Algiers, the town in Algeria where the novel is set. All are part of the "mechanism", that system of "implacable rituals", arbitrary conventions, customs and moralities that prevents the people of Algiers from recognizing the essential absurdity of existence (and hence living a truly authentic life) and Meursault is an outsider precisely due to his inability to partake in these illusions.

The entire juridical process that follows Meursault's shooting of an "Arab" is exposed as relying on conventional and arbitrary mores and the implication is that Meursault is being convicted not because of the murder of this man, but primarily because of his estrangement from society. At Meursault's trial, every little event is assumed to have immense significance. Meursault's association with Raymond, his "irregular" affair with Marie, his laughing at a Fernandel film after his mother's death and his acceptance of coffee and a cigarette at her deathbed are all pivotal factors in his eventual conviction. Meursault himself struggles to comprehend how the qualities of an ordinary man "could be used as damning evidence of guilt". But the point is that he is not an ordinary man, at least in the context of the Algerian society that Camus depicts. It seems that Meursault alone is authentic. He alone refuses to sentimentalize and mystify the truth and Camus's narration suggests that he consequently enjoys a greater freedom than those seeking external guarantors of meaning, his freedom deriving from his acceptance of absurdity and his consequent lack of interest in anything but life itself.

Conclusion

We have considered some of the most important influences on the existential thinkers to be considered in the main part of this book. Although a good case could be made for including Hegel in any such list, as Merleau-Ponty does in his essay "Hegel as Existentialist", this requires a rather strong reading of Hegel's work and it also obscures the foundational role that Kierkegaard's rejection of Hegel's systematic philosophy has in the history of existentialism. Literary figures such as Dostoyevsky, Tolstoy (who influenced Heidegger's understanding of death), Kafka and others have also been productively associated with existentialism. Characters in their novels, and even the movement of their novels as a whole, have been characterized as existential. This was historically the case in regard to the early secondary literature on existentialism, as the works of Kierkegaard, Heidegger and Sartre were first being translated into English, and there was good reason for this. Existential philosophers tend to have a developed literary style because of their desire for their texts to have an affective force on their readers rather than just being about the accumulation of knowledge. In my opinion, however, none of the above novelists were pivotal to the development of the four thinkers that this book will focus on, who take certain existential insights already given in the philosophical work of Nietzsche, Kierkegaard, Jaspers and Camus, and make them more systematic.

two

Heidegger and the existential analytic

Martin Heidegger's (1889–1976) relationship to existentialism is the subject of some controversy, not only because of his criticisms of Sartre's focus on consciousness and subjectivity in his 1945 essay "Letter on Humanism", but also because of some substantive philosophical differences between his project and those of his French contemporaries. At the same time, there can be no doubting the extent of Heidegger's influence on existentialism. In fact, an adequate understanding of it would be impossible without at least some comprehension of his work, particularly his enormously influential *Being and Time* (1927), so we will shortly consider the aspects of his thought that have been important for existentialism: largely the material that he calls the "existential analytic".

First, however, it is necessary to digress somewhat to consider Heidegger's broader philosophical project and there is no easy way to do this. Not only is Heidegger's language notoriously dense and difficult, and probably quite unlike anything that you will have encountered before, but the questions that guide and motivate his existential analytic are also, at first glance, highly abstract (the complication of his language is at least *partly* because of his attempts to escape the distorting effects of existing ways of thinking that Heidegger finds to be problematic). In the first few pages of this chapter, I hence attempt to lay out the basic impetus *behind* the more existential aspects of his work, as they are expressed in the "Introduction" in *Being and Time*, and his essay "What is Metaphysics?" Although readers might be tempted to skip this section of the chapter and begin with the more obviously existential material on "*Dasein*", if this is done it is important eventually to return to these first few pages and, better yet, to the "Introduction" in *Being and Time*, as they problematize any too-quick conflation of Heidegger and existentialism.

The question of Being

For Heidegger, the Western philosophical tradition has been imbued with problems. From the mind–body debate to the problem of the external world and the question of whether or not other people exist, it seems that we have been beset by a host of complications. This is no doubt the nature and allure of philosophy for some. For Heidegger, however, it is the nature of Western philosophy with its metaphysical bent (roughly, metaphysics seeks to establish what is the ultimate reality beyond appearances). Suggesting that the whole corpus of Western philosophy has posited the *presence* of things as the ultimate reality and therefore the proper object of philosophical investigation, he asserts that the entire tradition has thereby ignored the most fundamental philosophical problem in the process: the problem of that which allows things to be present at all, or what he calls the problem of Being.

Before this claim can be made to make any sense, a brief explanation about the term itself is called for. After all, the term "Being" has a long history in philosophy as the most universal but indefinable concept and it is also one of those words that is frequently thrown around but, on Heidegger's view, rarely understood. This is partly because it is not something that we can pin down or define; it exceeds all of our resources for attempting to describe it and Heidegger himself hence deliberately resists any attempt to define Being. Although Heidegger would loathe this, a tentative definition of Being might run as follows: Being is that which allows existence to be possible at all. On this understanding, ontology just means the study of Being, or the conceptually developed account of that which allows things to be, and Heidegger opposes his procedure of "fundamental ontology" (which is concerned with Being) to traditional Western metaphysics (which is concerned with what *is*, and focuses upon particular beings of the world, rather than Being *per se*).

While the question of Being is necessarily shrouded in darkness, Heidegger argues that all of us also have some lived understanding of the meaning of Being, albeit a vague one, and it is for this reason that our *own existence* is at issue in pursuing this apparently opaque question. Being is presupposed in all of our everyday practices and he also argues that it is precisely this tension between our lived understanding of Being and the philosophical tradition's inability to offer any cogent theoretical account of it that shows that there is a need to ask about the meaning of Being; on his view, this is the most pressing question of all, even if at first glance it appears to epitomise philosophical abstraction. Even if exactly what Being refers to is still unclear – and this would not be surprising given that Heidegger spent his entire career finding different ways to probe this question – it is important to note that Heidegger draws a famous and important distinction between beings and Being that is sometimes referred to as the ontico-ontological difference.

KEY POINT *The ontico-ontological difference*
- *Ontical enquiry* examines entities, or beings.
- *Ontological enquiry* examines that which allows entities to be, or Being.

(Following the translator's practice in *Being and Time*, when intended in an ontological sense "Being" will be capitalized throughout this book.) On Heidegger's view, ontical beings such as objects and entities of the world have Being in common, but there remains an ontological difference between all of these various beings and Being; despite beings partaking in Being, they are not the same thing. We might say that the Being of entities is not itself an entity.

Heidegger argues, however, that since the Greeks this difference has been covered over and ignored, and he suggests that this is because philosophers have been ill at ease with time (hence the title of his book), invariably construing Being as timeless, eternal and unchanging. He suggests that philosophers have sought to make Being present, *either* in empirical things (beings), *or* in the realm of that which is transcendent and "otherworldly" (such as the changeless and eternal world of Plato's Forms). Rather than consider the question of Being – the fundamental ontological question of what allows empirical things to show up for us, and for there to be a meaningful "world" – Western philosophy has frequently posited one special thing that makes all of the other empirical things possible. Most obvious among these explanations is God, but for Heidegger there are many ontologies that do not explicitly invoke God but retain the general form of having one kind of transcendent thing that makes possible all of the other things; he calls these philosophies "onto-theologies". Effectively, however, this is to forget the question of Being and to ignore the ontico-ontological difference between things of the world and their conditions of possibility. Heidegger argues that philosophical enquiry needs to focus on time, and what he calls "*Dasein*", to clear up, in so far as this is possible, the meaning of the question of Being. While some of the details of Heidegger's understanding of the question of Being and his recuperation of the philosophical project of ontology itself are not relevant to a book on existentialism, they do need to be discussed in a cursory way so as not to extract his findings from their main philosophical purpose and context; after all, this is what he accuses Sartre's existentialist appropriation of his work as doing.

"What is Metaphysics?"

In this respect, it is worth briefly considering another early text of Heidegger's that develops this contrast between his own project of fundamental ontology and the Western metaphysics that he distances himself from (BT: §1): his essay "What is Metaphysics?" In this text he argues that Being is necessarily non-being, in that it cannot be located in the world as beings can. He suggests that the Western philosophical tradition has ignored this lack, this "nothingness" that is Being, and as a consequence has struggled to free itself of the implications ever since. If this term "nothingness" is no clearer than the term Being, Heidegger's claim, put as simply as possible, is that the tradition, preoccupied with the desire to know and contain Being as a totality (consider the Socratic preoccupation with the question "what is?"), has failed to recognize absence as a precondition for presence. This kind of metaphysics is, by its very nature, excluded from the experience of Being, because it always represents Being only with an eye to what of Being has already manifested itself as beings, that is, as things or objects in the world (BW: 104). Cut off from the truth of being, metaphysics then has recourse only to truths of knowledge (epistemology) rather than fundamental ontology (BT: §13). Any ontological enquiry into the possibility of presence itself is ignored, and any experience of "the Being-question" is hence quickly followed, Heidegger suggests, by the "forgetting of Being".

The derogatory connotation that the term metaphysics bears in contemporary philosophical circles is partly due to this analysis (as well as to the Anglo-American rejection of metaphysics that arguably began with Bertrand Russell), which Heidegger forcefully brought to bear upon many of the most famous Western philosophers, including Plato, Aristotle, Kant and Nietzsche. For Heidegger, metaphysics is inevitably a *metaphysics of presence*: a metaphysics, or science, of that which *is*. To repeat his fundamental claim, Being has been understood as thing(s), as objectively present and "there", and any metaphysical account of "reality" is then constructed on the basis of this prior understanding of the meaning of Being. Indeed, Heidegger argues that there is a resultant prioritization of theoretical ways of knowing and understanding – of what he calls the "present-at-hand" – and this is, in fact, a distorted way of experiencing that is not fundamental to human existence.

At the same time, Heidegger does not want to insist crudely that the entire philosophical canon has been devoid of intelligence and unaccountably ignorant, and he must hence offer some kind of explanation about its "forgetting of Being". He does this by suggesting that Being cannot be positively affirmed for and by itself (BT: §13) and he attempts to get at the meaning of Being by examining the phenomenon of the forgetting of Being in the work of various figures in the history of Western philosophy. This suggestion satisfies what might seem to be competing needs. Being can be encountered, as we will shortly see, and yet it is understandable that it has generally been ignored by much of the Western philosophical tradition. In fact, Heidegger's work, particularly after *Being and Time*, uses a process that he terms "destructive retrieval" to show in detail why various philosophers were unable to fully approach the question of Being, while at the same time their work testifies to its existence. With a few important adjustments, this aspect of Heidegger's project has metamorphosed into Derridean deconstruction, but that cannot concern us here. It is enough to point out that Heidegger claims that the question of Being branches out into two questions: an interpretation of *Dasein* in terms of temporality; and a destructive history of ontology (BT: §8). We will only be concerned with the former in this chapter, because it is his interpretation of *Dasein* in terms of temporality, what he calls his "existential analytic", that most clearly relates to existentialism. Six main themes from Heidegger's "existential analytic" are particularly important to existentialism. These are:

1. the initial priority that Heidegger accords to "average, everydayness" and what he calls the "ready-to-hand";
2. his analysis of authenticity and inauthenticity;
3. his descriptions of fallenness, they-self and *das Man*;
4. his discussion of the significance of moods such as fear, anxiety and boredom;
5. his insistence on care as being fundamental to *Dasein*;
6. his famous ruminations on death and its ontological significance in Division 2 of *Being and Time*.

Dasein

Some further preparatory questions first need to be answered. In particular, what is *Dasein* and why does Heidegger think that an analysis of it allows privileged access to the question of Being? In *Being and Time*, Heidegger eschews references to consciousness, or humanity, and his anti-subjectivist account of existence instead employs the term "*Dasein*", which is literally translated as "being-there". On Heidegger's view, terms such as human, subject, object, consciousness, spirit, person and even the "I" bring metaphysical assumptions with them. To employ them in *Being and Time* would undermine his overall project of recuperating the question of Being and that is why *Dasein* is used instead of human consciousness, even if it is nevertheless the case that the term *Dasein* functionally serves to distinguish the human from the non-human in *Being and Time*.

Significantly, Heidegger suggests that *Dasein* is the particular being, or entity, that must be investigated in order to understand Being. This is because *Dasein* is the only being that can raise the question of its own being, is concerned with its own being, and, somewhat synonymously, for whom its existence is in question (Sartre will replicate these claims in the early chapters of *Being and Nothingness*, as well as the priority that is given to the phenomena of questioning). *Dasein* is a privileged site of enquiry because it has an understanding of the meaning of Being in general (Heidegger calls it a "pre-ontological" understanding), even if it is often repressed and concealed. In fact, in *Being and Time* Heidegger goes as far as to suggest that there is Being only as long as *Dasein* is – a formulation that Sartre will not accept – and he asserts that it is only through *Dasein*'s understanding of the world that we can have any access to the being of entities. Only through *Dasein* can the things show themselves as they are (BT: §4). Heidegger's eventual analysis of these aspects of *Dasein* in his "existential analytic" is the ground for the existentialist interpretations of his thought.

Although the privilege that he accords to an analysis of *Dasein* in *Being and Time* is one that he will abandon in his later work, it is also significant that Heidegger characterizes the mode of Being of *Dasein* as existence, or *existenz*, borrowing Kierkegaard and Jaspers's terminology, meaning that *Dasein* has no essence or fixed nature. In Heidegger's words, "the essence of *Dasein* lies in its existence" (BT: §9). This was clearly an inspiration for Sartre's famous existentialist motto that for human beings "existence precedes essence", even if Heidegger himself would later renounce this Sartrean formulation for being still too metaphysical. Heidegger's point is that *Dasein* stands out from mere immersion in the world, is self-interpreting (BT: §9), and does not have objective attributes or essences that can adequately define it. Heidegger also suggests that there are two other aspects of *Dasein* that are peculiar to it and are worth drawing attention to:

1. Only *Dasein* can "understand itself in terms of its existence, in terms of its possibility to be itself or *to not be itself*" (BT: §4). On Heidegger's view, there is something peculiar about a creature that is capable of not being itself, of being inauthentic. (Sartre will also analyse and draw attention to this feature of human existence in his discussions of what he calls bad faith.)

2. *Dasein* also has the character of what is sometimes translated as "mineness", basically meaning specificity and individuality but not an enduring sense of personal identity. Rather, the point is that for any particular case of responsibility and for any particular decision and so on, it can be said that it is *my* responsibility and *my* decision. *Dasein* names this individuality as it is lived as opposed to objectively described, and this emphasis on "lived" and concrete experience is retained in all existential thinkers.

Being-in-the-world

In *Being and Time*, Heidegger analyses the essential features of the structure of *Dasein*, and he refers to these features as *existentiale* (or *existentialia* in plural form). An existentiale is an element of the being of *Dasein*, and as such can be contrasted with *categories*, which are the essential features of beings other than *Dasein*.

The first and broadest set of existentialia discussed in *Being and Time* is termed "being-in-the-world" and in the chapter of the same name Heidegger examines the way that *Dasein* relates to other entities. It becomes clear that for Heidegger, unlike say Descartes and his project of radical doubt of the external world (which eventually culminates in his famous *cogito* argument, "I think, therefore I am"), we are essentially in the world and inseparable from it. Fundamentally, we are not abstracted from the world, as some scientific practice tends to assume – indeed the very concept of "methodology" is arguably based on the presupposition of a detachment of the observer from that which is observed – but rather are always immersed in the everyday lifeworld (*Lebenswelt* as Husserl called it). Arguably, Heidegger's thesis of the primacy of being-in-the-world also means that Husserl's own radical phenomenological reduction, which in some respects can be seen to continue to the Cartesian project, is itself untenable.

Without spending too much time on Heidegger's discussions of the ontological structure of worldliness (BT: Ch. 3), it is sufficient to say that an important feature of being-in-the-world is that it is concerned with *dwelling*, rather than with any more objective description of location. In other words, being-in-the-world is concerned with explicating that which makes the world our home, and only *Dasein* can be said to have a world, the notion of "world" here referring to a context, and an association of references and possible projects in the world that have meaning. In this regard, one very important thing to come out of this section of *Being and Time*, which we will now focus on, is the priority that Heidegger accords to what Macquarrie and Robinson translate as the "ready-to-hand". In different ways, his analysis of the ready-to-hand was very influential on both Sartre and Merleau-Ponty, as well as on various philosophers and scientists working in cognitive science and artificial intelligence.

The priority of the ready-to-hand

We have already seen that philosophy has traditionally prioritized the *theoretical encounter* with things, whether it be Descartes engaging in radical doubt as part of his search for clear and distinct ideas, or even the Husserlian reduction to the things themselves. On Heidegger's view, however, *Dasein* associates with things first and foremost on a *practical* and immediate basis that he calls the "ready-to-hand", which refers to the availability of things for our use and deployment in relation to the completion of tasks. For Heidegger, useful things are necessarily in a situation and are always related to other useful things by a network of association. Heidegger calls this connection between various objects and our potential use of them an "equipmental totality" (which is basically synonymous with the notion of the world) and he analyses it in detail.

An interrogation of this kind of practical "average everydayness" is prioritized in Division 1 of *Being and Time*, because here, Heidegger tells us, things are least distorted by metaphysical abstractions. For Heidegger, the problems of philosophy are rarely problems that we encounter in our practical existence. The scandal of philosophy is not that the problem of the external world has not been solved, but that it has persisted for so long. The metaphysical intent to know and contain the world has ignored the practicalities of our average, everyday existence where, according to

Heidegger, we are best placed to apprehend Being, in however necessarily limited a manner (BT: §5). This is because implicit in all of our activities is an understanding of what it means to be, even if this "pre-ontology" still needs to be adequately conceptualized.

Heidegger also argues that a kind of knowledge and intelligibility accompanies the ready-to-hand. In fact, he argues that all other modes of knowing are subsidiary to that of the ready-to-hand: the practicalities of everyday existence are epistemologically prior to any other consideration; they are also ontologically more significant. For Heidegger, in the derivative mode of knowing that he terms the present-at-hand, entities are forced to become material objects that are available for inspection (or mental constructs), rather than as tools for our use. A present-at-hand consideration of an object might delve into its size, shape, colour, configurations or molecular composition, but this will ignore the object's most fundamental relationship with *Dasein*. Against the Cartesian view, the world is not primarily the scientific world, but the practical one of everyday life. For Heidegger, the objects that surround us are tools for our use first and most fundamentally and the structure of human existence is hence best disclosed in practical activity. It has been said that *Dasein* is at home in the world as a labourer is in his or her workshop, and speaking of a hammer in this context Heidegger explains that, "the less we just stare at the hammer-thing, and the more we seize hold of it and use it, the more primordial does our relationship to it become" (BT: §15). In other words, being-in-the-world is a matter of manipulating things and engaging in practice, rather than abstracting from things in theoretical cognition. In this respect, Heidegger makes the following important distinction:

- *ready*-to-*hand* – a practical relation to objects and the world as an "equipmental totality";
- *present*-at-*hand* – a more abstract relation to objects in which they are not defined by their involvement in human activity and instead take on an "objective presence".

Questions might be raised regarding whether or not this distinction pertains equally to all cultures, but disregarding such anthropological considerations and presuming that objects are construed instrumentally Heidegger makes it clear that we cannot simply step outside this primordial relation of instrumentality (the ready-to-hand) to some realm of rarefied objects or, for that matter, thought, as metaphysics often aims to. For Heidegger there is no object outside human context and all present-to-hand theorizing must recognize that a condition of its possibility is this more primary and pragmatic comportment towards things that he labels the ready-to-hand.

This point is also important when it comes to the issue of perception. Heidegger's view means that we cannot see a broken beer bottle as simply the objective sum of its colour, shape, molecular composition and so on (present-at-hand), because the objects that we encounter in the world are first and foremost always objects of a certain kind and construed in relation to our possible use of them (ready-to-hand). As Heidegger states, "what we 'first' hear is neither noises or complexes of sounds, but the creaking wagon, the motorcycle" (BT: §34). In other words, a form of understanding is always already involved in our perception of the world, against what in the philosophical literature is called the representationalist account of perception. This paradigm of how perception occurs – a passive physical seeing something and then an active, mental interpretation of that brute physical perception – is a false model that does not recognize our essential being-in-the-world. As Heidegger makes explicit, "meaning is an existentiale of *Dasein*, not a property attaching to entities, lying behind them or floating somewhere as an intermediate domain" (BT: 19). The world exists in this practical way to our perception, not in some reified domain of pure sensory apprehension, of colours, shapes and the like, which later on comes to be mediated by thought and interpretation.

The breakdown of the ready-to-hand

Of course, we are usually unaware of this practical and habitual way of relating to things that is the ready-to-hand, and this is why we can make the mistake of taking rational reflection (the present-at-hand) as primary. How then can Heidegger offer the description of the ready-to-hand that he does, if in fact it is a background way of relating to things that is always presupposed but rarely the object of our explicit awareness? On his view, certain modes of what he calls "taking care" uncover the importance of the ready-to-hand and equipmentality for us. In particular, we experience our reliance on the ready-to-hand when it suddenly fails us, or breaks down. When we encounter unusable equipment that no longer fulfils its task it becomes akin to an objective presence for us, rather than something poised for our use (and scepticism becomes possible in this reflective mode but it feeds off the more primary experience of the ready-to-hand). A similar situation applies when we find that equipment is missing and on the recognition that objects can get in the way; in both cases objects again evince a kind of obstinacy that precludes their being absorbed into the ready-to-hand. In Heidegger's terminology, there are three main modes in which this "objective presence" of things is revealed to us – conspicuousness, obtrusiveness and obstinacy – but the important point to ascertain is that in its failure the tool becomes opaque rather than transparent; the tool is seen as a tool, and the nature of the ready-to-hand also becomes clear, at least from an ontic perspective.

In response to this, we might treat the tool as present-at-hand and analyse the various parts of the carburettor, for example, in order to ascertain why smoke is emanating from it. Although this is not necessitated, there are clearly often good reasons for this move; it can be very useful. Indeed, present-at-hand thinking is the basis for the considerable findings of modern science. However, for Heidegger problems occur when this mode is taken to be ontologically primary (see his 1953 essay, "The Question Concerning Technology") and his point is that both reflection and action emerge out of the more fundamental coping that is evinced in the ready-to-hand, a position that is quite closely related to the habitual equilibrium that Merleau-Ponty argues that the body perpetually seeks to cultivate, as we will see in Chapter 5.

Mitsein

As has already been noted in our descriptions of "being-in-the-world", Heidegger insists that there can be no isolated subject that subsequently encounters others. Rather, for him *Dasein* is always in the world, a being-with, or *Mitsein* in Heidegger's German (BT: §§26, 27). In fact, he argues that being-with is a necessary condition of *Dasein*. Although it is ontically a fact that some people may be alone, like a hermit in a cave, ontologically *Dasein* is always a being-with. On this view, one cannot be a self, or subject, without others. Heidegger also argues that when we see objects in terms of their use-value in the mode of the ready-to-hand, other people are also presupposed in this. For him, it is only in a world of others that things can be ready-to-hand and can give us an equipmental totality. The world is always already the one that we share with others, with the "they" (BT: §27).

KEY POINT

As we will see in Chapter 4, Sartre argues that Heidegger's understanding of *Mitsein* presupposes the existence of others – what Sartre calls a "crew" – rather than offering a phenomenological proof of them, and hence cannot be said to refute solipsism adequately without begging the question (BN: 244–50).

This section of *Being and Time* also offers a more detailed account of *Dasein* and it becomes clear that Heidegger thinks that the conception of the self as an isolated subject that remains constant in all experiences (as John Locke's memory criterion of identity arguably assumes) is to treat that person as a thing, or a brute object. This kind of analysis might be helpful in certain ways, and contemporary psychology is evidence of this, but on Heidegger's view it does not show us anything about *Dasein*, but rather just about *Dasein* as an entity. Both Heidegger and Sartre are vehemently against this kind of ontical self-enquiry that treats the self as an object with a pre-given identity or essence. Contrary to this view, Heidegger suggests that "*Dasein* is, initially and for the most part, not itself" (BT: §27) and the relationship that this bears to Sartre's own paradoxical formulations of what he calls "being-for-itself" – "it is not what it is, and it is what it is not" (BN: 79) – is far from coincidental. Moreover, as we will shortly see, *Dasein*'s tendency to ignore or to cover over this groundlessness, this way in which *Dasein* is *not itself*, is the basis for what Heidegger calls inauthenticity.

Das Man: the they

One of the more famous parts of *Being and Time* is its descriptions of what in German is called *das Man*, variously translated as the herd, the many, the they, the crowd, they-self and sometimes even "the one". This term's fame derives partly from Heidegger's complicated and at least partly complicit relation with Nazism, but it needs to be made explicit from the outset that he does not intend to use the concept of *das Man* as a normative principle by which to judge and evaluate human conduct, as many of his critics assume. It refers to the aspects of our lives that are average and anonymous and in which we tend to blend in with a crowd, indistinguishable from the multitudes, but, as would be apparent from the preceding discussion of *Mitsein*, for Heidegger there is no essential "I" that is distinguishable from the "they" (the feeling of "mineness" of which he speaks does not entail an enduring personal identity). In Heidegger's terms, since we are not for the most part ourselves, we are others and we are *das Man*. As he enigmatically suggests: "Everyone is the other, and no-one is himself" (BT: §27).

At the same time, Heidegger makes it clear that this realm of anonymity, *das Man*, is ultimately envisaged as inauthentic and as something that should be left behind as much as possible. He suggests that it is how each *Dasein* distances itself from the crowd that determines its sense of self, and Heidegger hence distinguishes the authentic self from the anonymous "they-self", where we are largely indistinguishable from anyone else. Although we can never be simply and unambiguously authentic for Heidegger (and authenticity itself requires inauthenticity in order to illuminate itself), the self of everyday *Dasein* is in fact this "they-self" rather than the authentic self. We will keep coming back to this famous and controversial distinction between the authentic and the inauthentic in what follows below, particularly in regard to Heidegger's analysis of fallenness. (Rather than addressing the authentic–inauthentic distinction in one section, Heidegger deals with different aspects of it in all of the key chapters of *Being and Time*.)

Being-in as such

Chapter 5 of *Being and Time* discusses three important and distinctive characteristics of *Dasein*:

1. mood (or state of mind, as it is sometimes translated);
2. understanding;
3. discourse/fallenness.

In the next chapter Heidegger argues that these different modalities of *Dasein* are all unified by what he calls "care" (BT: §41), but for the moment it is sufficient to note that these three categories are considered by Heidegger to be equally fundamental.

Moods

Most Heideggerian commentators find fault with the Macquarrie and Robinson translation of Heidegger's German term "*Befindlichkeit*", as state of mind. Basically, their worry is that "state of mind" carries connotations of subjective mental states, but Heidegger intends his concept to be broader than this and to have a public and social significance. For these reasons other translators have used the term "attunement", but for the sake of simplicity we might also simply translate it as mood, bearing in mind our earlier caveat about not making it purely a subjective feeling and also acknowledging that mood cannot be reduced to what *Dasein* believes when it has a mood.

For Heidegger moods are a vitally important and fundamental existentiale of *Dasein*; they should not be considered weaknesses or exceptions to the rule of rationality. Rather, moods confront us with an enigma that cannot be rationalized and they have tremendous onto-logical import (BT: §29); passions, desires and the like, are thought of as necessary conditions for reason, understanding and knowledge. Moreover, on Heidegger's view they can also disclose the world in a way in which reason cannot; to put the point crudely, the disclosure of Being in cognition is not as deep as the disclosure of Being in moods. This is one place where the public reputation of existentialism as being on about moodiness, despair, nihilism and so on, partially matches up with the philosophy itself. Heidegger does think that there is something sig-nificant about certain moods that reveals the more burdensome aspects of existence, particularly the mood that he calls *Angst* (which we will translate as anxiety), but also guilt, boredom and fear.

Thrownness

Heidegger argues that in moods we glimpse what he calls our "thrown-ness", which on his understanding refers to our being given over to a situation, to what he calls a "there", as well as to the further recognition that that very "there" is contingent and that things might have been otherwise; we could have been born somewhere else, with other parents and vastly different circumstances of innumerable kinds. Thrownness is meant to convey the fact of that being delivered over to contingency without rhyme or reason, and it emphasizes the unalterability of the past, which we are not creators of but which we must appropriate and make our own. Moods tend to only indirectly reveal this thrownness, because for the most part *Dasein* turns away from these burdensome revelations in inauthenticity and fallenness. It is also important to note that on Heidegger's analysis moods are largely independent of our con-trol. We find ourselves thrown into certain moods and this discloses *Dasein*'s submissiveness to the world. As we will see, Sartre's analysis of moods in *Being and Nothingness* does not emphasize this to the same extent. Sartre holds, for example, that consciousness affects itself with sadness as a recourse against a situation that is too urgent, and, even when nausea and anguish overcome us, there appears to be more control of these experiences than Heidegger's philosophy will admit.

On Heidegger's conception, ontologically important moods such as anxiety and boredom come neither from outside nor from inside. They arise out of our being-in-the-world, and he insists that we cannot make particular moods happen; nor for that matter can we do without moods altogether. *Dasein* always has some mood (a calm temperament is still a mood, as is indifference) and it is important to note that a mood is overcome only by means of a counter-mood; there is no overcoming of moods themselves (BT: §29). The authentic existence of which Heidegger so frequently speaks is hence not one that is free of moods. On the contrary, our thrownness is the basis for the world mattering to *Dasein*. If we were pure possibility (without mood, without contingency, and without a past), things would not concern us, motivate us, nor impel us with any sense of urgency. In this sense, Heidegger argues that it is moods that make it possible to direct oneself towards things and engage in meaningful projects in the world.

Although Heidegger is careful not to engage in any overt moralizing, it is clear that in relation to these moods that disclose our thrownness we should not simply lament the absurdity and ask "Why me?" Instead, we should ask, "How should I think about this?" Thrownness is envisaged as coexistent with the possibilities for freedom that are opened up by it. Although Heidegger's conception of freedom and possibility will not be discussed until the next section, it is important to recognize that contingency and thrownness are far from all that Heidegger insists on. Other aspects of his work (especially the existentiale of understanding) counter this emphasis upon "thrownness" and *Being and Time* is hence not simply a lament about being thrown into an unpredictable world, which is one possible interpretation of Camus's notion of the absurd.

Heidegger also insists that this emphasis on the omnipresence of moods has consequences for the practice of philosophy. It means that no theoretical position can leave moods behind and divest itself of feeling and affect. Descartes's famous clear and distinct ideas are themselves made possible and conditioned by mood and Heidegger suggests that it has been one of the merits of phenomenological research that it has again brought these phenomena (affects) more unrestrictedly into our sight. Although we have not so far discussed any particular moods in detail, in §30 Heidegger discusses the mood of fear at some length. He asserts that it reveals both the stark givenness of the world, and the way in which we are tied and attached to the world; our way of being is such that it is capable of being threatened. Ultimately, however, he suggests that moods such as fear are not as ontologically revealing as anxiety, which is considered at a later stage of *Being and Time* and which we will turn to shortly.

KEY POINT *Three essential characteristics of mood*
- Disclosure of thrownness and facticity (we cannot do without moods).
- Disclosure of being-in-the-world as a whole (this makes possible projects and directing oneself toward things).
- Disclosure that what *Dasein* encounters matters to *Dasein*.

Understanding

Whereas Heidegger suggests that moods are largely concerned with the past and with that which has been, in the existentiale that he terms "understanding" *Dasein* is thrown towards the future and it is this that makes freedom possible (BT: §31). On the simplest level, "understanding" is bound up with the recognition and projection of possibilities. *Dasein* is always already aware of possibilities and in the mode of the ready-to-hand, for example, the world presents itself in a particular light in relation to something that I am about to do, or in relation to some project that I am about to engage in. To offer a mundane example, a chair is significant because I am about to sit down and begin reading a manuscript. The important point to ascertain from this is that the world does not offer *Dasein* neutral objects that are subsequently interpreted. Rather, at the most basic level it offers *Dasein* possibilities and in this respect *Dasein* can never be reduced to mere actuality.

Although Heidegger states that "understanding" and moods are equally fundamental a structure of *Dasein*, this future orientation that is involved in understanding is arguably privileged in his work. While the actual and the possible cannot be reduced to one another, and although actuality has a tremendous existential significance as we have seen in the foregoing discussion of moods, possibility has an ontological priority given that *Being and Time* is directed towards understanding what it means to be. Moreover, his focus on the possibilities contained in "understanding" reinforces his fundamental definition of *Dasein* as primarily that which it is "not yet", including the various aims and ambitions that we all have for the future, whether or not they are explicitly conceptualized. Potentiality, or the possibility of being, becomes intimately associated with *Dasein*, more so than actuality or that which *is* (recall the ontico-ontological difference), and this is something that Heidegger's work shares with Sartre's similarly future-oriented vision of human existence.

That said, it should be acknowledged that, for Heidegger, as a thrown being, or what he calls a "thrown thrower" (BT: §31), we have only certain definite possibilities and our understanding of these possibilities is always at least partly determined by the past and our moods in a way that Sartre does not allow. For Sartre, there is a radical rupture, or break, between the past and the present (as well as the present and the future), and this means that our awareness of future possibilities cannot be circumscribed in the way that Heidegger allows.

Interpretation and the virtuous rather than vicious hermeneutic circle

On Heidegger's famous conception, analytical enquiry and "interpretation" are nothing more than the working out of the possibilities that are already projected by the "understanding" (BT: §32). In fact, he goes as far as to suggest that, "in interpretation, understanding does not become something different. It becomes itself". This means that all interpretation is at least partially grounded in something that we see in advance, in what he terms the "forestructure of our understanding". For Heidegger, this is because in interpretation there is "never a pre-suppositionless apprehension of something presented to us". Any appeal to what actually "stands there" is nothing other than the undiscussed assumptions of the person doing the interpreting. While interpretation is merely the "working out of possibilities projected in understanding" (BT: §32), the more explicit rendering of our immediate understanding, this working out of the possibilities already involved in understanding can be clarifying. Heidegger is hence not suggesting that we should acknowledge the futility of interpretation and analytic reflection and give them up, but he contends that the forestructure of our understanding grounds the possibility of interpretation, and he argues that this was ignored by many philosophers prior to the advent of phenomenology.

To offer a few examples of this structure of our understanding that he also terms the "existential-hermeneutical as" (BT: § 32), we inevitably hear a certain particular spluttering sound *as* a lawn mower starting up, we perceive the door *as* an escape route if we are being chased, we see the ruins *as* they were in their former glory, perhaps *as* evidence of the decline of the Roman Empire if they are in the relevant location, and Heidegger's fundamental claim is that we cannot get outside this mode of "seeing as". Moreover, although it is sometimes useful, the attempt to see something free of this "as" structure is also deficient and derivative: the object or experience is deprived of its world, and is, in a sense, no longer understood at all. This means that there is no such thing as a pure perception that is without theoretical and practical preconceptions. Rather, all perception is inevitably also an interpretation.

While Heidegger's account of the forestructure of our understanding is more nuanced than I can present it here, involving distinctions between fore-having, fore-sight, and fore-conception (BT: §32), for our purposes it is important to note that he rejects the suggestion that this position commits him to a vicious epistemological relativism. Although he admits that the structure of understanding and interpretation that he describes is circular, he argues that far from being a problem the mistake is actually to yearn for a stable form of knowledge that is independently justifiable and therefore not circular, which on his view inevitably falls foul of something akin to the learning paradox that Meno famously described.

> **KEY POINT** *Meno's learning paradox*
> If we have full knowledge of what we are looking for in our intellectual pursuits, then there is no reason to be looking (as anything found would already be known), but if we are ignorant of what we are searching for, then we could never know when we have found the object of our enquiry and thereby satisfied our intellectual pursuit.

Meno's paradox seems to suggest that there is something wrong with a conception of knowledge as capable of rigorous justification that is independent of human interests and preconceptions. What is decisive, Heidegger consequently argues, is not to get out of the hermeneutic circle, but to come into it in the right way. We must have a vague understanding of what it is we are looking for (i.e. as contained in the ready-to-hand and its pre-ontological conception of the meaning of Being), and this conception of interpretation heralds the renewal of a hermeneutical method that has since been productively explored by several of Heidegger's students, most notably Hans-Georg Gadamer.

Fallenness and inauthenticity

In the third existentialia that he terms "discourse" (BT: §34), Heidegger discusses idle talk, ambiguity and curiousity as they afflict the life of the "they-self". Interestingly, Heidegger discusses ambiguity in a predominantly negative light, unlike its positive explicit formulations in the work of Merleau-Ponty and de Beauvoir. For our purposes it is Heidegger's discussions of fallenness and inauthenticity that require attention. We have already seen that it is not the case that we can live permanently in authenticity. Rather, Heidegger insists that inauthenticity and absorption among the many is the condition for authenticity and cannot be simply done away with. This is because in utilizing objects in the mode of the ready-to-hand we act as anyone and everyone else acts. Moreover, he also argues that a structural feature of *Dasein* is characterized by what Heidegger calls its fallenness.

> **KEY POINT**
> *Fallenness* is the tendency for individuality and distinctiveness to get lost or reabsorbed into the anonymity of ordinary life, and the way in which *Dasein* inevitably flees its finitude and covers over its thrownness.

On this account, fallenness and immersion among the crowd are considered to be inauthentic, but at the same time all of us are fallen and Heidegger hence denies making a negative evaluation of inauthentic life. In precisely worded statements, Heidegger suggests that authenticity and inauthenticity are two basic modes of Being of *Dasein*, and not self-chosen possibilities. Most of Heidegger's "existential analytic" in *Being and Time* is concerned to analyse the way in which we are inevitably caught up and dragged into everyday banalities (fallenness and inauthenticity) and yet also to reveal the opposite movement in which this anonymity is exposed for what it is and we are radically individualized by the experience of anxiety when we are forced to make a difficult decision, or when confronting the possibility of our own death (authenticity). There is a clear relationship here to Jaspers's conception of limit situations, although it is not one that Heidegger acknowledges at any length. Although Heidegger's view of authentic existence can only be fully grasped following consideration of what he thinks is involved in resolutely facing up to our own death, it is nevertheless helpful to summarize a few general points about this distinction between authenticity and inauthenticity that will continue to be developed in subsequent sections of this book.

KEY POINT *Authenticity and inauthenticity*

1. Authenticity involves an individualizing sense of "mineness" – e.g. *my* decision – as well as a recognition of wholeness (BT: §12) because it assumes, rather than flees from, the finitude and groundlessness of *Dasein*'s existence.
2. Authentic existence is also grounded predominantly in possibility, whereas inauthentic existence is grounded predominantly in actuality (such as when the self is construed as an object or mere thing).
3. Authentic existence is aware of the meaning of existence, whereas the inauthentic is not.

We can deduce from the conjunction of claims 2 and 3 that the meaning of existence is inextricably bound up with the dimension of possibility, and Heidegger explicitly argues this in Division 2 of *Being and Time*. His various discussions of authenticity suggest that our lives are meaningful on account of that which might be (in the future), or even what might have been (in the past), more than on account of that which currently *is*. In this respect, Heidegger argues that *Dasein* tends to fall foul of three main flights from authentic existence: a reliance on various kinds of psychological determinism (the insistence that all behaviour is causally determined by the past); a conception of a particular future as inevitable; and a conception of ourselves as having an essence or nature.

Care as the Being of *Dasein*

As we have seen, being-in-the-world assumes many forms and Heidegger argues that these different modalities of *Dasein* are all unified by an underlying structure that he refers to as "taking care of", or care (*Sorge*) (BT: §41). It is this structure that is evident in, and underlies, all of the various existentials thus far considered. We might say that *Dasein*'s being is fundamentally one of care – care is the way that *Dasein* comports itself towards the world – although it is again important to note that Heidegger does not think that we are all enlightened Bodhisattva's caring for our fellow sentient beings. Rather, his insistence on the importance of "care" to *Dasein* is to say, among other things, that we are creatures for whom the kind of life that we are going to live is an issue for us.

On Heidegger's analysis, concern and solicitude are subcategories of care. *Dasein* is *concerned* with the job of hammering and is concerned in relation to entities, but the mode of care appropriate to others (*Mitsein*) is termed *solicitude*. Another way of expressing this distinction is as follows:

KEY POINT
Care is subdivided into *caring about* (i.e. concern: care about objects of the world) and *caring for* (i.e. solicitude: care for other people).

Although this distinction seems somewhat contentious in that it means that we cannot care *for* animals or the state of our essay, but only care *about* them, Heidegger's general argument that care underlies all of the different existentials thus far considered (fallenness, understanding, and so on), allows him to offer a first tentative answer to the question of what it means to be. For *Dasein*, to be means to care, in the distinctive sense that he gives to this idea, although it is important to recall that this answer remains on a different level from the question that he will ultimately return to regarding the meaning of Being itself. Heidegger's efforts to figure out what it means to be *Dasein* in Division 1 of *Being and Time* are merely the "preparatory" means for him to get to the more fundamental ontological question regarding what it means to be *per se*, which he examines in Division 2.

Anxiety and *Angst*

Heidegger's German term *Angst* is sometimes retained in this form in English translations. Other translators usually choose terms like dread, or anguish, and Macquarrie and Robinson prefer the more common term "anxiety" but divested of its medical connotations. Regardless of the translation, anxiety or *Angst* is a mood that has tremendous significance in *Being and Time* largely because of the individualizing role that Heidegger argues that it plays (BT: §40). On his view, the experience of pervasive anxiety existentially and dramatically reveals to us that social roles can never offer a complete, all-encompassing account of identity. We are confronted with the recognition that social mores and customs are not sufficient to make life meaningful for the individual in question, and in the process Heidegger argues that anxiety thereby intimates the potential for an individual and distinctive disclosure of the world.

In order to show why Heidegger thinks it does this, it is important to note that in the experience of anxiety the familiar world loses its normal significance; all of our habitual and everyday ways of relating to the world drop away and sink into insignificance. Forced to confront our own thrownness and finitude, anxiety individualizes us because we no longer feel at home in the world of the ready-to-hand, of *das Man*, and the many. Rather, *Dasein* is forced out of its "they-self" to consider itself and its role. By thus individualizing us, anxiety reveals *my* possibilities precisely as mine, but Heidegger also intimates that despite this feeling of "mineness" there is also a sense in which the self is annihilated in this process. Certainly any given essential self is annihilated and replaced by anxiety in the breakdown of the individual's life and his or her sudden recognition that nothing matters except that nothing matters. This is because on Heidegger's account, in anxiety *Dasein* finds that it has no essential possibilities of its own; the possibilities evinced for it in the ready-to-hand are there for everyone. They have no intrinsic or unique meaning for the individual in question and the recognition of this can jar us out of our habitual comfort zones; we find that things are uncanny (*unheimlich*), and this can provoke the awareness that we are free to either authentically or inauthentically confront the possibilities before us.

To develop this distinction between the authentic and the inauthentic, Heidegger discusses the moods of fear and anxiety as representative of two different ways in which we can face our past. In this respect, Heidegger is strongly influenced by Kierkegaard and essentially his point is that fear has a definite object, unlike anxiety, whose object, if any, is precisely no-thing-ness. Moreover, it is only the latter that forces us out of our habitual ways of being among the many and that *can* act as an impetus to authenticity. (As we will see, Sartre also argues that the experience of anguish reveals that the self has no essential possibilities and that whatever possibilities may be chosen are, in a sense, unjustifiable.)

Being-towards-death

The second division of *Being and Time* is devoted to an analysis of time. Although this division is more ontological than the material we have thus far considered, it is still engaged in a project that has ramifications for any existential analysis. This is because unlike Husserl, Heidegger did not think that we could consider time in isolation, or by performing a sustained phenomenological reduction. Rather, time and existence are necessarily co-implicated and this means that his discussions of time are intertwined with further analysis of *Dasein* in terms of care, and more importantly for our purposes, with what he calls being-towards-death and resoluteness. That a relationship obtains between time and death is clear enough, but Heidegger challenges the common understanding of this relationship.

While reflections on mortality were a large part of Greek philosophical thought, particularly in the Hellenistic period, in the Christian tradition and modernity they have been less common. Heidegger sought to redeem such questions, arguing, to put his point crudely, that the prospect of death grants unity and wholeness to *Dasein* (BT: §52). He also argues that a genuine comprehension of the inevitability of our own death recognizes something akin to an ontological truth of *Dasein*'s constitution. To accept that we are what he calls "beings-towards-death" is to be authentic, recalling that authentic existence is characterized by an explicit understanding of what it means to be.

At the same time, Heidegger accepts the obvious point – famously made by the Greek philosopher Epicurus – that as long as a subject exists it has "not yet" reached its end. In fact, for Heidegger the future orientation captured in this "not yet" is taken as characteristic of *Dasein*'s existence. *Dasein* is always "on the way", "ahead of itself", "what it is not" (a formulation that Sartre will use frequently), and projecting toward future possibilities that are "to come" (prefiguring the use of this phrase in the work of Jacques Derrida). The problem for Heidegger's account is that if this is the case then it seems difficult to refute the Epicurean "no subject argument", which implies that we do not, and cannot, experience our own death, but only the death of others. After all, as Epicurus' famous aphorism points out "where death is, I am not; where I am, death is". Other existential philosophers, including Sartre, consider this pretty much all that can be said on the matter.

However, Heidegger's position diverges quite dramatically from such a view. In fact, he argues that this tendency to avoid considering our own death is a major problem. To borrow an image for which I am indebted to my colleague Jonathan Roffe, it means that we act as if we are vampires; although we are not immortal, for all intents and purposes we act as if we are. We recognize that everyone dies sooner or later, but we consider this from an objective and impartial perspective. We do not take seriously the fact that we ourselves will die. In response to this attitude that he finds to be pervasive, Heidegger argues that although we cannot literally experience being dead, we nevertheless can and should confront it ahead of the event. In other words, we need to anticipate our own death, and not just the death of others. Why? Because this experience of "being-towards-death" reveals an important part of what it is to be human and Heidegger thinks that recognizing this has important consequences for the kind of life that we might lead. In order to understand this, it is best to proceed negatively, and to begin by establishing what Heidegger thinks is wrong with the understanding of death that he labels as "inauthentic".

The inauthentic apprehension of death

Heidegger suggests that there are two main inauthentic modes of understanding death – indifference and fear – and these ways of apprehending death are labelled as "inauthentic" because they do not fully recognize what it means to exist. The first of these ways of understanding death, indifference, itself breaks up into two different kinds. The less common of these is the indifference towards death that Epicurus' arguments attempt to foster. Epicurus' point is that no subject can experience the pain of being dead (as opposed to dying) so why worry about it?

At the same time, the vague and general recognition that all of us will *perish* biologically, which few of us would dispute, also exhibits an indifference towards death, albeit of a different kind, in that death is treated as something that indifferently comes to all of us; it is the ultimate egalitarian agent. This may seem to be a realistic way of confronting death, but for Heidegger it is to consider your own death as if it is the death of another. It is an inauthentic apprehension of death, as death in this instance is not understood as really your own; it afflicts someone else and is understood on an abstract and general level, and as something that will happen in the future at some indefinite point in time.

Of course, it might be argued (as Epicurus did) that this view is quickly replaced by fear on the inevitable occasions when these kinds of evasions and obfuscations are no longer possible. In other words, when confronted with illness, danger, old age, or any more intimate and probable relation to death, the indifference of abstraction and generalization is quickly supplanted by fear. In this regard, Heidegger agrees and suggests that the most common inauthentic apprehension of death for *das Man* is fear: that is, focusing on the actual event of our own *demise* and resenting or being scared by it. Why is this inauthentic? For Heidegger, the problem is that fear treats death as an empirical *actuality*, rather than as my "ownmost *possibility*" (BT: §52). This inauthentic view treats death only as a future actuality, but for Heidegger this future death is, paradoxically enough, a future possibility. Treating death only as an actuality again means that it is not thought of as happening to you. It is an empirical actuality that will end your life, but it is not part of your life, and this flees the finitude that is at the heart of *Dasein*'s existence. Heidegger argues that this attitude is typical of *das Man*, or the "they-self", who take more significance from what is actual than from what is possible (and from the conditions of possibility of the actual), and here you can see how the question of death returns us to the ontological question of Being that Heidegger thought the Western philosophical tradition had covered over and forgotten.

In a famous line, Heidegger argues against this view and suggests that: "death, as the end of *Dasein*, is *Dasein*'s ownmost possibility" (BT: §52), and he goes on to comment that "the more unveiledly this possibility gets understood, the more purely does the understanding penetrate into it as the possibility of the impossibility of any existence at all" (BT: §52). This raises several questions: first, how can we be directed towards something that can never be actualized (for us)? We can be towards our wedding day, or our graduation from the university, precisely because it can come about and be actualized for us at some date in the future. How can Heidegger accept the Epicurean "no subject" argument and yet nevertheless insist that we are a being-towards-death? How can death be my possibility when it is also, on his own admission, an "impossibility"? Sartre, whose work we will consider shortly, will simply respond that for this very reason death cannot be part of the structure of human subjectivity, but Heidegger insists that death is a possibility that is internal to the very being of *Dasein*. Death is an existential structure that defines human subjectivity and this means that the possibility of dying is part of the structure of our world as we experience it now, not just something that is deferred until later. In more philosophical language, we might say that death is a future possibility that is constitutive of the "now" of the present. We can understand this claim in the sense that my present is what it is, only owing to my understanding that this present is finite and that it will not go on forever. In other words, my understanding of a final "not yet", a final possibility, is what allows us to structure and organize our lives meaningfully. Awareness that I am going to die allows me to get a perspective on life as a whole because, as David Krell suggests, it "invades my present, truncates my future, and monumentalises my past" (BW: 22). Without this sense of the future as involving death, our motivations for pursuing certain kinds of projects would be lost; we would be vampires, still finite, as certain choices preclude other choices, but not mortal. In this regard, Heidegger insists that constraints such as death are a necessary condition for freedom and for individuality.

For Heidegger, our future possibilities become more focused by genuinely facing the prospect of our own death. Only if we are aware of our own finitude are we impelled to act now and with urgency. It makes it more likely that we will achieve the authentic mood that Heidegger calls "resoluteness". Without this recognition, Heidegger suggests that a life of inauthenticity and frivolity, and of uncritically believing what others believe, threatens to dominate. If Heidegger's understanding of death seems unrealistic, it is important to note that a confrontation with death *can* help focus us on what it means to be. It does not necessarily do so. Genuine recognition of impending death can transform the way that we view and experience life, but personal empirical experiences of being on the threshold of death and not feeling this way are not important here, and they are not sufficient to refute Heidegger. In this respect, it is also clear that Heidegger's account of an authentic attitude towards death excludes the possibility of seeking to immerse ourselves in some transcendent figure, such as God, or the promise of salvation. Any reliance on the prospect of an afterlife is to ignore the significance of death and human finitude, not to courageously and resolutely face it.

Interestingly, Heidegger also states that we should anticipate death, rather than simply expecting it. The distinction being drawn here is quite subtle, but for him, anticipation is authentic, whereas expectation is inauthentic because it treats death as an actuality (an objective thing that happens to everyone) rather than as our "ownmost possibility". For Heidegger, we must recognize that we are, right now, a being-towards-death. We must live our lives facing this recognition that our present is pervaded by the horizon of death because he suggests that it is antici-pation of death that individualizes *Dasein* and lends a wholeness and integrity to life. To show why this is so, it is necessary to reconsider the phenomenon of anxiety, or *Angst*, but this time in relation to the prospect of our own death.

Anxiety and the authentic apprehension of death

For Heidegger, an authentic apprehension of death tends to result in (or be motivated by) anxiety, bearing in mind that anxiety must be dis-tinguished from fear, as fear relates to the possibility of external things harming us, whereas anxiety is a trepidation before our many and varied possibilities. However, Heidegger's point is not to suggest that death itself is an explicit object of *Angst*. Rather, it is more that the prospect of death occasions anxiety in relation to our general manner of being-in-the-world. Again, he is not concerned with the event of death, but with life in relation to the prospect of that event, and against Sartre and Epicurus he holds that we need not be at an end to realize that we are going to end. That is why we are a being-towards-death, not a being-at-death or a being-in-death.

Why then does Heidegger think that in anxiety we authentically apprehend death? The experience illuminates that death is not chosen by us, but is thrown or forced upon us. As we have seen, we usually try to avoid a full understanding of what it means to die by immersing ourselves in common platitudes such as "everyone will die", and this is part of a more general tendency – fallenness – to consider ourselves as simply one among many. In *Angst*, however, Heidegger points out that we no longer feel at home in this world and in the anonymity of the masses. The anonymity of day-to-day life is torn away (Heidegger does not think this experience is particularly common) and we find ourselves alone with the "they-self" stripped away. In this regard, an authentic apprehension of death individuates us by destroying our illu-sion of having a fixed and stable identity that is grounded by societal mores, our status within that society and the various conventions that undergird daily social existence: idle chatter, vacuous politeness and so on. Anxiety forces us to retreat from the assumption that our identity is given by these forms of interaction and, in Heidegger's terms, it reveals *Dasein*'s "certain possibility of having no necessary possibilities", and thereby makes us see that the meaning of our existence is dependent upon us alone.

Death individuates us: no one else can die for me

Recognizing that I must die, rather than just that everybody dies, entails a way of comprehending myself as an individual, rather than simply one among the crowd. In order to understand Heidegger's point, imagine for a moment that you are condemned to death. Clearly that would be a very strange experience, and in this regard it is helpful to think again about Camus's *The Outsider*. Towards the end it becomes clear that being condemned to death liberates the main character, Meursault, but it could also be very frightening. And yet why is it that in our day-to-day lives we rarely experience this recognition? We all know we are going to die, just as Meursault does as he awaits his execution. The only difference is that we do not know exactly when we are going to die, whereas he does (of course, he may be pardoned while awaiting his fate). In this regard, Heidegger suggests that the "they-self" avoids an authentic comprehension of death by manipulating the indefiniteness of the time of death – we do not know when it is going to happen, and hence do not fully cognize that we are going to die – but he also argues that this is surely a sleight of hand.

It is important to note that when Heidegger comments that "no one else can die for me", he is not subject to empirical refutation, such as in the example of a historical martyr who died for their friend. He means that no one else can die for me, in the sense of living in anticipation of death for me. As we have seen, this idea of anticipating death is crucial to his account of an authentic and resolute apprehension of death, as well as for meaningfully organizing our lives and imbuing them with an individual significance beyond "average everydayness".

KEY POINT *Heidegger on death*
- Death is very much my own – it is my "ownmost".
- Death cannot be shared by others – it is non-relational.
- Death is a possibility that cannot be avoided – it is inevitable (no other possibilities are like this and retain their status as possibilities).

Conscience and guilt

We have seen that, for Heidegger, freedom is something of a burden, not least because it deprives us of our habitual comfort zones. As a result of this burden, and because of the anonymity that is necessarily involved in the ready-to-hand, we tend to avoid making choices and instead are carried along with the crowd. At least to some extent we are hence inevitably ensnared in inauthenticity. On what basis, then, can we be hopeful about possibilities for authenticity, given that Heidegger argues that authentically being-one's-self takes the form of an existential modification of the "they-self"? What resources can *Dasein* draw on to be authentic, recalling Heidegger's general principle that the source of authenticity must be available to each and every *Dasein*, and must lie within the range of that which is already partly understood? He argues that this potential for authentically being-one's-self is attested to by the experience of conscience. To put the point crudely, conscience and guilt are the bases that allow us to find our authentic self, bearing in mind that this self is not a static, pre-given identity of any sort.

Of course, the notion of a "conscience" has a long and complicated theological and sociocultural history, but Heidegger's understanding of conscience is importantly distinct from these moral perspectives. On his view, conscience is described simply as a "call", as an appeal to *Dasein* to take note of *Dasein*'s individual possibilities and potential: in other words, to take responsibility. This phenomenon of conscience gives us something to understand (much as mood does) and Heidegger insists that it cannot be reductively explained away by biology or psychology. Nor, he suggests, can an empirical proof of conscience be expected. On his view, that is to leave the ontological level and to attempt to make the phenomena something purely present-at-hand.

Heidegger comments that, strictly speaking, the call of conscience says nothing, and gives no information about world events. Rather, in a famous phrase he says that the self is summoned, or called, to its "ownmost potentiality-for-Being" (BT: §56). On his analysis, *Dasein* is simultaneously both that which is called and that which is doing the calling. While this formulation presents some logical difficulties, we might say that *Dasein* as its "ownmost potentiality" and radically individualized (D1), calls *Dasein* as fallen and a they-self (D2). No doubt this is overly schematic, but it is clear that on his view the caller (D1) is radically unfamiliar to the they-self and the everyday world. Indeed, it is this feature that allows Heidegger to explain how we can feel the call of conscience against our "will" and much to our own chagrin. As he says, "the call comes from me and yet beyond me" (BT: §57), and he makes explicit that the call of conscience either addresses *Dasein* as guilty, as possibly guilty (e.g. a warning) or as conscious of no guilt (e.g. a good conscience) (BT: §58).

Importantly, Heidegger also consistently reaffirms that conscience paradoxically discourses in the mode of keeping silent (BT: §58), as Kierkegaard had argued at length before him in *Fear and Trembling* and Derrida has also more recently emphasized in *The Gift of Death*. For Heidegger, the call cannot be reported and he even suggests that the concept of a world conscience, or a public conscience, is a dubious fabrication. He goes on to argue that the more the call is understood non-relationally (as death must also be understood), the less *Dasein* is perverted by considerations of acceptability, prudence in a context, or fitting in within a society (BT: §58). Conscience hence individualizes in much the same way as anxiety and Heidegger reaffirms that authenticity is non-relational. This individualism is arguably a defining trait of existentialism despite the transcendental rejection of solipsism in the work of Heidegger (see the idea of *Mitsein*), as well as in Sartre's analysis of the experience of shame.

The experiences of conscience and guilt make the "I" concrete and give it a lived and existential significance, and the important question then becomes one regarding how we should respond to guilt. We could deny that our behaviour was free by pointing to external causes or some version of psychological determinism, but that would be inauthentic on Heidegger's view. That said, authentically confronting guilt is also far from simply engaging in self-flagellation and accusing ourselves of past misdeeds. These are both fallen interpretations of conscience. Seeking to find others, or ourselves, guilty of infractions of rules and regulations, for past mistakes, is what the "they-self" inauthentically does. To be authentic we must want to have a conscience, but not a good conscience. We must be ready to be appealed to, and ready for *Angst* and conscience, but not too quick to establish that we are either forever empirically guilty (i.e. indebted) or forever liberated from guilt.

Heidegger also claims that ethics and morals emerge from a consideration of guilt, rather than the other way around, as has been traditionally supposed by various philosophers who have argued that the experience of guilt presupposes an ethical code that has been transgressed. In this respect, Michael Gelven captures the issue at hand well when he asks: "Is it that I first find out or learn what I ought to do, and then feel guilty if I violate that maxim; or is that I first feel a call to be good or authentic, and then establish a moral order to satisfy this desire?" (Gelven 1989: 161).

For Heidegger, the latter is the case, but we do not feel impelled to be good for selfish or hedonic reasons, such as in order to maximize happiness, or even to maximize the welfare of all sentient beings, as some utilitarians hold. Rather, we all have a tacit understanding of authenticity and an awareness of what it means to be from the "beginning". This ontological priority of guilt over morality is what ensures that his project remains one of fundamental ontology and it also means that the experience of guilt is not reducible to the fear of reprisals from those who have been harmed, or to a feeling of indebtedness to them or to society at large; an understanding of guilt must be detached from any understanding of law, moral obligation or the "ought" because it is the basis on which these are constructed.

Resoluteness

"Resoluteness" is Heidegger's term for authentically being-one's-self. For English speakers, it carries connotations of having made up our mind and of decision-making resolve. This impression is not altogether false in regard to Heidegger's understanding of the term, but at the same time it needs to be emphasized that the experiences of conscience and guilt are the grounds for resoluteness and this means that resoluteness will never be arrogant self-assertion or dogmatism. Moreover, although it comes from, and is motivated by, the individualizing of conscience and guilt, resoluteness does not detach *Dasein* from the world. In fact, Heidegger declares that it is nothing other than being-in-the-world and that resolute *Dasein* "frees itself *for* its world" (BT: §60). He goes on to argue that it is resoluteness that brings us to solicitude, because it is only through authentically being-one's-self that we can authentically be with others. This is a sentiment that also plays a large role in the work of de Beauvoir, but in order to clarify what he means by resoluteness Heidegger also suggests that only for the resolute is there what he calls a "situation". The "they-self", on the other hand, know of the generality of the habitus but know nothing of the situation, as a situation is always particularized by an individualized being that anticipates various possibilities. Anticipating is very important to establishing the mood of resoluteness, as it involves actively going toward futural possibilities and always already taking action, rather than passively waiting for things to come to you. Ultimately, Heidegger suggests that to be authentic is to exist in anticipatory resoluteness.

"Letter on Humanism"

Heidegger's 1945 essay "Letter on Humanism" was, among other things, a response to Sartre's *Existentialism is a Humanism* and to a quick reading of *Being and Nothingness* (nearly all of the pages of Heidegger's copy of this book were not cut, as they needed to be in those days before the book could be read). Basically, Heidegger argues that this version of existentialism that focuses on human consciousness bears no relation to his own thought, which in *Being and Time*, and more obviously beyond this text, had left such anthropological commitments behind. He also suggests that Sartre's favoured existentialist formula – existence precedes essence – simply reverses Platonism and is therefore still a form of metaphysics rather than a fundamental ontology. "Letter on Humanism" has been a very influential text in contemporary French thought, influencing both structuralists and poststructuralists alike in their appraisals of Sartre and existentialism, and this reception will be examined in Chapter 7.

Summary of key points

The ontico-ontological difference
- Ontical enquiry – examines entities, or beings.
- Ontological enquiry – examines that which allows entities to be, or Being.

Dasein
- *Dasein*'s essence is its existence (*Dasein* stands out from mere immersion in the world, and does not have objective attributes or essences that can adequately define it).
- *Dasein* understands itself in terms of its existence (its possibility to be, or not be, itself).
- *Dasein* is in each case mine, in that there is a specificity and an individuality about experiences (*my* decision, *my* responsibility, etc.).

The ready-to-hand and the present-at-hand
- Ready-*to*-hand – a practical relation to objects and the world as an "equipmental totality".
- Present-*at*-hand – a more abstract relation to objects in which they are not defined by their involvement in human activity and instead take on an "objective presence".

Three essential characteristics of mood (state of mind)
- Disclosure of thrownness and facticity (we cannot do without moods).

- Disclosure of being-in-the-world as a whole (this makes possible projects and directing oneself toward things).
- Disclosure that what *Dasein* encounters matters to *Dasein*.

Authenticity and inauthenticity
- Authenticity involves an individualizing sense of "mineness" – e.g. *my* decision – as well as a recognition of wholeness (BT: §12), because it assumes, rather than flees from, the finitude and groundlessness of *Dasein's* existence.
- Authentic existence is also grounded predominantly in possibility, whereas inauthentic existence is grounded predominantly in actuality (such as when the self is construed as an object or mere thing).
- Authentic existence is aware of the meaning of existence, whereas the inauthentic is not.

Anxiety
In the experience of anxiety, we are forced to confront our own thrownness and finitude. This individualizes us because we no longer feel at home in the world of the ready-to-hand, of *das Man*, and the many.

Death
- Death is very much my own – it is my "ownmost".
- Death cannot be shared by others – it is non-relational.
- Death is a possibility that cannot be avoided – it is inevitable (no other possibilities are like this and retain their status as possibilities).
- An authentic existence requires the recognition that we are beings-towards-death

three

Condemned to freedom:
Sartre's phenomenological ontology

According to several commentators, Jean-Paul Sartre (1905–80) has been read more widely in his own lifetime than any other philosopher in the history of philosophy, and around 100,000 people paid tribute to him at his funeral in Paris. He is also arguably the only self-proclaimed existentialist, at least of the major historical figures associated with the tradition, even if it is true that his initial acceptance of the label consisted largely in a begrudging assent to the media proliferation of the term with which Marcel had first described him and his partner, de Beauvoir. That said, Sartre is rightly considered to be the canonical existentialist, both in terms of public reception (he regularly graced the pages of *Vogue* in the US in the 1950s and was synonymous with French intellectual life), and academically, where his opus *Being and Nothingness: An Essay on Phenomenological Ontology* (1943) still stands as the iconic and defining work of the tradition.

Being and Nothingness was partly inspired by Sartre's encounter with Heidegger's *Being and Time* while he was a prisoner of war. Sartre's main influences in this work are Heidegger, Husserl and Hegel, but it is difficult to determine to what extent each of them influenced him, largely because Sartre's interpretations of them are always creative and do a certain violence to their texts (this is perhaps why Heidegger's response to Sartre in "Letter on Humanism" is so scathing). Although it is true that Sartre had published philosophical work of great acumen before *Being and Nothingness* – most notably his monograph, *Transcendence of the Ego* (1938), as well as work on the imagination and the emotions, and the enormously popular novel *Nausea* (1938) – it was *Being and Noth-*

ingness that established his reputation philosophically speaking, and that gave French existentialism its foundation. It is also with this text, which he published in 1943, that we will primarily be concerned here, although his later book, *Critique of Dialectical Reason* (1960), engages in a sophisticated rapprochement of his existentialism and Marxism.

All of the previously mentioned existential themes dominate this book: freedom; death, finitude and mortality; phenomenological experiences such as anguish, nausea and so on; an emphasis on themes pertaining to authenticity, responsibility and the denigration of bad faith; a pessimism regarding human relations; and a rejection of any external determination of morality or value, including conceptions of God and the emphasis on rationality of the Enlightenment. Indeed, more than is the case with Heidegger, Sartre emphasizes the importance of the individual and attributes to human existence an ontological freedom that cannot be diminished. In the process, these main existential themes are also emphasized to a greater extent than was the case with Heidegger (with the exception of death), and they are also cast in a starker light. This partly explains the unprecedented popularity and public recognition that Sartre enjoyed in the 1940s and 1950s, although his works of literature and ongoing political engagements were also significant in this respect.

The method of phenomenological ontology

Sartre's subtitle to *Being and Nothingness* is "an essay on phenomenological ontology", and this reflects his indebtedness to Heidegger, who argues that the only genuine ontology is a phenomenology. Sartre argues that there is a distinction between his own method of phenomenological ontology, which describes the structures of existence, and metaphysics, which speculates about what is beyond or behind appearances. However, "phenomenological ontology" remains a curious description of Sartre's project. After all, he seems to begin this book with a quite elaborate metaphysics, or, more generously, ontology, in that he names and describes several different kinds of being. This includes his guiding distinction between Being and Nothingness, but on the human level he also makes ontological distinctions between being-for-itself, being-in-itself and being-for-others. These are held to be fundamental categories from the beginning of his enquiry, or they are presupposed as categories (except for being-for-others, which is introduced at a later stage in his book, and might be said to be "discovered" via the more traditional phenomenological method of attending to experience). Recall that phenomenology, at least for Husserl, claims to bracket away any unnecessary theoretical postulations (including any preconceived metaphysics), and instead aims at attending to experience, before discerning the essential aspects, or necessary conditions, of that experience. At least in places, Sartre's method in *Being and Nothingness* seems to move in the opposite direction and this is something that Merleau-Ponty has argued at length. Can Sartre reconcile his elaborate metaphysical system with his position as an avowed phenomenologist, and a Husserlian phenomenologist at that? There is no clear answer to this question, but a couple of things need to be pointed out. First, and most obviously, Sartre does not think that any sustained reduction to the things themselves is possible. This is why he, like Merleau-Ponty, portrays his method as one of existential phenomenology as opposed to "pure" phenomenology. Moreover, despite problematizing the reduction he nevertheless holds true to Husserl's technique of argumentation in other ways, and this will become apparent as we consider the details of his philosophical position.

Existence precedes essence

Somewhat after Sartre had become a famous philosopher, novelist and playwright, but well before he turned down the Nobel Prize for Literature in 1964, some conservative French newspapers began to lament that he was pushing a nihilistic philosophy of anguish and despair. In a public lecture in 1945, subsequently published as *Existentialism is a Humanism* in 1946, Sartre responded to such claims and in the process he offered perhaps the defining account of existentialism, while also giving it an ethical impetus – declaring that no one is free until all are – that although not so apparent in *Being and Nothingness* would soon be developed by de Beauvoir's *The Ethics of Ambiguity* (1947). He argued that existentialism is typified by a relatively simple dictum: that man's existence precedes his essence (EH; cf. BN: 25, 568). In more gender-neutral terms, this simply means that human beings have no soul, nature, self or essence that makes us what we are. We simply are, without any such constraints making us exist in any particular fashion, and it is only later that we come to accord our existence any essence.

Sartre develops his point by comparison with a triangle and a pen. Both triangles and pens have a form, essence or function that precedes their concrete existence. For example, for something to be a triangle it must first have a certain essential form: it will involve three corners and all of the corners add up to 180 degrees. Against Plato and his various successors, Sartre argues emphatically that this is not the case for human beings, whose way of being-in-the-world is distinct from all else, hence the humanism mentioned in his essay title (Sartre does not deal with either the question of animals or issues to do with childhood development, unlike, for example, Merleau-Ponty). For Sartre, human existence precedes essence, which is to say that we exist first and thereafter define our essence by the way in which we live.

KEY POINT
Triangles (and all objects) have a form, essence or function that precedes their concrete existence. For something to be a triangle it must have three corners, and all of the corners must add up to 180 degrees. For something to be a pen, it must potentially be able to perform the function of writing. Sartre argues that this is not the case for human beings. Our *existence precedes our essence*, which is to say that we exist first, and thereafter define our essence by the way in which we live.

This suggestion that we do not come into the world with a predefined self, soul or essence runs counter to much of the Western philosophical tradition. Indeed, in his early essay *Transcendence of the Ego*, Sartre explicitly targets the Cartesian "I think therefore I am", which emphasizes just such a self, as well as its contemporary Husserlian manifestation. Against these accounts, Sartre argues that there is a disjunction between the "I think" and the "I am" in the Cartesian *cogito*, such that the consciousness that says "I am" is not, or at least is not necessarily, the consciousness that says "I think". In other words, he thinks that there are two fundamentally different and irreconcilable modes of consciousness (which he will term the reflective and the pre-reflective), and that Descartes has conflated these into one without any supporting arguments. For Sartre, the original or primary mode of consciousness is what he calls the pre-reflective cogito, which is where we experience the world without a conception of the self, or ego, betrothed to it. The second mode of consciousness is the reflective cogito, which posits a self in order to reflect on past experiences.

KEY POINT
Sartre distinguishes two modes of consciousness: the *pre-reflective cogito* (which does not involve an ego or self); and the *reflective cogito* (which posits a self and unifies past disparate experiences).

The main point to take from this is that in our primary way of encountering the world, there is no self. We simply pre-reflectively gaze out the window, for example, and have no phenomenological experience of our own selfhood, nor any access to ourselves as a metaphysically enduring subject. On the other hand, when through memory we recall events, such as our gazing through the window a few hours previously, we retrospectively give ourselves a self by imposing a unity on the temporal sequence (reflective cogito), but this has no ontological or metaphysical status. But what precisely is Sartre's view of consciousness? To some extent the answer to this question depends on our forthcoming discussion of negation, but his view can be represented as in the following key point.

KEY POINT *Sartre on consciousness*

For Sartre, all consciousness and every intending act is both: (i) positionally (or thetically) aware of the object that it posits – consciousness is directed at and has a bearing towards some object, such as the scenery being observed; and (ii) non-positionally (non-thetically) aware of itself as awareness – it is indirectly aware that it is *not* that object that it is perceiving or positing.

Note that although the second aspect of consciousness means that self-consciousness is involved in any and every aspect of consciousness – as consciousness is always aware of itself, "aware of being aware" – there is no substantive content to this awareness. Moreover, this awareness does not entail, or require, that an ego be involved with a conscious relation to the object, and phenomenological description of this mode of consciousness hence cannot establish the existence of a self or ego.

In some respects, this is a Humean position on the subject, but Sartre does not go as far as to suggest that the self is just a bundle of perceptions, or that it is a bundle of drives as Nietzsche, for example, thought. For Sartre, there is a unity to consciousness, although his eventual explanation of why this is so requires elaboration on the significant role that he accords to the idea of a fundamental project in the final chapters of *Being and Nothingness*. For our present purposes it is enough to point out that one of the main consequences that Sartre draws from this lack of self, essence or nature is that human existence is completely and irrevocably free. For him:

> Human freedom precedes essence in man and makes it possible; the essence of human being is suspended in his freedom. What we call freedom is impossible to distinguish from the being of "human reality". Man does not exist first in order to be free subsequently; there is no difference between the being of man and his being free … (BN 25)

For Sartre, with no essence defining us we are free to pursue whatever essence we desire, at least within an intersubjective world, and it is this philosophy of absolute freedom that has been Sartre's most famous and enduring contribution to the history of philosophy. His philosophy of freedom pervades the entirety of *Being and Nothingness*, roughly separating into three main aspects that will be considered in what follows: ontological arguments for freedom; phenomenological apprehensions of freedom; and discussions of "concrete" or situated freedom.

Humanity is condemned to be free

Not only are we free but, as Sartre expresses it multiple times, we are "condemned to be free". This may seem somewhat contradictory considering that he holds that it is human existence that inaugurates value in the world, but all Sartre means is that we cannot relinquish this freedom even if we want to. Given this declaration of our radical freedom, it needs to be pointed out that Sartre is not ignoring the fact that we are born in a situation, with certain physical and social dispositions. We might be poor, oppressed by the Nazi regime, enslaved by colonialism, or in any other situation you can imagine. However, for Sartre, this is what he terms our "facticity" – the sum of "facts" about us, including our social situation and physical circumstances – and it in no way undermines our freedom. This is because, according to Sartre, we cannot have freedom without a context, and we can always rebel against this oppression, and struggle to interpret it in several different ways. Perhaps a good example of this is that even while we are being tortured, Sartre argues that we still have several different possible modes of action open to us. For example, we may want to immerse ourselves completely in our pain and, indeed, consider ourselves as nothing but this pain. On the contrary, we may also attempt to ignore this pain and look defiantly into the eyes of our persecutor, and there are innumerable other examples of the different ways we can behave in such a situation. For Sartre, the situation we find ourselves in does not limit our freedom but, according to his definition of freedom (which has clear antecedents in Descartes and Kant), simply provides the context for us to exercise this freedom. Freedom then is something absolute, which cannot be compromised or limited. Even when imprisoned, we are still free in that we can form different intentions to act, as well as the values that motivate those actions. On this account we cannot either gain or lose our freedom, which is constitutive of human existence, and his more sustained arguments for this position are considered below in the section "Tripartite argument for freedom".

KEY POINT

Sartre declares that we are "*condemned to be free*", which is to argue that our freedom is not something that can be either gained or lost, but is a necessary aspect of being human.

In Sartre's own more complicated terminology, freedom is the condition of human existence, which is defined by, as he says, a "being which is what it is not and is not what it is" (BN: 79). This statement has a temporal significance that will be explained throughout, but part of what this phrase means is that we are not just the facts of our lives because we choose the meaning of these facts about ourselves. Human existence, for Sartre, is hence typified not only by what he calls our facticity, but more by the negation of this facticity: by the suggestion that I am *not* just the sum of facts about me at this present moment. We are getting into somewhat difficult territory here, but this is simply Sartre's suggestion that a human being is never just his or her history, or his or her circumstances. To clarify why he thinks this is the case, it is necessary to turn to his ontology.

Ontology of human existence

I have attempted to make the early parts of this chapter reasonably accessible, but it is time to explicate a couple of more difficult terms, as well as the fundamental ontology, or system of metaphysics, that Sartre constructs in *Being and Nothingness*. Ontology in the traditional, non-Heideggerian sense refers to the structure of that which *is*, or the study of the way things are, and in Sartre's case it is closely related to a traditional metaphysics, which is summarized in the following key point.

KEY POINT

Sartre thinks that humanity is fundamentally composed of two different, but often inseparable, aspects: our *facticity* (i.e. our past, our biology, our possessions, the society we are a part of, etc.); and our freedom to negate and, sometimes, to interpret this facticity, which he describes elsewhere as our *transcendence*.

It is part of our *facticity* that we are born into a certain society, with certain physical and social attributes, and that we find ourselves in situations not directly of our choosing. However, for Sartre, human existence always *transcends*, or moves beyond (negates, or nihilates to use Sartre's term) these facts about our circumstances. We are always *free* to think of other possibilities, other kinds of lives, and to negate the given situation that we are currently in. Human existence must always transcend these brute facts about our lives that we cannot change. We can, and must, always leap beyond these facts to create further projects, and we are always free to interpret these facts in various different ways. The fact that we may be blind, or poor, does not, according to Sartre at least, fix our identity or causally determine us to react to this in any one particular way. Sartre claims that for us to be able to interpret these facts in a different way we must put them at a distance from ourselves: in Sartre's terms we negate, or nihilate, our facticity.

The glossary of definitions written by Hazel E. Barnes (the translator) in *Being and Nothingness* is a helpful resource for clarifying some of the technical terms that Sartre employs, but Sartre's fundamental claim is that human consciousness functions through *negating* these facts. In other words, I am *not* just the sum of my past successes, not just a certain job or role that I fulfil, and any human subject, for Sartre, is always aspiring towards and projecting future goals, and this is only possible by negating that which *is*. As we will see, a human being who simply rested content with their past would be in bad faith for Sartre: that is, they would be denying their freedom, and he thinks that they are exercising their freedom in their very attempt to deny it.

Being-for-itself and being-in-itself

To introduce some terms that have not yet been considered, and that are not exactly synonymous with this distinction between transcendence and facticity, Sartre argues that there are two fundamental categories involved in human existence – being-for-itself and being-in-itself – although a third category that is irreducible to the above two will be introduced in Chapter 4: being-for-others. Unlike the relationship between Being and Nothingness that we will soon consider, the for-itself and the in-itself are envisaged as completely separate.

Being-for-itself, as the term suggests, refers to creatures that are something for themselves, that are self-reflective, but it cannot be restricted merely to reflective consciousness. Rather, the for-itself refers to all consciousness. Sartre suggests that the being of the for-itself is freedom, and it functions by negating the in-itself; in his own terms, the for-itself is continually determining itself *not to be* the in-itself. It is not a substantive entity and exists only by knowing what it is not, by "judging" other beings. To re-employ some of our earlier terms, the for-itself transcends the given, or that which *is*, and negates our facticity. But if consciousness exists only by negating the in-itself and facticity (these are not synonyms), then consciousness is always and necessarily situated in terms of its being-in-the-world.

Being-in-itself, on the other hand, refers to objects and more generally to everything that is not consciousness. It is a "pure plenitude" and, according to Sartre, we cannot properly speak of it. To refine our earlier definition, our facticity is the relationship between the for-itself (transcendence) and the in-itself (brute objects). For Sartre, we can talk about and describe our facticity, but we cannot speak of the object as it is in-itself: that is, as it is outside certain human ways of understanding and comprehending that object. In this respect Sartre is feeding into a long tradition of philosophy that dates back to Kant's discussions of "the thing in itself". For Kant, there is a brute thing, or a brute reality out there, but we always encounter it through specific human faculties for understanding and, as Husserl emphasized, in terms of our various aims and intentions in the world. This means that we cannot neutrally perceive reality as it is, although such a reality is there notwithstanding our inability to access it.

KEY POINT

- *Being-for-itself* – free and transcendent consciousness, which negates both our facticity and objects.
- *Being-in-itself* – pure objecthood, or "pure plenitude", about which we cannot say much, except that it is contingent and without reason.
- *Facticity* – refining our earlier definition, it designates the relationship between the for-itself and the in-itself, and this incorporates our social situation.
- *Being-for-others* (to be discussed in Chapter 4).

Recall that ontology is the study of Being, or, less esoterically, the study of the way that things are. For Sartre, this for-itself and in-itself structure is the way that things are in human existence. Now there is a sense in which this appears to be a dualism in that there is a subject–object distinction being drawn here. It is for this reason that Sartre's work is often considered Cartesian, despite his own protestations to the contrary, and this is something that Merleau-Ponty also argues, as we will see in Chapter 5.

Tripartite argument for freedom, and the ontology of Being and Nothingness

The key to understanding the early parts of *Being and Nothingness* is to pay particular attention to Part 1, Chapter 1, "The Problem of Nothingness". (The introductory chapter "The Pursuit of Being" is notoriously difficult to read and best avoided until one is familiar with the rest of Sartre's philosophical framework.) On reading "The Problem of Nothingness", you will notice that there are three main arguments that Sartre proposes for why we are free, which revolve around the themes of: (i) questioning; (ii) absence; (iii) destruction. All of these depend on the for-itself's capacity for negation. Sartre's project of foregrounding the importance of Nothingness and negation has forerunners, most obviously in Hegel, but also in Heidegger. In *Being and Time*, for example, Heidegger asks, "Has anyone ever made a problem of the ontological source of notness, or, prior to that, even sought the mere conditions on the basis of which the problem of the 'not' and its notness and the possibility of that notness can be raised?" (BT: 332). It could be suggested that Sartre attempts this very project.

(i) Questioning (BN: 1–8, 23–4)

One of the first things worth noting in Sartre's "Introduction" is that he thinks that there is something profoundly important about the ability to pose a question. Now, this should immediately remind us of the father of "modern" philosophy, René Descartes. Descartes famously argued that the simple fact that I can never doubt my own existence provides the only possible certainty. When I doubt or question my existence in the world, I cannot nevertheless doubt that I am thinking. For Sartre, it is this posing of the question itself that is ontologically important, not epistemologically important; in other words, the question that concerns him is not the Cartesian one about knowledge and its limits. Even in more recent times, Sartre is not original in according such importance to the question. We have seen that Heidegger also argues that questioning is a constitutive aspect of *Dasein*. *Dasein* is the only being for whom its being is in question, and this is also why Heidegger accords philosophy, or at least a certain kind of thinking in his later work, such an important role. Heidegger thinks that the question "Why the why?" as in "Why ask the question why at all?" is one of the more profound that we can ask, although some other philosophers have accused Heidegger of navel-gazing in this respect. While it is important to recall that Sartre does not want to say that we have any universal human essence, there are neverthe-less universal ontological truths of the human situation, of which the phe-nomenon of questioning highlights an important one: negation. Sartre argues that the question introduces negativity into the world or, as he says, reveals non-thing-ness in the world, in at least three different ways, which will be explored below and can be characterized as follows:

1. *Every question contains the possibility of a negative reply.*
   First, Sartre argues that every question presupposes two things: something that is questioned and someone that is doing the ques-tioning. A question also always expects a reply. Among other possibilities, it can be a yes or a no. The reply may be negative, and therein lies the first negation, or non-being, that the ques-tion introduces. If I ask "Are you enjoying this book?", the answer may simply be "No" (although hopefully not), and that is the first and most obvious negation. Sartre suggests that even the question that he is posing in this first chapter of *Being and Nothingness* – Is there a fundamental relation of humanity to the world? – neces-sarily admits the possibility of a negative answer; there may be no fundamental relation of humanity to the world (BN: 5).

2. *Every genuine question presupposes a state of indetermination, of not knowing the answer.*
   There is a second type of negation brought into play by the ques-tion. It is not just that the answer to a particular question might be "No", but it is also significant that by asking a question the questioner puts themselves in, or at least admits, a state of indeter-mination (BN: 5): that is, a state of not-knowing what the answer is (second negation).

3. *Every question has an answer, and that answer imposes a limitation on the world.*
   Finally, Sartre suggests that any question also presupposes that there is, in fact, a truth of the matter (BN: 5). By asking "What time is it?" we tacitly accept that there is a truthful time, even if we cannot currently figure out what that truth is. That is why scepti-cism is incoherent on a lived and practical level. You cannot live

doubting everything, even if Descartes could briefly do so theoretically (and this is also arguable). This fact that the question presumes that there is a truth of the matter and that the answer to a particular question is "Yes" or "No", means that whatever answer may be given, a limitation is introduced into the world (this is the third negation).

If this is not obvious, consider the following question: are there unicorns in Australia? If the answer is "No, there are no unicorns in Australia", a limitation is set on the world. If the answer is "Yes, there are unicorns in Australia", then indeed there are unicorns in Australia, but that also limits the world: Australia cannot be a place where there are not unicorns.

KEY POINT
Sartre concludes that the question introduces a triple negation or non-being into the world: negative reply; indetermination, or not knowing the answer; and it creates a limitation on the world.

Sartre concludes from this that there is negation, non-being, and he will go on to argue that we are encompassed by Nothingness. This need not be some mystical state; simply read "Nothingness" as it sounds: nothing-ness. Questioning and the capacity for negation are not reducible to *things*, or objects that have an essence, and Sartre hence argues that within Being (defined as the totality of that which *is*) it is necessary that there be some kind of gap, or Nothingness, and it is this Nothingness that allows negation and nihilation to take place. This then, is an ontological point. By analysing human existence it becomes apparent that we negate, and Sartre argues that this is only possible if Nothingness is part of the ontological structure of the human–world relation.

Now this is a difficult point that we will come back to, but there is an obvious response to this claim that Nothingness is a part of Being but is nevertheless not reducible to it. Someone might respond, "Sure, Jean-Paul, there is negation, but it is human judgement that introduces the negation". To use one of Sartre's own examples (BN: 6–7), when we open our wallets and find a certain amount of money missing, it is only through reflective judgement that we realize that we are missing something. In other words, the negation is imposed by human reflection and perhaps there is hence no need to talk about some ontological category called Nothingness that makes negation possible. The proponent of this type of theory, which has a long history in philosophy, could claim that Being is just positivity and that Nothingness does not exist in its own right. Nothingness is not part of the ontological structure of our world, as Sartre claims that it is, but is simply the secondary absence of something, in this case Being.

So the question that Sartre must ask is: does the human capacity for negation introduce Nothingness, or is the human capacity for negation only possible because there is an ontological category called Nothingness? Sartre concludes the latter. He does not dispute that negation depends upon human *anticipation*, but he thinks that it is pre-judicative; that is, he argues that we have an apprehension of Nothingness prior to reflective human *judgement* (BN: 7). He points out that we can question (or negate) simply by a look, or a gesture, and without reflectively considering it. Moreover, for Sartre we also question things, or objects, when they break down. For example, we peer inquisitively at the carburettor, or spark plugs, or the fuel tank, when our car is not performing as well as it should, or has broken down (BN: 7). According to Sartre, questioning in this way is inconceivable if we cannot disassociate from the causal order of the world. The questioner must affect a kind of withdrawal from the thing that is being questioned; for example, when you are peering at the fuel tank to see if it has run out of petrol, you distance yourself from the fuel tank (nihilate it in Sartre's language) and place it is a state of neutrality in order to judge it. In that sense, human beings are the being through which Nothingness comes to the world. More importantly though, to do this, to disengage from the given and to question objects as well as other people, he argues that we must be free. Sartre's rhetorical point goes something like this: how could we pose a question at all if we were determined? What resources could we use to reflect on, or distance ourselves from the situation, if the situation itself determines us? If you are not convinced by this attempted proof of our freedom, Sartre also provides two more examples to illustrate that Nothingness can be said to be an ontological category, and these are a little easier to grasp than his questioning example.

(ii) Destruction (BN: 8–9)

Imagine that the university building that you are currently studying "existentialism" in is suddenly destroyed by a storm, earthquake or a natural catastrophe of some magnitude. On a certain level it might be said that there is no destruction or, rather, that the mass of the university is simply redistributed. As Sartre suggests, on one level there is not *less* after the storm, just something else (BN: 8). What we apprehend on a pre-reflective, or a pre-judicative level – that is, before judgement

– is this destruction. Generally, we do not have to reflectively judge that a building has been destroyed, even if this sometimes undoubtedly is the case. We disengage from the "given" (that mass of rubble) to see it in terms of that which it is *not*: that being the university in its former glory (BN: 8). For him, human beings introduce the possibility of destruction into the world (and they simultaneously apprehend and introduce fragility into the world) as objectively there is just a change. But his claim is that this is not through an act of judgement. Rather, we apprehend the Nothingness, and we disengage from the given, prior to reflection. And again, Sartre's question is: how could we accomplish this if we were not free? How could we disengage from what is before us (i.e. simple rubble) to posit that which is not (i.e. the university intact), all in a single perception, if we were not free?

(iii) Absence (BN: 9–11, 27)

Sartre's example of Pierre's absence at a café is the most famous of his three examples of negation, although it is a little more difficult to understand than his destruction example. Basically, Sartre walks into a café, perhaps the famous "headquarters of existentialism" at Café de Flore on the boulevard St Germain, and finds that his friend is not there to meet him, as he had promised to be. Analogously, just imagine if it was 2.30pm, and your lecturer, who was due to begin the class at 2pm still had not shown up. It is not so much that you would have to make a reflective judgement that they were not there. While you might well do this at times, Sartre argues that when he walks into the café expecting his friend Pierre, he immediately has an intuition of Pierre's absence rather than making a rational, calculative judgement that Pierre is not present. When he looks at the next person to come in the door, he nihilates them; that is, he immediately sees them in terms of what they are not: Pierre. And nor is it that Sartre can find Pierre's absence in some precise spot in the café. His point is that this absence pervades the entire room and everything in it.

Now Sartre's expectation for Pierre to be there obviously in some sense caused the absence of Pierre to occur. But Sartre argues that he discovers the absence, again pre-judicatively. He finds it in the café, and it is, he says, an "objective fact for that moment" (BN: 10). Sartre says that if we try to play some kind of mental game, and flippantly judge, for example, that the pope or the president is also not in the café, while this is logically true it does not engage us in the same way (BN: 10). According to Sartre, this shows that judging that someone is not there through reflective thought is entirely different from phenomenologically finding and feeling that someone is absent. His point, again, is that we could not apprehend absence and perceive that which is not in the café were we not free, were consciousness not radically separate from the realm of things (BN: 27).

These, then, are the foundation for Sartre's later insistence on our radical freedom. All of his various examples of negation (i.e. questioning, destruction and absence) involve a rupture, or a break, from what is given, or from that which *is*, to posit that which is not given. He concludes from this that particular instances of negation are made possible by non-being (or Nothingness) and not the other way around. Nothingness is part of the ontology of the human–world relation, although it is human beings who are the beings by which Nothingness comes to things. Sartre hence argues that there are two fundamental ontological categories, which are, as the title of his book indicates, Being and Nothingness (BN: 21–5). It should not be too quickly assumed that this is a simple dualism, however. A dualistic ontology says there are two divided and separate sides (for example, the idea that good and evil are separate forces in the world). On the other hand, a monism argues that all is one, or that everything is made of the same stuff. Sartre wants to argue that Nothingness is an interruption within being, or in his own more literary terms, Nothingness "lies coiled in the heart of being like a worm" (BN: 21); it is like a monism with an internal split or divergence. Do not worry too much about this, however, as many philosophers argue that Sartre is actually dualistic and on the level of his concrete analysis of human beings he is more obviously so.

Concrete freedom (BN: 433–89)

In order to comprehend the radical implications that this ontology has for the question of human freedom, it is worth examining some of the more concrete examples of freedom that concern Sartre in the later stages of *Being and Nothingness*. Here Sartre discusses the technicalities of action, asserting that freedom is the first condition of action, and he again emphasizes that the freedom of which he speaks requires a *situation*. His account is against any strict causal determinism about action, but interestingly he also distances himself from traditional arguments for the freedom of the will on the grounds that freedom cannot be restricted to the mere exercise of the will, or of rational, calculative judgement. Rather, he insists that we are always and forever free, and that the decision to reflect and engage what is traditionally called the "will" is itself the result of a prior freedom and choice (BN: 444). His emphasis on the human capacity to "choose" the significance of a situation is not to suggest that every such choice implies a reflected-on decision. While Sartre does not want to refer to an unconscious life, the day-to-day choices that we make are often not reflected-on, rationalistic decisions, but according to Sartre, they are nevertheless choices. A choice, according to his definition, is said to be free, if it is such that it could have been other than what it is (BN: 453). Later on, he distances himself even further from any voluntaristic understanding of freedom as concerned with rational choice, provocatively stating that "voluntary deliberation is always a deception" (BN: 450). His arguments for freedom are hence not simply a modern rehashing of old themes.

According to one of Sartre's famous examples, we have the free capacity to interpret the cliff face that we encounter (and also all other objects and "facticity" of our world) in a number of different ways. Rather than being something that is a simple fact of the world, it is we who can determine what he terms, following Gaston Bachelard, the "coefficient of adversity" of the cliff face. However, this is not to suggest, in an idealistic manner, that we construct the world through our perception. For Sartre there is a reality there, but his point is that we can never see these purely physical attributes of a cliff; on the contrary, we always perceive the cliff in relation to its use for us, and our possible modes of conduct toward it. Sartre suggests that if we have made of ourselves an efficient climber, we see the cliff itself differently to the manner in which an inexperienced climber might see it. And we certainly see it vastly differently from how a landscape artist might view it, to offer merely some of the more obvious examples of how our perception of the cliff can differ (BN: 488).

We will come back to this example as Merleau-Ponty takes issue with it, but to put the suggestion in different and admittedly slightly less contentious terms, Sartre is arguing that as hard as we may try, we cannot see the broken shards of a beer bottle as simply the sum of its colour, shape and so on. The whole background apparatus of what that bottle is used for, what consuming the liquids contained therein means for different people, and even the social significance of what it is for something to be "broken", comes with, and not behind, our perception of that bottle. Perception, for Sartre (and the existentialists generally), is not a process where we attain access to some rarefied, pure object, or have a brute sensation following an encounter with that object, which is subsequently interpreted. Rather, we see objects in terms of their function, and the objects we encounter are always objects of a certain kind and construed in relation to ourselves. To return to Sartre's example of the cliff face, this simply means that it is we who have chosen to see the cliff in a certain way, both over a period of time in that we have rendered the cliff either climbable or unclimbable by the training we have undergone, and in the immediate instant that we approach the cliff, in that we choose whether the cliff is something to be climbed, appreciated for its aesthetic beauty or whatever else (BN: 482, 88–9). It is only in the light of the ends that we have posited through a free act of consciousness (climbing the cliff, appreciating its beauty, etc.), that the difficulties and constraints of that project are revealed to us (BN: 482).

But let us consider another example of this freedom and choice that Sartre argues for. In the later stages of *Being and Nothingness*, Sartre discusses two hikers who have been walking for hours on end and who are consequently very fatigued (BN: 453–7). According to Sartre's example, their fatigue is roughly equivalent, as are their respective physical capacities. Despite this, one person will inevitably give in to their pain and collapse to the ground before the other one, who might persist through the "pain barrier", see it as a challenge and keep walking. For such a person, Sartre comments, "doing is a method of appropriating" (BN: 455), anticipating his later account of the structure of action along the initially tripartite lines of doing, being and having (doing is soon revealed as reducible to the modes of being and having). More often than not, the person who has not given in to their pain will reproach their friend who has, suggesting that they were free to go on and implying that their act of dropping to the ground was not determined by any thing or person, and that they could have resisted their fatigue longer. They could, Sartre says, have done otherwise, and hence there was a choice. Fatigue by itself cannot cause the decision to stop walking (unless it induced fainting, but in that case there is no decision), and Sartre's point here is analogous to that which he was making in the torturer example. We suffer pain in both situations, but that pain does not determine how we will respond to it and whether it will be envisaged as a challenge that reveals the adversity of the mountains in a new light, or as an insurmountable impediment that is to be resented. For Sartre, fatigue is generally experienced as an indirect (non-positional or non-thetic) consciousness of the body. It *can* also become a direct (positional or thetic) object of our consciousness, in that we can deliberately reflect on the pain our body is undergoing (and this is what we tend do if we adopt a new end, such as the desire to rest rather than persist in the hike), but nothing can causally determine this ontological shift in perspective. As Sartre says, "no factual state whatever it may be is capable by itself of motivating any act whatsoever" (BN: 435, 459).

But there is a further important question that Sartre poses that complicates this account: could the bushwalker who collapsed to the ground have done otherwise without modifying the "organic totality of projects which they are" (BN: 454), or would it, on the contrary, have required a radical transformation of their being-in-the-world, a transformation that is possible but highly unlikely? In line with the latter possibility, Sartre admits that it might be responded that the person who gave in to their fatigue is a "sissy", and *essentially* so, while the other person who presses on is not. Of course, this kind of response will not satisfy Sartre. We do not have a given character, or essence, that determines our behaviour (as the for-itself is literally no-thing). As a consequence, no one is essentially courageous or cowardly; in the case we have considered, "sissy" is just a name given to the way that one person generally suffers their tiredness and fatigue, but for Sartre there is nothing dictating that this will be so in the future. Without contradicting this comment, it is worth noting that the final chapters of the section of *Being and Nothingness* entitled "Existential Psychoanalysis" go on to develop the notion of a fundamental project (BN: 557–75). In these passages, Sartre argues that although a fundamental project is freely chosen, it has a firm and relatively stable disposition. An inferiority complex is one way among others of choosing ourselves, but in the above example of the hikers it may well be likely to perpetuate itself.

Responsibility

It is important to recognize that, for Sartre, this freedom from being determined, this recognition that we alone confer meaning on an alarm clock in the morning, that we alone decide on what is moral or otherwise, that we alone decide on our own future (or at least its significance) entails heavy responsibility. Indeed, it is partly for this reason that he suggests that humanity is condemned to be free, for we bear entire responsibility for the events that befall us, since we alone have contributed to being there in that situation, with our particular capacities or otherwise, and we retain our capacity to negate our facticity. By not removing ourselves from a situation, for him, we have chosen it. He uses the example of war, and suggests that while we may have become involved in a war for many reasons, such as money, recklessness born of boredom, pressure from our family, patriotic fervour or any other reason that you can think of, at some level all of them involve a choice (BN: 554; EH). For Sartre, even our birth is chosen in the sense that we endow this fact of our existence with meaning – whether it is to be lamented or celebrated (BN: 556) – and this massive responsibility is confirmed when Sartre, somewhat provocatively, suggests that "there are no accidents" (BN: 554).

Sartre's concept of radical freedom may seem to be an extreme one, and for many contemporary philosophers it is overly so. Many hold that consistent oppression, or perhaps the omnipresent influence of capitalist ideology, can inhibit our ability to see different alternatives and can hence prevent the full expression of our freedom, as de Beauvoir argued in relation to the oppression of women. For Sartre, at least in *Being and Nothingness*, this is not the case (a consciousness that could not negate the "given", and their facticity, would not be human) and in this regard it is important to recognize the historical context of the Second World War and the German occupation of France, which motivated much of his theorizing. Sartre had been horrified at people disavowing responsibility for their situation, and his notion of absolute responsibility is an effort to awaken these people from their lethargy and their offhand acceptance that things are just happening to them. He wanted people, and the people of France in particular, to recognize that ultimately they could change their situation and were responsible, both collectively and individually, for the circumstances that befell them.

In fact, according to Sartre, we are responsible for everything except for the fact that we are responsible for everything (BN: 554). It is easy to see how the recognition of this absolute freedom and responsibility could be frightening or, as Sartre suggests, could tend to induce what he terms the experience of anguish, which bears many similarities with the Kierkegaardian and Heideggerian conceptions of dread, anxiety and *Angst*. After all, if humanity is conceived of as being absolutely free, then an individual cannot blame another person, or even misfortune, for the predicament they are in. Indeed, Sartre goes on to suggest that when we realize this it becomes senseless to complain since nothing foreign can decide what we feel, how we live and what we are (BN: 554). In other words, he wants us to live without appeal to fate, history, God, rationality, society or any such concept, but to assume ultimate responsibility for our every course of action, and this is an ethical insistence that he shares with Camus, notwithstanding their many other differences. It is difficult to see how this could be anything but intimidating and it is worth contemplating what the phenomenon of anguish means, for Sartre, since this will shed some light on exactly what significance the experience has for his philosophy. In this respect, it is important to remember that Sartre is still doing phenomenology; that is, describing the experiences of consciousness, and then seeking to explicate what is essential to, and necessary for, such experiences. Moreover, as an existential phenomenologist who is aiming to make Husserlian phenomenology less abstract and more "concrete", he is committed to the idea that Being will be disclosed to us by some kind of immediate experience, such as through the experiences of boredom, nausea, shame and, in the case to which we now turn, anguish (BN: xxiv).

Anguish

If, as Sartre suggests, the no-thing-ness of consciousness condemns us to freedom, and given that consciousness is always also consciousness of itself (indirectly or non-thetically), then there ought to be some kind of phenomenological apprehension of this freedom. For Sartre, that experience is anguish.

> **KEY POINT**
> The experience of *anguish* is a phenomenological apprehension of our own freedom, not a philosophical proof of it. It is in anguish that freedom is, in its being, in question for itself (BN: 29).

According to Sartre, anguish is importantly different from fear, as Kierkegaard and Heidegger have also argued. Sartre suggests that "fear is fear of beings in the world whereas anguish is anguish before myself" (BN: 29). In other words, we can fear being hurt by others, or fear a certain external situation conspiring against us, but we feel anguish before the prospect of how we might respond to a certain situation.

> **KEY POINT**
> *Anguish needs to be distinguished from fear*, although the adoption of the one attitude tends to be born in the failure of the other. Fear is an unreflective apprehension of the possibility that something in the world (and outside us) might harm us; anguish involves a reflective apprehension of the self and our freedom to respond to an external situation in any number of different ways.

Sartre's most famous example of anguish is an extreme one, but it involves a person walking along a vast cliff top. For him there are two main experiences we can have in this situation: we can be afraid of falling, of the path crumbling and ourselves falling to our deaths (this is fear of an external harm being done to us); or we can experience anguish at the possibility of jumping into the abyss, afraid, that is, of our own absolute freedom within a situation (this is anguish at the prospect of what we might ourselves do, and distrust of our own response to a given situation). Sartre describes the latter situation thus: "If nothing compels me to save my life, nothing prevents me from precipitating myself into the abyss. The decisive product will emanate from a self which I am not yet" (BN: 32). Do not worry too much about Sartre's terminology here. His references to different selves is part of his suggestion that what I currently am is not the foundation of what I will be in the future; the past does not cause me to act in any manner whatsoever, so each moment is perpetually a new one.

Another example that Sartre offers helps to clarify what is at stake in anguish. Rather than being afraid of being killed by the opposing soldiers, a new army officer on reporting for duty at the outbreak of war might be more "afraid of being afraid", filled with anguish before himself or herself (BN: 29). Anguish hence involves the recognition of freedom, as well as the realization of our own responsibility for our every possible course of action. It is the realization that nothing external can compel us to be or do anything (BN: 31–2), and consequently that the failures and successes of our lives depend only on ourselves.

The anguish associated with this responsibility can be quite intimidating, and this is so even without contemplating the fact that, for Sartre, despite being responsible for all humanity, no individual can have absolute control over the situation they are in. Responsibility for everything would probably be a lot more bearable if we were God and did have this control, but we are in a situation and we cannot simply click our fingers and make the world as we would have it. We cannot, axiomatically, decide to be a millionaire and have the world accord with this desire immediately, and perhaps even ever. There are other subjects beside ourselves and while we are free within a situation, we cannot simply determine the situation, and because of this we feel anguish before this world, for which we are responsible and which nevertheless eludes our control.

It is important to note that Sartre distinguishes two main senses of anguish: *anguish in the face of the future* and *anguish in the face of the past* (BN: 32–3). The person walking along the precipice captures anguish in the face of the future (they are aware that they could do anything in the future, even jump off a cliff, and that nothing prevents them from doing this), but he uses an example of a gambler to illustrate what is at stake in anguish in the face of the past. Imagine that a man has lost a lot of money and jeopardised his marriage because of ongoing gambling. He then decides and promises to never gamble again.

For Sartre, the next time that man passes a place of gambling it is likely that he will experience the recognition that his past decision no longer binds him and that he could simply rescind it. He might then experience anguish at the realization that his past decision must be reinvoked and committed to anew. Being conscious of a past decision in this direct positional way (thetically) implies a distance or withdrawal from the self that so decided.

This kind of anguish in the face of the past is also embodied in Antoine Roquentin's behaviour in Sartre's novel *Nausea*. Nearing the end of the book that he is writing on a historical figure, Monsieur Rollebon, Roquentin admits that he does not want to go on. While others might "make" themselves complete their book by reminding themselves that they have promised and committed to finish it, signed certain contracts and so on, Roquentin will not let past resolutions confer meaning on the present. Refusing to do this, however, means that questions regarding how to act cause Roquentin the most grief. Reflections such as "Shall I have to go away again, leaving everything behind – my research, my book?" trouble him, and this sense of anguished urgency, aware that anything can happen, is for Sartre an apprehension of the nature of consciousness (BN: 36–7).

Sartre also suggests that anguish and fear are born in the failure or destruction of the other (BN: 30). For example, fear can turn into anguish when we stop panicking about something external harming us and instead attempt to decide what to do when confronted with this perilous situation. In that respect, we tend to oscillate between the two experiences. But if this is so, an important question looms: why is it that Sartre also says that anguish is rare (BN: 35)?

Bad faith

According to Sartre, we generally flee this anguished apprehension of our responsibility in what he terms "bad faith". He asserts that there exist many "guardrails against anguish": alarm clocks to which we automatically respond in an attempt to evade the troubling question about whether or not we want to go to work, but also signposts, tax forms, policemen and so on, all of which fulfil a similar function (BN: 39). In its indictment of "normality", Sartre's novel *Nausea* provides many examples of the various ruses and evasions that people, in particular the bourgeoisie, adopt in order to avoid recognizing their own freedom and responsibility. In *Being and Nothingness*, Sartre makes it clear that there are two fundamental ways of being in bad faith. The most obvious of these is by denying our freedom (transcendence) and pretending that we have no choice but to go along with a certain situation. Perhaps in a bar, we might, for example, tell ourselves that we must fight this person who has insulted us. For Sartre, such an attitude would be in bad faith because we are never compelled; if we do respond with violence then this is our choice and we must bear responsibility for that choice. A person is also in bad faith if they identify themselves with their belongings or any other part of their facticity. If we tell ourselves that we are a better person than somebody else merely because we wear the right clothing, listen to certain CDs, have a powerful position in society or have a lot of money, we are identifying ourselves with our possessions and our facticity.

If we take our identity as given by our situation, or even by a previous choice that we have made, such as heroically fighting in a war some twenty years ago, then we are in bad faith. Identity, as we have seen, is never given but must always be continually created in our actions and not in some fact of our circumstances. Any attempt to immerse ourselves completely in our facticity is in bad faith, as is any attempt to affirm only our free transcendence, although Sartre pays less attention to this second phenomenon. Although his complicated example of a waiter who "plays" at being a waiter – he holds himself apart from his activity and treats what he does as having no definitive role in his life – could be said to be in bad faith for this reason (BN: 59), the clearest example of someone being in bad faith for exclusively emphasizing their transcendence (and refusing to acknowledge their facticity) is his somewhat problematic example of a homosexual who refuses to admit that they are a homosexual (BN: 63–4). As a free transcendence, they do not take their past homosexual behaviour to in any way define them and they refuse to take responsibility for it. They claim not to be a homosexual in the same way that a chair is not a table (BN: 64), but for Sartre this is a false analogy and they are not acknowledging that their actions *do* have a social significance that cannot be ignored, and are a part of their facticity. The structure of human existence for Sartre is one of *both* facticity and transcendent freedom, and bad faith is the denial of, or the failure to coordinate, these two aspects of our lives (BN: 56).

Probably Sartre's most famous example of bad faith, however, is one that has raised the ire of various feminists; women feature in *Being and Nothingness* twice, and both times they are in bad faith, and one of them is "frigid" (BN: 54). Any reservations regarding its sexism notwithstanding, it is certainly worth considering his example in order to gain a better understanding of this concept. A woman is on a date with a man and is uncertain about how to proceed, given that it is a first date and the man is beginning to make advances to her (BN: 55–8). However, according to Sartre she deliberately concerns herself with only what is respectful and discrete in the attitude of her male companion. If he says to her "I find you so attractive", Sartre suggests that the woman divests this comment of all significance and especially of its sexual connotations. The man then tries to hold her hand and to initiate something more romantic. The woman wants neither to willingly hold his hand nor to rebuff his attempt to hold her hand. Instead, she casually allows her hand to be held by her partner, thereby denying, or at least pretending (for Sartre) not to make a choice herself. Of course, she is making a choice (she chooses not to choose), and Sartre concludes that she is in bad faith precisely because she denies this. Sartre suggests that the woman in this example has affected a divorce between her body and her mind, or between her desire and her decision. She wants to take the hand, but will not admit it to herself. The woman hence leaves her hand there, but does not notice that she is leaving it there. She does not notice because, as Sartre somewhat facetiously says, "it happens by chance that she is at that moment all intellect" (BN: 56).

Various writers have offered feminist criticisms of the sexism inherent in this account, perhaps most notably Michele Le Doeuff in *Hipparchia's Choice* (1991). Le Doeuff's complaint with this example is that it is the man, as in Sartre, who presumes that he knows what is going on in the woman's mind. Sartre presumes that he has privileged access to the situation. But the second, and in my mind more telling, objection to this example that has been raised is that Sartre offers no account of why women might need, and certainly might have needed in 1940s France, to play this kind of covert game, the obvious reason for this being that the social situation is structured very differently for men and women. To some extent, sexually active women are sometimes still considered promiscuous or tainted by some similarly pejorative term, whereas the equivalent man is frequently designated more positively. If that kind of thing is impressed on women from a young age, then it is no simple decision to just take the hand of somebody who offers it or not take the hand.

We will return to such points in our forthcoming discussion of de Beauvoir, but it is important to see that, at least to some extent, Sartre considers bad faith to be inevitable (BN: 48). Indeed, Sartre even suggests that any attempt to be sincere is in bad faith, as it means that someone attempts to be *essentially* sincere, true to what they are, as if there were a thing-like essence to a person (BN: 58–67). Of course, on his view there is no truth to what one is in this sense – on the contrary we are no-thing-ness – and hence the project of sincerity is misguided in much the same way as the project of trying to be courageous (BN: 65–7). This is important as sincerity is sometimes confused with authenticity or good faith, which it should not be.

Although Sartre does not discuss authenticity as much as Heidegger and de Beauvoir do (except in his *War Diaries*), by implication good faith entails recognizing that our project is never founded and that we never attain a permanent decision. Our marriage vows, to take one example, are in an important sense enacted again in every instant. This may sound overly dramatic, but all he means is that our project is never founded externally, even if we ourselves choose to thus found it. We must choose and choose again. Imagine that we have eaten too much chocolate and decide that we will not have any more for the remainder of the week. Pretty quickly we realize that this choice that we have made is nothing but a choice from our past and that if we do not choose it again there will soon be no chocolate left. Now, there is anguish at the prospect of this permanent choice, at least in relation to things more substantial than a chocolate addiction, and so we pretend we cannot choose. Perhaps we tell ourselves that we must become a medical practitioner, because all of the rest of our family have been doctors, in an attempt to refrain from considering the situation again. For Sartre, however, such conduct would once more be in bad faith for refusing to acknowledge that we necessarily transcend our situation and circumstances, as well as the various social roles that we contingently assume.

It becomes apparent that while Sartre thinks that humanity has no intrinsic nature, the recognition of this does not simply license an "anything goes" kind of relativism, or an ineffectual pessimism. There is a type of ethics – the question of how we should act – involved in Sartre's philosophy of absolute freedom. It is a personal ethics about refusing to allow our humanity to ever be defined, but to create it, and, arguably, also to allow other human beings the same opportunity (Sartre emphasizes this ethical aspect in *Existentialism is a Humanism* and in his abandoned *Notebooks for an Ethics* (written 1947–8), more than in *Being and Nothingness*). Perhaps it could be summarized as: act so that you would never say of yourself or your actions "it just happened". In other words, Sartre wants us to stop pretending that our hormones, our biology, or anything else, is a determining factor in our behaviour.

Against psychoanalysis

Even the suggestion that our past forces us to take a certain course of action is ruled out by Sartre, and this denies all psychological explanations of behaviour if they suggest that because of childhood events the adult develops a complex that forces him or her to enact a certain event, or deviate from a certain norm. In fact, Sartre's chapter on bad faith (BN: 47–70) contains a sustained discussion and rejection of Freudian psychoanalysis, which he describes as obsessed with the past, although he also acknowledges that psychoanalysis is an important influence on his own conception of existential psychoanalysis. For Sartre, the psychological and psychoanalytic attempt to describe the psyche mechanistically and scientifically, as if it were constituted by myriad thing-like forces acting on a person that they cannot control, is an elaborate and "permanent game of excuses" (BN: 40); it is an example of bad faith because we treat part of ourselves as "not us" and create a conscious–unconscious dyad. For Sartre, the main way of fleeing anguish is by apprehending ourselves as determined and as a plaything of forces outside our control, and for him both psychology and psychoanalysis do this; they do not reconcile our transcendence with our facticity. Instead, they insist that we are passive before our instincts and drives that are unconscious and they thereby divorce ourselves from the most troubling parts of us.

As an aside, Sartre also argues that psychoanalysis is incoherent on its own terms, because the hypothesis of the censor presupposes that the censor must be aware of what it is repressing, as well as the more general deceiver–deceived dyad, in order to effectively complete its task (BN: 52). If this is the case, the censor becomes the seat both of consciousness and of bad faith, and the problem of how this is possible still remains to be explained. The technicalities of this rather nuanced argument cannot be considered here, but it is important to note that, on Sartre's account, consciousness affects itself with bad faith. It is not a state that overcomes us (BN: 49), as the drives might overcome the pathological for a Freudian. This means that although bad faith is considered to be inevitable to greater and lesser extents, it is also thought to be self-defeating as the lie to oneself occurs within the structure of a unitary consciousness. At some level we must know what we are fleeing in bad faith, because on

Sartre's understanding of consciousness there is no "second self", such as the Id or the unconscious, to make the lie more readily comprehensible. It is for this reason that Sartre describes bad faith as "metastable", or subject to change (BN: 50, 57, 68).

Towards the end of *Being and Nothingness* Sartre offers his own version of existential psychoanalysis that does without the concept of the unconscious and instead has recourse to the idea of an original, or fundamental, project that plays a role in our behaviour but never reductively causes us to behave in any one particular way as some traditional psychoanalysis has it. A detailed discussion of that, however, is beyond the purview of this book, as Sartre's most sophisticated material on existential psychoanalysis occurs in his later books on Gustave Flaubert and Jean Genet, and in *Words* about his own childhood.

The body

In *Being and Nothingness* Sartre has a long and very complicated account of the body that it is important to take seriously because of both the role that it plays at the mid-point in this text as it endeavours to move towards a "concrete" understanding of freedom, and its significance for existentialism. After all, from Plato to Descartes the body has been denigrated by the Western philosophical tradition, arguably until at least Nietzsche. French existentialism, however, emphasizes the importance of the body, of desire and so on, and Sartre has one long and technical chapter devoted to analysing the body that had a significant impact on Merleau-Ponty, whose own revolutionary work on the body has been influential. Merleau-Ponty has argued that Sartre does not take our embodied situation seriously enough (and that his account of the for-itself and in-itself is tacitly dualistic – that is, the mind, or freedom, transcends the body) – but before considering this position an exposition of Sartre's work is first required.

There are some obvious and important things to derive from what Sartre has to say about the body. Notably, Sartre describes human embodiment as comprising the body-for-itself (that is, the body as we experience it – the body as *lived*), as opposed to the body-for-others (that is, the way in which my body appears to others, and the Other's body appears to me). The scientific treatment of the body as an object or a thing – as something to be analysed and dissected – derives from, and is the reflective instantiation of, the more basic and pre-reflective aspect of our body-for-others. To make things more complicated, Sartre also describes a third ontological aspect to embodiment, which although not labelled explicitly in *Being and Nothingness* other than as "the third ontological dimension of the body", has come to be designated as the body-for-itself-for-others. It involves a pre-reflective recognition that the body-for-itself and the body-for-others are separate and incommensurable; it is an apprehension of the disjunction between my own experience of embodiment and how the Other (including science) construes my body, and this is also what is experienced in the phenomena that Sartre calls the look, which we will examine in Chapter 4 on relations with other people.

KEY POINT
Human embodiment comprises the *body-for-itself* (that is, the body as we experience it), the *body-for-others* (that is, the way in which my body appears to others, and the Other's body appears to me) and the *body-for-itself-for-others* (which involves a pre-reflective recognition that the above two modalities of the body are forever disjunct).

For our current purposes it is sufficient to distinguish between the first two ontological components of the body. In this respect it is important to note that Sartre repeatedly says that the body-for-itself and the body-for-others (crudely the body-as-object, albeit a particular kind of object) are on different and incommunicable levels; in other words, they cannot be reduced to one another and neither is satisfactory in isolation (BN: 304–5). Of course, the question of what relation they actually bear to one another is a pivotal one that we will come back to.

Body-for-itself

Sartre begins his long analysis of the body-for-itself by distinguishing it from what it is not. In this regard, he insists that the body that science describes – which he characterizes as the body of others, the body-for-others – is not the body as we experience it. Sartre suggests that my body, as it is for me, "does not appear in the midst of the world" (BN: 303) subject to causal determination and independent diagnoses. Instead of advocating this kind of "objectifying realism", for Sartre the body is first, and most importantly, that from which we have a point of view. He argues that we cannot successfully take a third-person, scientific point of view on our body while we are a lived body that is engaged in projects in the world. To illustrate this point, Sartre uses the example of somebody surveying their surroundings from the top of a hill. While they can survey all that is around them, they nevertheless do not have a perspective on their own body; the body is the point of view on whatever is actually being surveyed but it cannot itself be seen. Even if there were some Archimedean spot outside the world from which we could see everything, it would nevertheless still be the case that we would not be able to see ourselves seeing.

Now it might be responded that Sartre is simply incorrect because on some level we can see our bodies "in the midst of the world". For example, we can see a video of ourselves being operated on in a hospital. Sartre argues that in these cases we do not really see our body, or at least we do not see our body as it actually is *for us*. In such cases, we see the body as an object, and can have knowledge of it, but this is not the way we actually experience our own bodies. For Sartre, when we watch ourselves being operated on, it is nevertheless difficult to identify with that body; we initially see the body on the operating table as a thing of the world and only later infer that it is *our body* through rational processes, or the testimony of the doctor, or through other means. But Sartre suggests that even when we do make this inference that that the body on the operating table is us, we still do not really recognize our body as our own; we treat it as an object. According to Sartre's analysis, these two ways of understanding our body – the body-for-itself (lived) and the body that is treated as a medical or scientific object – are mutually exclusive.

> **KEY POINT**
> To put Sartre's point aphoristically, we might say that it is not possible to fully know the body that I experience, or to experience the body that I know.

Sartre's next major philosophical point in this chapter of *Being and Nothingness* is to argue that *when we say that there is a world, we are also necessarily saying that there is a body* (BN: 307, 325). He thinks that the body is always given over to the world that it is a part of, and neither the world nor the body is conceivable without the other. This means that Sartre cannot conceive of the possibility of various thought experiments that divorce the mind (or brain) from the body that some "analytic" philosophers play around with. One famous example of such a thought experiment is proposed by Hilary Putnam, who tries to envisage a brain that is sustained in a vat that would have no need of a body. Sartre would not countenance such a possibility, as he repeatedly states that we cannot have a world without a body. The brain in the vat, which does not have a body, and consequently does not have a world either, at least according to Sartre could not be said to be human.

But why exactly does Sartre argue that "to say that there is a world, or that I have a body, is one and the same thing"? His first reason for making such a claim is because he thinks that without the body, there would be no orientation of objects, since all orientations would be equivalent. What exactly does Sartre mean by orientation? He means that objects are not presented to us in just any order, but that objects within our perceptual field all presuppose the body as the central point of view, and that particular objects or instruments are given to us as necessarily relating to other objects and instruments. In order to understand this idea, it is worth considering an example that Sartre uses in *Being and Nothingness*. He argues that if our general project is one of fixing a door, then the nail that we are looking at will, in turn, pre-reflectively refer us to the hammer that is needed to make use of that nail. Moreover, that hammer also refers us to the bit of wood that needs to be stabilized, and this in turn refers to the arm and hand that will hold the hammer. In other words, our perception of objects is structured according to their probable use for us. Even the initial perception of a single nail comes with all of these myriad possibilities and potentialities attached to it, and this means that there is no pure perception that can subsequently be interpreted. From the start, perception is meaningful and organized in terms of possible projects in the world, and in this regard perception solicits us towards action. This idea is explored in detail by Merleau-Ponty.

Sartre's transcendental argument is that it is only because we have a body that objects in a perceptual field are always oriented towards us. Without the body as this centre of reference, objects would have no particular orientation and no projects in relation to those objects would then be possible. Instead, all instrumentalities would become equivalent and objects would not have this meaningful structure in which they appear connected to other similar objects. If this was the case, we would have no way of deciding which instruments to use and why. The series of references would be infinite: for example, paper refers to pen, pen refers to something else, which in turn refers to something else, which in turn refers to something else, and the chain of associations would have no end. For Sartre, every perceptual field presupposes a hand, or a body, that ends any such chain of reference or association. It is this fact that we have a body that is within this world of objects (although it is not simply an object itself) that narrows this range of phenomena down and allows us to have meaningful projects in the world. It is important to emphasize that the body is not itself *in* the perceptual field and is not simply another instrument that we can utilize, as we cannot get a perspective on the body in its entirety as we can with other objects. In our most basic relationship to the world, the body is not an object (and hence is not the body of science) but is the presupposed end of the chain of objects. As Sartre says, the hand is the "unknowable and not utilizable term that the last instrument of the series indicates" (BN: 323).

For Sartre, this is phenomenologically the way we experience our bodies, and he argues that on the level of the pre-reflective consciousness we do not have direct or positional consciousness of our body. Think about gazing through the window of a train, or a car, observing the scenery. Generally we do not have direct consciousness of our body when doing this. Sartre also points out that when writing something down on a notepad we tend to be aware of the pen, but are not usually aware of the various contortions of our hand. We can, of course, make a reflective attempt to focus on our hand inscribing the lecture notes (and hence treat the body as an object), but Sartre's point is that this is not usually the case. It is the pen that you are usually aware of and not the workings of your hand muscles. Now this seems phenomenologically true and it reaffirms that the body is, in Sartre's words, "the inapprehensible given", or the centre that cannot be known.

At the same time, it needs to be remembered that the body, for Sartre, is not reducible to the body-for-itself. Sartre also argues that we have another aspect of our bodies, which is the body-for-others, or, on the reflective level, the body-as-object. There are hence two modes of being of the body. First, the body is in one sense objectively defined by the world and subject to many causal laws, but if we restrict ourselves to this we do not figure out how it is that there is actually a meaningful world for us. To account for this, Sartre thinks we need to focus more intently on the body as it is lived: hence the importance of the "lived body", which is also affirmed by Husserl and Merleau-Ponty.

KEY POINT

The Scottish philosopher David Hume (1711–76) once asked a fellow philosopher how they could know that they have a body. His colleague replied that he knew he had a body because when he lifted his arm he had "a sensation of effort". For Sartre, however, the lived body is actually not known in this way (BN: 324). It is not really known in any way at all. The only response to Hume's question is to point out that without a body we could not have a world. But we do have a world in which we can engage in meaningful projects, and Sartre's analysis suggests that a necessary condition of this is that we also have a body.

But it is not that Sartre wants to hold that one particular conception of the body can exist on its own. The body-for-itself (the lived body) also needs the more objective aspect of the body-as-object. If your lecturer is facing you in the classroom, for example, it is necessary that the blackboard (or whiteboard) is behind them, and that you are in front of them. It is also necessary that if they turn around the reverse will be the case. This just means that consciousness is always situated. The for-itself cannot project just anything at all, but within every situation there are alternatives. To use philosophical terms, it is *necessary* that objects appear in such an objective way, but it is *contingent* whether I focus on this or that particular aspect of the blackboard. As Sartre says, "if definite rules did not determine the use of instruments, I could never distinguish within me desire from will, nor dream from act, nor the possible from the real" (BN: 327). So this objective aspect of embodiment is necessary or else no projects would be possible for the very reason that everything would be equally attainable. This might sound like a contradiction, but if there were no certain objective rules pertaining to the objects of the world, then there would be nothing for the for-itself to act on or against, and we would have no motivation for adopting one course of action rather than another. As we have pointed out earlier, freedom is not possible without constraint.

That is a complicated part of *Being and Nothingness*, but the main point to take away from this discussion is that there is a double relation of the body and that the terms of this relation are on separate and "incommunicable" levels. There is a relation with the things *on which* the body is a point of view (body-as-object) and there is a relation with objects *for whom* the body is a point of a view (body-for-itself). The first aspect of the body is an objective relation and the second aspect of the body is an existential or lived relation. Sartre thinks that these two realms remain separate, although if we are realists then we have a tendency to want to say that they refer to the same thing. Indeed, it remains the case that on the ontological level Sartre's account leaves several questions unanswered, most notably in explaining why there often appears to be a unity between these different "aspects" of embodiment.

Moreover, on the level of Sartre's own work, there are two main questions about this account of the body-for-itself and the body-in-itself. First, does it reinstate a dualism? Secondly, if not, then how does it relate to his account of our absolute ontological freedom? At times, there is still a sense in which, for Sartre, the body is the surpassed, or the transcended (BN: 309, 326). Although Sartre argues that the body is there in each project and perception of the for-itself, even that it *is* the for-itself, he also suggests that it is always there in the form of the immediate past (BN: 301, 326). Moreover, the body is not only a point of view, but it is also "a point of departure", and it hence seems to be more akin to facticity than transcendence (and note that the section on the body-for-itself is subtitled facticity). If we recall that Sartre holds that I cannot be crippled without choosing myself as crippled (BN: 328) there are elements in his account that seem to suggest that by nihilation, or negation, we still escape the body.

On the other hand, Sartre also claims in this chapter that the body-for-itself is wholly consciousness and wholly body. To be more precise, he states that "being-for-itself must be wholly body and it must be wholly consciousness", but then he goes on to add the very important proviso, "it cannot be united with a body" (BN: 305). This suggests that being-for-itself is both body and mind, but it is not simply body. There is still this dual aspect in which the mind can transcend or negate the body, but this all occurs in the body-for-itself (the lived body). Is this a dualism or not? It is difficult to say because Sartre is not precise on this point and it requires more textual analysis than we can devote to the problem here. It seems that we transcend only the in-itself aspect of our bodies, the brute scientific fact, or the body-as-object, and that we never transcend our bodies entirely. This seems to imply that consciousness is affected by the body and hence not as free as Sartre argues. Does such an account of the body fit with his philosophy of freedom, as the body, after all, can inhibit us, can develop habitual ways of relating to the world that we do not, strictly speaking, choose? We will come back to such questions in our consideration of the work of Merleau-Ponty.

Death is not *my* possibility (BN: 531–48)

Although Heidegger was a major influence on *Being and Nothingness*, there is one notable point of disagreement between the two philosophers and that is on the issue of death. In the section titled "Freedom and Facticity: The Situation", Sartre challenges Heidegger's insistence on the importance of being-towards-death to any authentic existence.

For both of them, an authentic existence involves recognizing and living in accord with certain truths of the human situation – crudely, Sartre encourages us to assume our freedom, whereas Heidegger encourages us to assume our mortality – but they have decidedly different perspectives on what role death plays in human existence. For Heidegger, death is *Dasein*'s "ownmost possibility", and it is that which establishes us as a radically singular individual. To be authentic, or to be differentiated from *das Man* (the herd), demands recognition of our being-towards-death. Although Sartre is reluctant to use the term "authentic", the clear implication of his work is that we should affirm certain truths of the human situation, but he insists, unlike Heidegger, that death is not part of this human situation but is rather an unknowable limit. Being-towards-death is literally an impossibility on Sartre's conception of consciousness (which functions by negating that which *is* – and death *is not*), but let us proceed more slowly in order to show why this is so.

According to Sartre's representation of Heidegger's view, death is an event that constitutes the meaning of the entire process of life; it is like the final note of a melody that confers meaning on all of the notes that have preceded it. On this view, death becomes the phenomenon that makes life personal and unique, and individuals become responsible for their death, as well as for their life. Against this view, Sartre emphasizes the absurdity of death and the ways in which it is *not* analogous with the end of a musical symphony that sheds light on everything that has preceded it. Sartre argues that when an individual dies is a matter of luck, or chance (BN: 537), and this absurdity does not allow a life to be neatly concluded like the end of a symphony; instead it may just be cut off in ignominious and inappropriate fashion.

Although it is far from clear that Heidegger's position requires death to be an "end note" in this extreme sense, Sartre discusses an up and coming young novelist to help make his general point that death is not that which bestows meaning on our lives. According to his example, the author has written one novel that shows considerable talent, even has the hallmarks of greatness, but on its own that is not sufficient to definitively establish his greatness. To be a great novelist requires that he can produce another work of similar breadth and genius, but suddenly, in the flush of his first literary success, death interrupts his career and prevents him having the opportunity to test himself with that difficult second novel; we are left abandoned, unsure whether his subsequent novels would have shown him to be a literary giant or merely a flash in the pan (BN: 539). Against Heidegger, Sartre hence suggests that death is never that which gives life its meanings; rather, it is that which on principle removes meanings from life, as it does with the aspiring novelist. In Sartre's own words: "we can no longer even say that death confers a meaning on life from the outside; a meaning can come only from subjectivity. Since death does not appear on the foundation of our freedom, it can only remove all meaning from life" (BN: 539). Sartre holds that rather than giving totality to my life, death abandons it in a state of indetermination.

"No one else can die for me": Sartre's response

Sartre also confronts Heidegger's famous suggestion that "no one else can die for me", and he uses on old technique in philosophy called *reductio ad absurdum*, which simply means to draw out the logical consequences of a position until it is revealed as absurd. Sartre argues that you can say exactly the same things that Heidegger says about death – no one else can die for me – in regard to love, and potentially also many other experiences (BN: 534). In one sense, it is also true that nobody else can love for me, but Sartre says this is banal, and he insists that another person can always do what I do, when considered from the point of view of their function and their result (another person, hard as it is to accept, could make our lover feel happy and secure). In other words, Sartre suggests that another person *can* always love for me and even die for me (consider a martyr) when considered from a functional perspective, and yet they *cannot* die for me, or love for me, in the sense that they are inside me in the experience of anticipating death or loving. For Sartre, however, this final point amounts to nothing more than the tautologous recognition that another person is, by definition, another person, and on his view death is hence no longer conceived of as having any special significance in terms of individuating us.

Against Heidegger's view that he characterizes as involving waiting for death, Sartre also suggests that we can only await death on condemnation to a death-sentence, and even then we may be granted a presidential reprieve, or killed by a respiratory bug while we are awaiting the gallows or a lethal injection (BN: 536). Sartre's account of Heidegger's position is somewhat caricatured here, in that Heidegger is not arguing that we should sit around and literally just wait for death. Heidegger does not think that we should wait for or expect death, but anticipate it, and this distinction is significant. But these problems with Sartre's interpretation of Heidegger aside, there are some substantive philosophical differences between them. For Sartre, death is fundamentally that which cannot be foreseen and cannot be waited for. On his view, we cannot even say that each minute that is passing brings us closer to death, and he argues that waiting for an undetermined death is absurd. For Sartre, Heidegger's focus on death is life-denying, perhaps even a version of what Friedrich Nietzsche called "slave morality": a disgust or resentment for life that occurs in those who cannot achieve all that they aspire to.

Sartre acknowledges that waiting for death at old age would *seem* to be to accept finitude. However, he points out that biologically sudden death at a young age is no different from death at an old age, and he asserts that this indetermination between death at old age and death at another time means that "one can wait for death from old age only blindly or in Bad Faith" (BN: 536). At a later stage, Sartre suggests that, "since the for-itself lays claim to an after, there is no place for death in the being which is for-itself" (BN: 540). His fundamental point here is that death cannot be part of the structure of subjectivity, and therefore that we are lying to ourselves if we allow our life to be saturated by the horizon of death. In some respects, Sartre's position in this regard has a famous precursor: Epicurus. As we saw in Chapter 2, Epicurus argues that death is something that should not concern us unduly, and that we should be indifferent to it. This is pretty much Sartre's ultimate position and in Epicurean fashion he also uses a version of what is called the "no subject argument" – which suggests that there is no subject around to experience being dead, so in that sense it cannot be said to harm anyone – arguing that "death is outside my possibilities and therefore I cannot wait for it; that is, I cannot thrust myself toward it as one of my possibilities" (BN: 545).

In contrast to Heidegger, Sartre hence prefers to talk about our finitude, rather than our mortality. For Sartre, even if we were immortal we would still be finite, as opportunities for certain experiences would be missed and choices would be made that preclude other possibilities (BN: 546). Authentic behaviour, or good faith, requires an acceptance of our finitude (the irreversibility of time), but he argues that we do not experience our own mortality and this sense of being-towards-death that Heidegger argues pervades the entirety of any authentic life. On the other hand, there is little doubt that Heidegger would claim that Sartre's indifference to death is a failure to fully assume the constant possibility of death occurring to the individual themselves; he would suggest that it is to pretend that death occurs to someone else.

"To be dead is to be prey for the living"

There is a final aspect of Sartre's view of death that is worth briefly considering. On Sartre's account, in death you are given over to the perspective of the Other, and to the judgements of posterity (see Sartre's autobiography, *Words*, for further ruminations on this). To be dead, Sartre suggests, is to be defenceless "prey for the living" (BN: 543). Death represents a "dispossession" and Sartre's point here is simply that while we are alive we can challenge the way in which we are construed or represented by our friends and by the populace at large, but in death we are given completely over to the whims of the Other; they remain free to characterize us however they wish, but we no longer have the possibility of reply. The fact of death gives victory to the Other in the ongoing battle that he envisages, following Hegel, as occurring between self and other (BN: 544). Sartre hence concludes that to live as Heidegger suggests we should, as a being-towards-death, is to live my subjectivity towards the Other and with regard to the other person's point of view, but he insists that this is not possible. For Sartre, we can never be sure what the other person thinks of us, as we will see in detail in Chapter 4, and so how could we live for the *Other* and for a perspective that we will never know? Sartre's individualism becomes apparent here (living authentically is about oneself, more than about behaving well towards others), and far from death being our own peculiar possibility it is considered to be that which on principle continually escapes us.

Summary of key points

Existence precedes essence
While triangles, pens, and objects generally have a form, essence or function, which precedes their concrete existence (for something to be a triangle, it must have three corners and all of the corners must add up to 180 degrees), Sartre argues that this is not the case for human beings. We exist first, and thereafter define our essence by the way in which we live.

Consciousness
- Sartre distinguishes two modes of consciousness: the *pre-reflective cogito* (which does not involve an ego or self); and the *reflective cogito* (which posits a self and unifies past disparate experiences).
- All consciousness and every intending act is both: (i) positionally (or thetically) aware of the object that it posits – consciousness is directed at, and has a bearing toward some object, such as the scenery being observed; and (ii) non-positionally (non-thetically) aware of itself as awareness – it is indirectly aware that it is *not* that object which it is perceiving/positing.

Ontology of human existence
- Humanity is composed of two different, but often inseparable aspects: that is our *facticity* (i.e. our past, our biology, our possessions, the society we are a part of, etc.); plus our freedom to negate and, sometimes, to interpret this facticity, which he describes elsewhere as our *transcendence*.

- *Being-for-itself* (free and transcendent consciousness, that negates both our facticity and objects)
- *Being-in-itself* (pure objecthood, or "pure plenitude", about which we cannot say much, except that it is contingent and without reason)
- *Facticity* (designates the relationship between the for-itself and the in-itself, and this incorporates our social situation)

Negation

Three main phenomena show that human consciousness functions through negation (and the condition of possibility for this negation is an ontological Nothingness that "lies coiled in the heart of Being"): questioning, absence and destruction. The negation involved in these experiences presupposes that consciousness is disjunct from the realm of empirical objects and things.

Anguish

- Anguish is a phenomenological apprehension of our own freedom, not a philosophical proof of it. It is in anguish that freedom is, in its being, in question for itself.
- *Anguish needs to be distinguished from fear.* Fear is an unreflective apprehension of the possibility that something in the world (and outside us) might harm us; anguish involves a reflective apprehension of the self and our freedom to respond to an external situation in any number of different ways.

Bad faith

Bad faith is the denial of, or failure to coordinate, our freedom (transcendence) and our facticity. If we reject either of these aspects of ourselves, we are in bad faith because we are refusing to recognize what it is to be human.

The body

Human embodiment comprises the *body-for-itself* (that is, the body as we experience it), the *body-for-others* (that is, the way in which my body appears to others, and the Other's body appears to me) and the *body-for-itself-for-others* (which involves a pre-reflective recognition that the above two modalities of the body are forever disjunct).

Sartre's critique of Heidegger's view of being-towards-death

- Sartre thinks that what Heidegger calls "being-towards-death" is a structural impossibility of the for-itself. Authentic behaviour, or good faith, requires an acceptance of our finitude (the irreversibility of time), but we do not experience our own mortality and this sense of being-towards-death.
- Sartre argues that Heidegger's comment that "no one else can die for me" is either unconvincing or banally true (a tautology), and the prospect of our own death does not play a special role in individuating us.

four

Sartre: hell is other people

In his play *No Exit* (1943), Sartre's character Garcin famously asserts that "hell is other people". This declaration has also been taken to exemplify his philosophical account of our relations with others and in what follows we will see that this is at least partly accurate. But first it is helpful to delineate a problem that Sartre's account of relations with others was working against: the problem of solipsism.

The reef of solipsism

In recent times, there have sometimes been complaints that phenomenology does not deal with the Other in their absolute difference, or in their genuine alterity; the term "alterity" is basically synonymous with otherness, although it also has connotations of change and transformation. One reason for this complaint against phenomenology is that it suggests that the perceived object, such as the mountain that I am looking at outside my window, cannot be entirely foreign to those who perceive it. In other words, I bring something to bear upon the appreciation of the mountain, and you might remember that Sartre insists that we never encounter a pure object, or the thing-in-itself. That is just to say that we never encounter the mountain as it really is, but always in relation to the intentions and projects that we have towards it. Or, as in Heidegger's example, we never hear a pure noise but always a noise of some kind of activity, such as a mower starting up, or a motorbike roaring past. It seems to follow from this that when we see another person, they too must be encountered in relation to the intentions and projects that we have towards them. One important question for phenomenology is hence the following: in what sense is our perception or experience of the other person genuinely recognizing their otherness? Can phenomenology talk about the other person in their difference? If phenomenology assimilates objects to the terms of reference of the perceiver, then the phenomenological treatment of the other seems to incline, at least potentially, towards being unable to show that other people really exist. After all, how do we know the other person really exists if the person that we are engaging with is at least partly constituted by our intentions and we have no access to them outside our intentions? Phenomenology hence *threatens* to be solipsistic, and to leave us with no means of establishing the existence of other minds.

> **KEY POINT**
> *Solipsism* is the doctrine that we cannot know or access the minds of anybody else. It is the idea that we know only our own perspective, and one epistemological consequence of this is that we cannot prove that other people exist.

While solipsism is undoubtedly a counter-intuitive position, it is far from an unheard of position in the history of philosophy. In fact, in *Being and Nothingness* Sartre suggests that all realists and idealists either inadvertently commit themselves to solipsism, or in fleeing it they abandon their own theoretical presuppositions and contradict themselves (BN: 230). He points out that idealists, for example, frequently end up abandoning their conviction that the mind constitutes and makes the world meaningful by relying on a common-sense realism about the existence of the other person ("Of course we know that others exist!") that is devoid of an argument. Either that, or they are forced to accept solipsism (BN: 229), because from an idealist perspective that reduces subjectivity to the mind, there is consciousness and, diametrically opposed to this, there are the objects of the world, the body included.

In this respect, it is worth again briefly considering Descartes. For him, the mind is the meaning-bestowing agent and the body is that which potentially misleads us. From such a starting-point, it is difficult to figure out how Descartes could know that other people exist and he tacitly admits this himself, stating:

> If I chance to look out of the window onto men passing in the street, I do not fail to say, on seeing them, that I see men ... and

yet what do I see from this window, other than hats and cloaks, which cover ghosts or dummies who move only by means of springs? But I judge them to be really men, and thus I understand, by the sole power of judgment that resides in my mind, what I believed I saw with my eyes. (M: 85)

The problem is that if an individual thinks of their mind as constituting or giving meaning to the world, then the other person who they see in that world presumably also constitutes and gives meaning to the world. However, this possibility is inconceivable because the other person is external to them and within the realm of objects. Their consciousness cannot be directly accessed, so the existence of the other person, on this line of argument, remains unconfirmable and subject only to the problematic speculation of arguments by analogy that basically proceed as follows: I have firsthand experience of my own feelings, emotions and subjectivity, and I also have a body that generally reacts in ways reflecting those feelings, emotions and so on. You have a body that looks and acts somewhat like mine. Therefore, by analogy, you must have feelings, emotions and, more generally, subjectivity.

Now it is worth noting here that there seems to be a clear link between the mind–body problem and the problem of other minds; at the very least, ways of thinking about the body have a significant impact on how we can conceive of our relations with others. If we consider the mind as transcending the body it is difficult to prove that other people do in fact exist. If mind and body are separate, when I see your body I have no idea whether or not you do, in fact, also have a mind. The only way I can attempt to establish that you do have a mind is to argue by analogy and this is not a satisfactory proof of the other; it presupposes that which it is being asked to explain. After both criticizing and using the insights of Husserl, Hegel and Heidegger – who he argues managed to install the other at the heart of consciousness, and thereby made an important contribution to the debate, notwithstanding the other flaws in their accounts – Sartre goes on to propose his own solution to the issue in the chapter of *Being and Nothingness* entitled "The Look".

Being-for-others

On what basis, then, can Sartre phenomenologically show that other people do in fact exist, bearing in mind that phenomenology should not entertain assumptions derived from the natural attitude and simply presume that there is an outside world or that there are other people? In order to answer that question, it is first worth examining the three main modes in which Sartre argues that we encounter the existence of the Other (Sartre often capitalizes the term and we will follow this protocol for the remainder of the chapter).

KEY POINT *Three kinds of relations with others*
- The Other can be an object that I appropriate and use as an instrument.
- The Other can be that which takes a perspective on objects that I am looking at, and can hence induce an "internal haemorrhage" in my own perspective.
- The Other can appear as he or she who looks at me, who can judge me, and I hence experience my own "objectness".

The Other can be an object that I appropriate and use as an instrument

In relation to the first kind of relation with other people that Sartre describes, we must remember that he assumes that we have an appropriative relationship with objects; that is, we generally manipulate objects to accord with our purposes. Sartre also argues that we can, and in fact frequently do, treat other people in much the same way. When we approach the shopkeeper and just want the completion of a certain transaction but resent them having any meaningful conversation with us, in some sense we are treating them as an object. That is, we are treating them instrumentally and in relation to the role they serve, or what we can get out of them. We are not treating them as a person in their own right, or as an end in themselves, as Kant suggests we should. In this case, though, there is nothing to distinguish the experience of a person from the experience of a well-disguised robot. When we treat the Other as an object that we use instrumentally, we still do not have any concrete proof that the shopkeeper is not a robot (as Descartes acknowledges in the above quote), and this is especially so because we are actually treating him or her like a robot. However, this is not the case in Sartre's last two examples that make up his phenomenological proof of the Other.

The Other can be that which takes a perspective on objects that I am looking at

The second mode of relating to others that Sartre describes is best captured by considering an example that he uses. Imagine that you are peacefully gazing at the flora in a park when you see another person suddenly enter your surroundings (BN: 254). Sartre suggests that it is not the case that this person's presence is of a "purely additive type" that can be comprehended as being just another object that is in one's immediate vicinity (BN: 254). Rather, the Other's presence fundamentally alters one's appreciation of the environment. Our relationship to the world, and to the park, becomes ontologically different given the presence of another person and Sartre suggests that this is the case even if the Other does not look at us, or even realize that we are in the park with them. Sartre claims that when the other person enters the park, we feel the world "drain" away from us and reorient itself around the other person's perspective, creating a new organization or metamorphosis of our world. In Sartre's words, we apprehend that "there unfolds a spatiality that is not my spatiality; for instead of a grouping toward me of objects, there is now an orientation which flees me" (BN: 254). When alone in the park, our perceptual field was structured directly in relation to our intentions, but the phenomenological organization of objects drastically changes with another person's presence. According to Sartre, we also resent this. We want to appropriate the world and to have things ordered to accord with our own perspective.

Another example might help to make this clearer. Consider that you are listening to a band that you have always loved and you spy a rather critical music journalist friend who is also listening to the same band. Your relation to that band and their music would most probably be changed by the recognition that your friend will also have an opinion about the music in question, and also by the recognition that exactly what your friend's perspective is escapes you. Somehow it is difficult to recapture your immersion in the music. The presence of another has changed your relationship with the world. The question then becomes one regarding how we could have this experience, this "internal haemorrhage" as Sartre calls it, if other people did not exist.

However, this second mode of relations with others, Sartre tells us, is not the original mode of relating to the Other. In his park example, it is still only probable that the other person is actually in fact a person. The Other is still an object of some kind within my perceptual field, albeit a particular kind of object that we cannot treat as just another object that can be manipulated. So we are still after the proof of the existence of the Other that Sartre is seeking.

The Other can appear as he or she who looks at me, who can judge me, and I hence experience my own "objectness"

Sartre argues that the third mode of relating to the Other is the primary or original one and it is called "the look", which is when we realize that we are ourselves an object in the eyes of another person, or the object of another's judgement (it need not entail a literal look, as we will see). Just as Sartre argues that there are experiences like anguish in which we are conscious of our freedom, so he argues there are some experiences in which we are incontrovertibly confronted with the consciousness of others and the primary one of these experiences is the look.

> **KEY POINT**
> In the look, we momentarily lose our subjectivity and experience ourselves as the object of another's judgement (we experience ourselves as defined by what Sartre calls our "being-for-others"). For Sartre, this experience is alienating and we hence seek to avoid it.

Let me run through his famous attempted proof of the existence of the Other in the anecdotal way that Sartre himself presents it (BN: 259). Sartre describes a person peering through a keyhole at something on the other side of the closed door, captivated by whatever is going on. They may be motivated by jealously, curiosity or some perverse vice. All of this occurs on the level of pre-reflective consciousness; the person is peering through the keyhole, entirely caught up in their activity, absorbed in the world. Suddenly they hear footsteps in the corridor and they are aware that somebody is now watching them. No longer concerned with what is going on behind the door, they are aware only that they are the object of another's look and that they are being evaluated and judged in ways that they cannot control. They are reduced to an object in that other person's perceptual field, and this, for Sartre, is the look, and it is, according to him, the original meaning of relations with others.

Interestingly, Sartre also argues that when this person is caught peering through a keyhole, a self comes to haunt their unreflective consciousness. Recall that unreflective consciousness is generally just consciousness of the world and is not aware of itself as having an identity or ego (although consciousness is nevertheless indirectly or non-thetically "aware of being aware"). Sartre suggests that this lack of direct self-awareness is the case with the person peeking through the keyhole *prior* to them being caught. However, after being caught they then become unreflectively aware of themselves as the object of another's gaze; they become aware of themselves as an objective existence that is something other than the centre of the world and this is still on a non-reflective level (BN: 260).

Another way of thinking about this claim is that, according to Sartre, when we are alone we are generally not conscious of the particular posture of our body; for ourselves we do not feel defined by the fact that we are sitting down. Sartre's claim, however, is that the presence and look of another does in fact so define us (BN: 262). The look of the Other defines us as a "peeping Tom", if we are looking through a keyhole, and it can also define us as a person seated, whichever the case may be. The Other defines us based on what we are on the outside and, according to Sartre, the Other can hence judge us in a way that we cannot judge ourselves. The person caught peeping realizes, for example, that this other person who has just arrived on the scene undoubtedly thinks of them as strange, or perverted. All of a sudden then – Sartre describes it as an "immediate shudder without discursive preparation" – they are conscious of their identity as escaping them in ways that they cannot control and they are ashamed of this fact. According to Sartre, the experience of shame recognizes both that we are that object that the Other is looking at and judging, and that we have our foundation outside ourselves; the Other sees an aspect of us that we cannot control and that requires their mediation. As Sartre suggests, "pure shame is not a feeling of being this or that guilty object, but in general of being an object" (BN: 288). In being ashamed in this manner, the world again "flows" towards the Other's consciousness; objects in our perceptual field are reoriented and given to us in a different manner with this person's presence on the scene. The look of the Other instigates a metamorphosis of our world; it denies physical distances from objects and unfolds its own distances. We are no longer aware of the activity going on behind the door and everything takes its significance from the fact that we have been caught peeping.

Unlike the second mode of relating to others described in the park example, Sartre suggests that in the experience of the look, our identity also flows to the Other. In the park scenario, the presence of another person altered the perspective on the park of the person who had previously been alone, but it did not fundamentally alter that person's self-apprehension. However, in the third mode of relating to other people, exemplified by the keyhole example, the look of the Other does fundamentally alter the looked-at person's self-apprehension. Before hearing footsteps in the hallway, the "peeping Tom" was unreflective, with no self; they were just immersed in peering through the keyhole. Once the Other arrived, though, they realized that they had been defined in a certain way and that the Other "holds the key to their existence". As Sartre says, "to be looked at is to apprehend oneself as the unknown object of unknowable appraisals". The important philosophical point to take away from this example is that the Other who catches the person peeping and causes them to feel ashamed, cannot just be another object. Rather, they must also be a subject. Why? For Sartre, it makes no sense to say that you have been objectified by another object. After all, a tree does not make you feel like an object, and does not make you feel ashamed if you do something untoward in front of it. Even a dog arguably would not make any of us feel embarrassed if it saw us peering through a keyhole (although the ascription of human qualities to domestic pets is common and complicates this account). This experience of shame means that the Other who induced it must be a subject; for us to experience ourselves as objectified when someone catches us at the keyhole (or in any of innumerable other circumstances) it is necessary that there be a subject who makes us an object. In other words, Sartre argues that this experience of shame, and of feeling like an object, could not happen if other people did not exist.

Now it is possible that the person caught peering through the keyhole might be mistaken when they think that they have been caught in this precarious position. They thought that they heard footsteps behind them, and then had this experience of shame, but in fact no one was actually there. Indeed, it is clear that another person does not actually have to be present for them to experience the look (BN: 275–7) and this seems to suggest that perhaps Sartre has not refuted solipsism and the epistemological scepticism that engenders it; perhaps we might still claim that we cannot know if other people exist. Sartre's response to this kind of position is to say that while there may not be someone literally there at a particular time and place in which we feel shame, at least one other person must exist for the experience of shame to be comprehensible at all (BN: 280). More empirically, Sartre also points out that it is significant that on realizing that our shame was initially "mistaken", in the sense that there was actually nobody observing us prone and in an abject position, our feeling of vulnerability before the look of the Other is actually far from dissipated; on the contrary, it is more likely that we will experience ourselves as an object all the more intensely. On Sartre's view, this cannot be explained without granting the existence of others. In rudimentary logical form, Sartre's argument goes something like the following key point.

KEY POINT *Sartre's phenomenological proof of other people*
1. Shame happens. We have phenomenological experiences of the look, of being an object in the eyes of another. (If you do not grant Sartre this premise, then his argument is ineffectual.)
2. Such experiences are only possible if other subjects exist.
3. Therefore others must exist.

Shame then, has a foundational role in Sartre's attempt to provide phenomenological evidence of other people and to deny solipsism, but there may well also be other emotions that play the same kind of role as the shame that Sartre's analysis focuses on. Pride perhaps has this social significance, and Sartre suggests this, although he also thinks that pride is a contradictory attitude that tends to be in bad faith (BN: 261, 290). I will leave you to think about whether other emotions might also provide phenomenological evidence of other people, but to return to the main issue, this experience of "being-seen-by-another" cannot be deduced from the structure of the for-itself, or from simply treating others as objects. It is a third ontological category that fits with being-in-itself and being-for-itself. Sartre calls this category "being-for-others". It has a different structure from these other modes of being and is an ontological category in its own right.

Sartre suggests that this third mode of relating to the other is the primary one, and he also argues that the second mode is ultimately actually based on this third mode. In other words, Sartre claims that we are disoriented when we see another person enter the park that we had previously inhabited alone primarily because we tacitly realize that this means that they can also see us and therefore they can also judge us. At one stage, Sartre enigmatically states that, "being seen by the other is the truth of seeing the other" (BN: 257), and this simply means that when we see another person, at some level we also apprehend that we are vulnerable to the Other's look and can never control the exact way in which we will be judged.

Of course, it needs to be emphasized that the look need not happen all the time. We may more often relate to other people in one of the other two modes, and not every empirical and literal exchange of glances is a look in Sartre's grand sense. More often than not the look is deliberately evaded through artifice and bad faith (we treat others as automatons), but in this respect it is important to recall that, for Sartre, the self-deception involved in bad faith contains the germ of its own destruction and we cannot forever avoid the dramatic and uneasy recognition of the Other's freedom that the look evinces. If you are looking for some kind of empirical proof of Sartre's theory of the look, then the fact that people often avoid eye contact in public places seems to suggest that there is at least some truth to what Sartre has to say, although it must be remembered that the look, understood as that which induces a change from subject to object in the person looked upon, can be manifest in experiences other than a literal look or glance. Sartre also discusses how a door opening, a murmur, a curtain fluttering, even the appearance of a building on the horizon in a wartime scenario where a soldier is wary of potential enemies, can all be apprehended as the look. Similarly, another person's scathing character assassination of me on the other end of a phone line might also induce this transformation from subject to object that Sartre so evocatively describes.

Now the introduction of the look, and this category of being-for-others more generally, seems to curtail the freedom of the for-itself that Sartre insisted on in the early stages of *Being and Nothingness*. After all, we lose our ability to judge the world because our own perspective is usurped by the recognition that someone else is judging us. However, Sartre claims that this experience of the look is only momentary. After having been judged in a certain way, we remain free to return the look and to subject the other person to our own judging gaze. In other words, the look is only a temporary impingement on our freedom. If we are caught staring through the keyhole we can quickly regain control by staring imperviously back at the person who has just surprised us, or we might just glare at them. Merleau-Ponty and de Beauvoir dispute some of these ideas, but Sartre's claim is that the look only impacts on us in that instant where we first feel alienated. He suggests that if we keep feeling alienated after that, then that is our own choice. If we pretend it is not our own choice, then we are in bad faith.

Sartre's insistence that we can return the look and attempt to regain control of the situation helps to explain why Garcin's dramatic declaration in *No Exit* that "hell is other people" is also representative of the philosophy of *Being and Nothingness*. Essentially, Sartre believes that relations with others are conflictual and this is primarily because we are always, for Sartre, trying to control the impact of the look. It is only the Other who can, in Sartre's terminology, transcend one's own transcendence. It is only the Other who can see us in a way that we cannot ever understand or know about ourselves (BN: 354), and this necessitates that an individual has their foundation outside themselves. We are dependent on a freedom that is other than ours, and, in this minimal sense, Sartre suggests that we are "enslaved". Moreover, according to Sartre we seek to protect ourselves and to secure our identity by reducing the impact of the other's look. The for-itself, or consciousness, seeks naturally to be the foundation of itself – in fact, Sartre suggests that the for-itself seeks to be God and to achieve an impossible synthesis of the for-itself and the in-itself – but this goal of being able to control our own identity could only be attained if we could control our being-for-others and control the way in which other people see us. Since this being-for-others dimension of our existence is obviously dependent on others, it necessitates any attempt to control this part of ourselves entailing an attempt to control Others.

This problem is reinforced by the fact that Sartre's notion of the look precludes two people simultaneously "looking" at each other, bearing in mind that by "looking'" he does not mean eyes simply following one another but the rendering of a subject as an object. This means that Beings-in-the-world are necessarily separated into a dichotomy; we are either the looker, or the looked upon. According to Sartre, this represents the main structure of experiencing the Other and depending on which mode the self has manifested itself in (for example, looking), the other must on principle be the opposite (that is, being looked at). As Sartre shows, any systematic elaboration from this position must fundamentally involve conflict. Because the experiences of the social self (shame, fear and alienation) are so disorientating, Sartre explains that people adopt variations on either sadism or masochism in an attempt to control it. In other words, we become a master or a slave. Again, Sartre leaves us with two main options. We can constantly objectify others and thereby seek to prevent the emergence of our social self, or we can try and induce the Other to see us exactly as we wish to be seen and thereby control their subjectivity. There seems to be no possibility of mutual recognition between individuals in this picture of human relationships. If we are inevitably a subject or an object, sadistic or masochistic, a master or a slave, then human relationships can only oscillate between these two polarities without ever approaching a more complementary or reciprocal intersubjectivity. Although it must be acknowledged that his abandoned *Notebooks for an Ethics* leaves more space for the possibility of love and reciprocity, in *Being and Nothingness* these are the two fundamental modes of relating to the Other, according to Sartre, although there are many variations within these main structures. Interestingly, Sartre also suggests that the positions of master and slave are both untenable and doomed to failure. They both divest the Other of their true relation to us and yet both positions are envisaged as inevitable.

KEY POINT

Sartre suggests that there are two main responses to the alienating effect of the look: we can attempt to transcend the Other's transcendence (what he calls the *second attitude towards others*); or we can attempt to appropriate the freedom of the Other by identifying with the way they view us and by incorporating their perspective within us (*first attitude towards others*).

First attitude towards others:
love, language and masochism

The first attitude towards others that we will consider can be referred to as the masochistic, slave, looked-upon, and objectified paradigm. Despite the subtitle of this section – "love, language and masochism" – Sartre does not talk much about language, other than to say that it is co-extensive with being-for-others, so I will leave out that aspect of the "first attitude" in favour of a more detailed consideration of his other two examples.

Love (BN: 364–77)

Notwithstanding his own lifelong open relationship with de Beauvoir, as well as less-enduring love relations with others (he claimed that de Beauvoir was his necessary love, while the others were contingent), Sartre basically considers love to be doomed to failure. Before it becomes clear why he thinks that this is the case, we need to consider his definition of love.

KEY POINT

Love is the project of trying to be seen as the most beloved object in the eyes of another.

In other words, to love is to want to be loved. Although it might be protested that this is not really what love is about, on Sartre's view love is a complicated ploy to ensure that the other person will view us in a way that is not alienating and that does not cause us to feel objectified by the look; love is basically a project of seducing somebody else into seeing us in a way that we are comfortable with and the impetus motivating it is that if we are consistently viewed by this one person favourably then we will not need to be worried about what they are thinking of us. This means that in love we are encouraging the other person to look at us as an object, but only in a certain way, and such that they will not consider loving anyone else.

In fact, Sartre argues that what we want in love, whether we recognize it or not, is to be seen as not only the most valuable object, but also that object from which all other objects derive their worth and significance (BN: 367). In love, he suggests that the beloved object demands that they are put "beyond the whole system of values posited by the Other and to place the lover as the condition of all valorisation and the objective foundation of values" (BN: 369). As phenomenological evidence for this, Sartre suggests that the beloved often wants their partner to, and sometimes will even enquire as to whether their partner would, sacrifice all other moral considerations for them (steal, kill, etc.).

But, of course, love cannot simply follow automatically from some kind of psychological determinism. It must nevertheless be freely agreed to. For Sartre, there is a paradox, or a tension, involved in love, because it involves trying to "possess a freedom *as* freedom" (BN: 367). This means that while we want the person to freely assent to love us, this love must nevertheless be so absolute that they do not judge us in any manner other than that which we are happy and comfortable with. This can obviously vary: one person may want their partner to see them as intelligent and deep; another may want their partner to think of them as wild and dangerous. The problem with this is that if someone loves us to such an extent that they seem to have no choice in the matter, then they are no longer a free consciousness and their love would not be satisfying. Or, to phrase the problem another way, if the other person is totally in love with us then they become simply an object for us (a person who is defined by their loving us), and that means that we must become a free consciousness and lose our status as the most beloved object (which is what we seek in love).

On the other hand, while we want the other person to freely engage lovingly with us, at the same time this also cannot be too free. Imagine if your partner offers an account of their feelings for you and suggests that "I love you because I freely choose to love you" (BN: 367). Somehow this is not satisfying on account of the other person not being sufficiently enslaved. So love involves us wanting the Other to freely see us as a beautiful and privileged object, but at the same time it also wants the Other to be enslaved by how beautiful we are. For Sartre, *the ideal of love is the appropriation of the Other as Other* (BN: 374). Love wants to divest the Other of their genuine otherness by trying to control the way in which we are seen by them. This project inevitably fails because we end up getting forced back into being a subject against our wishes; to repeat, if the Other is completely enslaved by their love for us, then they become an object, and we are forced to be a subject, rather than the beloved object. Sartre also argues that in love we are still tortured by wondering what the other party really thinks of us. While love is a "ruse" designed to overcome this problem, for him, we can never know what the Other thinks of us (and this is constitutively so), and we can hence never really be sure that we are, in fact, being seen as the most beloved object in the world, and as wild and dangerous, or however else we might want our partner to see us.

Finally, love's fragility and destructibility is also compounded by the fact that this reification of one person as the beloved object, and source of all value, depends on a dyadic two-person relationship (BN: 377). When a third party comes to interact with the loving couple, as inevitably happens, Sartre argues that the couple find their tacit agreement to view each other in a particular favourable way (as lover and beloved) transcended by this different and third perspective. While love requires that the beloved be the source of all value and is hence absolute, the presence of that third party inevitably reveals that this love is relative and the entire lover–beloved framework is thereby made unstable.

Masochism (BN: 377–9)

We have seen that, according to Sartre, when we love someone we actually want to be seen as an intrinsically worthy object in their eyes. In other words, we want them to look at us in a non-alienating way and we have seen how fragile he argues that this project is. However, we have yet to consider the masochistic project in a more general sense, which is an attitude towards others that tends to follow from the failure of this project of love.

KEY POINT
Masochism involves wanting to be a *degraded object* in the eyes of another, rather than being a *privileged object* for another person, which is what love seeks.

In other words, we might aim to have masochistic relations with others in which we are treated like an object and an instrument to be used. Why would anyone want this? To put Sartre's point crudely, the idea is that if we make it known that we do not mind being treated like just any object then perhaps the look of the Other will not be alienating. We might not feel ashamed about doing certain things in front of other people, because we are explicitly asking them to look at us doing these apparently embarrassing or crude things. Masochism is about deliberately making an object of our body for the look of the Other. On Sartre's definition, it need not be about making an object of our body so that a sadist can inflict pain on it. Rather, anybody overtly concerned with their body as the Other sees it, or their character as the Other sees it, can be said to be behaving masochistically.

To repeat, the main idea behind masochism is that we give ourselves completely over to our objectness, hoping that this will mean that the look of the Other will no longer induce shame and alienation. However, Sartre thinks that masochism is also doomed to failure. We can never successfully see ourselves as the object that we are in the eyes of another; it is only from the perspective of the Other that we might be seen as obscene, or passive, and this cannot be controlled or directly known by us. Masochism is also considered to be untenable because the very attempt to try to be nothing but a degraded object suggests that the masochist still has some subjectivity left (in order to commit to this very project), and that they are aware of what the Other *might* be thinking of them. In this respect, Sartre points out that when we attempt to ignore our own subjectivity we often actually become highly self-conscious and aware of our own subjectivity in the very attempt to evade it, and liable to the experience of anguish (BN: 378). Sartre also points out that while the masochist wants the other person to be the subject who sees them as an object, there is a sense in which the masochist is actually manipulating the Other in order to encourage them to appraise them in this way. If the masochist is manipulating the other person, then they are making them an object or an instrument for their own purposes (BN: 379). This suggests that their own subjectivity is in fact free (such that they can manipulate the situation), and they hence lose their sought-after masochistic status as an object. In other words, for Sartre the masochist inevitably finds they are not merely an object, despite their best attempts, and yet being an object is exactly what masochism seeks. So the masochistic project is also inherently unstable. Both masochism and love are typified by wanting to be the looked at, by deliberately attempting to be an object in the eyes of another person.

Second attitude towards others: indifference, desire, hatred and sadism

The second set of attitudes towards others that Sartre describes (BN: 379–413) is primarily about the consciousness that judges and treats the other people that are encountered as the objects of their look (although this is not quite so clearly the case with desire, which is somewhat more subtle, as we will shortly see).

Indifference (BN: 380–82)

Indifference seems to be a tempting way to treat the Other given the failure of love and masochism. One comment from Sartre indicates clearly what is at stake in indifference and is hence worth quoting in its entirety:

> In this state of blindness I concurrently ignore the Other's absolute subjectivity as the foundation of my being-in-the-world and my being-for-others. In a sense I am reassured, I am self-confident: that is, I am in no way conscious of the fact that the Other's Look can fix my potentialities and my Body. I am in a state the very opposite of timidity or shyness. I am at ease; I am not embarrassed by myself; for I am not outside myself.
>
> (BN: 381)

As Sartre suggests, the basic impetus behind indifference is that we deny that the Other can have a perspective on us that actually gets a grip on who we are; we do not recognize that their judgement gets at our subjectivity in any way. This is clearly a somewhat solipsistic position, as the indifferent person is basically saying to themselves that the Other cannot know or understand them, so consequently who cares what they think? Predictably enough, Sartre also thinks this attitude towards the Other is problematic and unstable. First, Sartre claims that even if we are completely indifferent to the Other, we nevertheless will continue to have an underlying awareness that they are, in fact, radically different from us. So no matter how indifferent we may attempt to be, we will have this perpetual feeling of uneasiness. A second problem with indifference is that if we were genuinely indifferent to other people, we also would not have any meaningful relations with those others at all. Admittedly, this seems difficult on Sartre's account, but genuine indifference might inhibit our quality of life. Lastly, and perhaps most significantly, indifference would seem to be in bad faith because it attempts to completely deny one aspect of the ontological structure of our existence – that is, our being-for-others – and there will inevitably be moments when our indifferent demeanour breaks down and we experience the alienating effects of the look all the more severely.

Desire (BN: 382–98)

According to Sartre's more nuanced analysis of desire, desire is an elaborate, if ultimately unsuccessful attempt to move beyond this fundamental looker–looked-upon dynamic, which does not truly understand the Other's freedom. On his account, sexual desire arises as a disruption to love (and vice versa), and he insists that it is very different from other forms of desire such as hunger (BN: 387). It has a passivity that these other forms of desire do not, in that it involves an attempt to momentarily embrace our facticity and contingency.

> **KEY POINT**
> In desire, Sartre suggests that consciousness makes itself body, but only in order to appropriate the Other's body as what he calls "flesh" (BN: 389).

What Sartre refers to as "flesh" is pure contingency, or brute being-there, that is deprived of transcendent situation and movements. On his analysis, the desirous caress seeks to reveal the Other's body as flesh that is divorced from context and situation. In other words, desire wants to make the Other's consciousness an incarnate object (BN: 389); that is, to make their subjectivity evident on the surface, and in this way desire makes the other person the object of our look, gaze and judgement.

But there is a paradox, or problem here, which is the reverse of, but is also structurally similar to, that which afflicted love. In desire, Sartre suggests that we want the desired object under our control and such that our freedom is what is being recognized, but we also want the Other to still be a free consciousness and not purely a body or an object (BN: 385–6). After all, even if we were to physically express whatever we wanted in desire, this still offers no evidence that the consciousness of the other person is itself enraptured and enslaved (BN: 385, 393). The other person, whatever the situation of their body, might still be dreaming about someone else. Moreover, were the objects of our desire like that, letting us do simply anything at all, then we would, for Sartre, pretty quickly start desiring someone or something else. What is needed in desire is that the Other's consciousness be sufficiently present for us to feel that we are possessing them in their freedom, but that their consciousness and freedom not be so apparent that we can feel ourselves simultaneously being judged in our desirous activity. If we feel ourselves being judged, then we are experiencing our being-for-others (our own objectness) and this is the antithesis of what desire seeks. On the other hand, desire also fails because if we were to genuinely master another person's consciousness by revealing it as a special kind of object, as "flesh", then we possess them simply as an object rather than as a free consciousness.

Apart from this tension that is built into the concept of desire, there are also some other problems with desire that concern its particular efforts to incarnate another's consciousness. First, Sartre points out that in desire we have to turn ourselves over to our body. Particularly if it progresses towards the level of nudity and sexual activity, this means that the desiring person also has to expose themselves as an object for the Other's gaze in their attempts to possess the Other's consciousness. As Sartre succinctly points out, "I disrobe the other only by disrobing myself" (BN: 395). While this comment should be understood ontologically, not literally or empirically, it is also the case that because of this physicality of desire, the desirer perennially risks being overwhelmed by that physicality and "losing themselves in the moment" (BN: 397), hence becoming an object for the look of the Other, rather than the subject who is getting the other person to recognize their transcendent freedom. In desire, Sartre hence argues that we are trying to get hold of not just a body, but also a free transcendent consciousness, and this is analysed as a paradoxical and impossible ambition.

Against Epicurus and hedonists of all sorts, Sartre asserts that we must abandon the idea that desire is fundamentally a desire for pleasure (or a desire for the cessation of pain). Although he admits that the average man through mental sluggishness and conformity can conceive of no other goal for his desire than orgasm, Sartre contends that desire does not imply the sexual act, or posit it as the ultimate end aimed at. On the contrary, Sartre suggests that "pleasure is the death and failure of desire" (BN: 397). For him, the sexual act and pleasure turn us inwards and away from that Other who is desired; pleasure ruptures the (relative) reciprocity of the Other's incarnation as flesh. Rather than being concerned with incarnating the Other's free consciousness in the caress, Sartre thinks that in the sexual act we instrumentally appropriate the Other's body for our own pleasure. The Other becomes an instrument for our use, an object rather than flesh, and we are returned to the conflict of the looker–looked-upon framework.

> **KEY POINT**
> Sartre also argues that desire and repulsion are ontologically fundamental aspects of our being-for-others and not something that derives its force and compulsion from the particular contingent biological sex that we happen to be (BN: 384).

Sadism (BN: 399–406)

The word "sadism" derives from the Marquis de Sade, a French writer who was imprisoned for his literature, as well as for his advocation of, and engagement in, various sadistic practices. For Sartre, sadism is the reverse of masochism. To different extents, indifference, desire and hate all fall under the broader category of sadism. What unifies these different varieties of sadism is the desire to be the subject, or to be the looker, rather than the object that is looked-upon. Sadism proper, however, takes this attitude to an extreme, and it is generally motivated by the failure of desire. As Sartre enigmatically suggests, "sadism is the failure of desire, and desire is the failure of sadism" (BN: 405).

KEY POINT

Sadism seeks the *obscene incarnation* of the Other, whereas desire seeks the incarnation of the Other *per se*. Sadism seeks to reveal the Other's unjustifiable facticity; the ungraceful and the obscene.

Although pain is not a necessary means of accomplishing this, in inflicting pain the sadist wants the Other's facticity to invade their consciousness (BN: 399). The obscenity is emphasized when the sadist, who is inflicting the pain, does not feel desire but is instead neutral.

On Sartre's view, the fundamental problem with sadism is that it can never be guaranteed success. The chained and tortured might still look back at their torturer with peaceful and forgiving eyes, which might momentarily cause their torturer to feel remorse. Alternatively, the tortured might still be defiant, even as they are about to die. In other words, the torturer can never completely efface the possibility of the tortured looking back at them in a certain way and hence making them experience their being-for-others (BN: 405). Even if the sadist kills the Other, this also fails because they have no longer enslaved the Other's consciousness precisely because it no longer exists. If the consciousness does still exist, then it always and necessarily retains the potential to look back at the sadist, thereby reminding them of their own objecthood in the eyes of another.

Hatred (BN: 410–12)

Rather than wanting to possess a free consciousness, hatred abandons any pretence to union with the Other. In an attempt to avoid feeling alienated or worried about the judgements of other people, in hating we take the initiative and judge all people first in a negative way. The supposition seems to be that the judgement of the other person cannot harm us if we consistently judge all others negatively. In this respect, Sartre makes the interesting claim that in hating any particular Other we are also tacitly hating all others (BN: 411). For him, hate understands that being looked at by another person is a suppression of my freedom, and it does not matter which Other thus suppresses my freedom. All suppressions of our transcendent freedom are resented, and in hating we try to completely eliminate this aspect of our being (our being-for-others).

However, hate is also seen to be inevitably unsuccessful, most obviously because hate actually recognizes that very Other whom we mean to suppress. This is because hate, as is commonly recognized, is not indifference, and substantial energy is in fact devoted to hating the person in question. The more we hate them, the more we recognize and imbue them with significance in our lives. The second main reason that hate fails, for Sartre, is that even if we did hate a-nd somehow efface all others from playing any role in our lives, we will nevertheless have remembered or internalized their perspective. In other words, we still retain the possibility of seeing ourselves as others see us (being-for-others is still a part of us), and we are still susceptible to the potentially alienating impact of the look.

Conclusion

To sum up, no mode of relating to the Other can be stable and ultimately successful. For Sartre, this means that most people are flung between these different ways of relating to the Other, seeking an equilibrium or moment of equal reciprocity with their lover and partner but never quite finding it. Sartre's point is *not* that we are forever and perpetually a masochist or a sadist, but rather that we oscillate between them in an ongoing master–slave dialectic – the failure of one modality refers to and motivates the adoption of another (BN: 408) – and there is no overcoming this. These are some disturbing themes. Do you think that human relationships are limited in the way that Sartre suggests? When it comes down to it, are we destined to conflict? Is love impossible? Can we only oscillate from looker to the looked-upon without ever approaching reciprocity in human relationships? Is respect for the Other's freedom an empty word, as Sartre famously suggests (BN: 409)?

Summary of key points

Being-for-others
A mode of human existence that is irreducible to being-for-itself and being-in-itself

Three kinds of relations with others
• The Other can be an object that I appropriate and use instrumentally.

- The Other can be that which takes a perspective on objects that I am looking at, and can hence induce an "internal haemorrhage" in my own perspective.
- The Other can appear as he or she who looks at me, who can judge me, and I hence experience my own "objectness".

The look
In the look, we momentarily lose our subjectivity and experience ourselves as the object of another's judgement. For Sartre, this experience is alienating and we hence seek to avoid it.

Sartre's phenomenological proof of other people
1. Shame happens. We have phenomenological experiences of the look, of being an object in the eyes of another. (If you do not grant Sartre this premise, then his argument is ineffectual.)
2. Such experiences are only possible if other subjects exist.
3. Therefore others must exist.

Two main responses to the alienating effect of the look
- We can attempt to transcend the Other's transcendence (what he calls the *second attitude towards others*).
- We can attempt to appropriate the freedom of the Other by identifying with the way they view us and by incorporating their perspective within us (*first attitude towards others*).

First attitude towards Others
- *Love* is the project of trying to be seen as the most beloved and privileged object in the eyes of another. *The ideal of love is the appropriation of the Other as Other.*
- *Masochism* involves wanting to be a *degraded object* in the eyes of another, rather than being a *privileged object* for another person, which is what love seeks.

Second attitude towards Others
- In *desire*, Sartre suggests that consciousness makes itself body, but only in order to appropriate the Other's body as what he calls "flesh" (BN: 389).
- *Sadism* seeks the *obscene incarnation* of the Other, whereas desire seeks the incarnation of the Other *per se*. Sadism seeks to reveal the Other's unjustifiable facticity; the ungraceful and the obscene.

five

Merleau-Ponty and the body

Maurice Merleau-Ponty (1908–61) completed his philosophy education at the École Normale Superieure in 1930 (with Sartre and de Beauvoir) and has frequently been associated with existentialism, although he never propounded quite the same extreme accounts of death, freedom, anguished responsibility and conflictual relations with others for which existentialism became both famous and notorious. Instead, he spent much of his academic career contesting and reformulating many of Sartre's positions, including a sustained critique of what he saw as Sartre's dualist and ultimately Cartesian ontology. He also came to disagree with Sartre's rather hard-line Marxism and this was a major factor in what was eventually a rather acrimonious ending to their friendship and editorial collaboration on the influential political, literary and philosophical magazine, *Les Temps modernes* (for Merleau-Ponty's assessment of their differences see "Sartre and Ultra-Bolshevism" in *Adventures of the Dialectic*, but for Sartre's version of events see "Merleau-Ponty Vivant" in *Situations*).

Merleau-Ponty argues that phenomenology is essentially, and necessarily, existential philosophy (PP: xiv), which is to say that any attempted reduction to the "things themselves", or experience, will actually end up by revealing the way in which experience is always permeated by the existential and social situation of which we are a part. In other words, the attempted phenomenological reduction is necessarily incomplete, but for Merleau-Ponty this inability to complete it actually reveals much about the human situation, and he thought of his project, at least in *Phenomenology of Perception* (1945), as both continuing Husserl's and also extending it so as to take into account our embodied and historical situatedness. His work is heavily based on accounts of perception, and tends towards emphasizing an embodied engagement in the world that is more fundamental than our reflective capacities. Although he is often associated with the idea of the "primacy of perception", rather than rejecting scientific and analytic ways of knowing the world Merleau-Ponty simply wanted to argue that such knowledge is always derivative in relation to the more practical aspects of the body's exposure to the world. While it is difficult to summarize Merleau-Ponty's work into neat propositions, he sought to develop a radical re-description of embodied human experience, and this chapter will consider his position on ambiguity, bodily motility, habit, relations with others and ontology, particularly as his discussions of such concepts challenges Sartre's more canonical version of existentialism. Before Merleau-Ponty's contributions to existentialism can be made clear, however, it is necessary to provide some background on his general philosophical project of emphasizing the body.

The body-subject

Good arguments can be put forward to suggest that a denigration of embodiment tacitly governs most philosophical thought, until at least Nietzsche, and this is something that the post-Heideggerian existentialists have tried to address. For Merleau-Ponty, there is no aspect of his phenomenology that does not implicate the body, or what is often termed in the literature the "body-subject".

In his major work, *Phenomenology of Perception*, he sets about exposing the problematic aspects of traditional philosophical dichotomies and, in particular, that age-old dualism involving the mind and the body. It is no accident that consideration of this dualism plays such an important role in his work, since the constitution of the body as an "object" is also a pivotal moment in the construction of the idea of an objective world that exists "out there" (PP: 72). Once this conception of the body is problematized, so too, according to Merleau-Ponty, is the whole idea of an outside world that is entirely distinguishable from the thinking subject. For him, this fundamental presupposition was responsible for the tendency of Western philosophy to fall within two main categories, neither of which is capable of shedding much light on the problems that it seeks to address. He was preoccupied with refuting both empiricism – the doctrine that all knowledge comes from sense experiences – and what he called "intellectualism", a broad term that in his usage encompasses what is commonly referred to as rationalism and idealism (rationalism is the view that we can know things that are not dependent on experience, a position that in its more extreme form can lead to idealism). It is not difficult to see why Merleau-Ponty would be preoccupied with undermining such dichotomous tendencies, which Foucault has termed the "empirico-transcendental doublet of modern thought" (OT: xiv). It ensures that one exists as a constituting thing (subject) or as a thing (object). Moreover, that perennial philosophical debate regarding whether humanity is free or determined is closely related, and this ontological dualism of immanence and transcendence – consider mind–body, thought–language, self–world, inside–outside – is at the forefront of all Merleau-Ponty's attempts to reorientate philosophy.

Although Merleau-Ponty does not deny the possibility of cognitive relations between subject and object, he does reject the suggestion that these are phenomenologically the most primitive. Following Marcel's lead, *Phenomenology of Perception* is united by the claim that we are our bodies, and he also holds that our lived experience of this body denies the detachment of subject from object, mind from body, that both rationalism and empiricism endorse in different ways (PP: xii). Virtually the entirety of his book is devoted to illustrating that the body cannot be viewed solely as an object, or material entity of the world.

One idea of central significance for Merleau-Ponty is the fact that the body is always there, and that its absence (and to a certain degree also its variation) is inconceivable (PP: 91). It means that we cannot treat the body as an object available for perusal, which can or cannot be part of our world, since it is not something that we can possibly do without. It is the mistake of classical psychology, not to mention the empiricism of the "hard" sciences, that it treats the body exclusively as an object, when for Merleau-Ponty, an object "is an object only insofar as it can be moved away from me … Its presence is such that it entails a possible absence. Now the permanence of my body is entirely different in kind" (PP: 90). The omnipresence of our body prevents us treating it simply as an object of the world, even though such an apparently axiomatic position is not always recognized by traditional philosophy.

Another factor against conceiving of the body as being completely constituted, as an object in-itself, is the fact that it is that by which there are objects. The body cannot be the mere servant of consciousness, since "in order that we may be able to move our body towards an object, the object must first exist for it, our body must not belong to the realm of the in-itself" (PP: 139). In this way, Merleau-Ponty emphasizes that the aspects of an object revealed to an individual are dependent on their bodily position and his further more general claim is that the body-subject is not given to us by the analyses of the sciences, but is the condition for us to experience objects at all. Our body should be conceived of as our means of communication with the world, rather than merely as a brute object in the world, which our mind orders to perform varying functions.

"I can" and "I think"

Merleau-Ponty has another important and related point to make about the status of our bodies, which precludes them from being categorized simply as objects. According to him, we move directly and in union with our bodies. As he points out, "I do not need to lead it (*the body*) towards a movement's completion, it is in contact with it from the start and propels itself towards that end" (PP: 94). In other words, we do not need to check to see if we have two legs before we stand up, since we are necessarily with our bodies. The consequences of this simple idea are more extensive than one may presume. On a more complicated level, the experience of playing sports testifies to this being with our bodies, as does the wave to a friend, or other gestures: our bodies simply respond to given circumstances without the intervention of traditional philosophical conceptions of thought and/or intention. Our actions are solicited by the situations that confront us, in a constantly evolving way.

Moreover, if this purposive action without a purpose (other than best accommodating ourselves to the situation in which we are immersed) is interrupted or forestalled, say if a particular golfer starts to ponder the intricacies of their swing, where their feet are positioned, mental outlook and so on rather than simply responding, it is certainly probable that they will lose form. "So what?", one may ask. According to Merleau-Ponty, the point is that "whether a system of motor or perceptual powers, our body is not an object for an 'I think', it is a grouping of lived-through meanings which moves towards its equilibrium" (PP: 153). The philosophical tradition's emphasis on rationalistic thought and the deliberative will, along with a tendency to dissect human behaviour through the "I think", can conspire to turn us away from the body's acclimatization to its own environment, which is more practical and, like Heidegger's conception of the ready-to-hand, is better characterized as an attitude of "I can". Merleau-Ponty hence explores a more basic motivation for human action than is usually taken to be the case. Rather than focusing on our desire to attain certain pleasures, or achieve certain goals, his analysis reveals the body's more primordial tendency to try to achieve an equilibrium with the world.

The habituality to which he is referring is far from being merely a mechanistic or behaviouristic propensity to pursue a certain line of action, but we may want to ask, as Merleau-Ponty does, "if habit is neither a form of knowledge nor an involuntary action, what is it then?" According to him, "it is knowledge in the hands, which is forthcoming only when bodily effort is made, and cannot be formulated in detachment from that effort" (PP: 144). Merleau-Ponty suggests that this type of "knowledge in the hands" is primordial. He implies that if we disregard this practical basis of knowledge, we risk embarking on philosophic and scientific endeavours that are of no practical benefit, and that might also reinforce and legitimize the mind–body dualism in the wider cultural context of which they are a part. In this respect, it is important to emphasize the distinction that Merleau-Ponty draws between a practical way of relating to things, the "I can", and the reflective mode of the "I think", the latter of which renders the body capable of being treated as an object. In some ways this repeats the distinction between the reflective and pre-reflective cogito that was such a major aspect of Sartre's work but, unlike Sartre, Merleau-Ponty attempts to legitimize this through empirical and psychological analysis.

Schneider and the difference between grasping and pointing

At various different points in his text, Merleau-Ponty discusses a patient by the name of Schneider who, on account of brain damage sustained during a war, is unable to perform bodily movements in the normal flowing manner (PP: 103–10). For example, while he can blow his nose if he feels that need, or *grasp his nose* if it has been bitten by a mosquito, he cannot perform equivalent actions if his eyes are shut and he also cannot *point to his nose* if asked to. If he watches his hand, eventually he can guide it to his nose, but it is a laborious and awkward process.

When confronted with a practical task such as cutting paper, however, Schneider does not have to first locate his hands before moving them; the scissors on the table and the task of cutting paper immediately and unreflectively mobilize potential actions and solicit him to react to them in certain ways. Concrete movements and acts of grasping, such as the blowing of his nose, enjoy a privileged position for him and, Merleau-Ponty will argue, for all of us; it is the main example of what he calls "motor intentionality". The grasping movement is from the outset at its end and involves anticipation, and the understanding of space involved in grasping is basic, even though it largely resists our explicit thematization and understanding.

On the other hand, when Schneider is asked to accomplish some abstract activity such as pointing to his nose we have seen that things are far more problematic. These kinds of reflective activity go through the intermediary of the objective world and Schneider cannot perform movements that are not a response to an actual, present situation. When attempting to point, Schneider is like a distanced observer to himself. In fact, he appears as a paradigm case of what it would be like to have a mind that ordered the body to do things and we can hence practically see just how problematic this model is. Schneider does treat his body as such an object and it makes actions such as pointing to his nose almost impossible.

In response to this case, Merleau-Ponty asks, "If I know where my nose is when it is a matter of holding it, how can I not know where it is when it is a matter of pointing to it?" (PP: 104). He suggests that the problem is that Schneider either has an ideal formula for a particular movement that he works out in his head before acting, or he launches blindly into movement. There is no feedback between these two very different attitudes, whereas for most of us active movement is indissolubly both movement and consciousness of movement and we presuppose a mutual presence of body and object in our pointing. While this example serves to reaffirm his distinction between the unreflective grasping body (the "I can") and the reflective pointing one (which admits of an "I think"), Merleau-Ponty is also keen to point out that Schneider's difficulties cannot be accounted for on the basis of either empiricism or intellectualism. Martin Dillon effectively summarizes Merleau-Ponty's point in this regard as follows:

> The patient cannot be understood as suffering from a purely physical disability (as empiricism would have it) because he can perform the physical movements; but neither can he be incapacitated in a purely psychical way (as intellectualism claims) because he can understand the goals to be achieved.
>
> (1988: 138)

Touching–touched

Whereas Sartre does not attach any special significance to the phenomenon of what is sometimes called "double-touching" and in fact explicitly denies it as a possibility (BN: 304), for Merleau-Ponty so-called double-touching is very important, as it reaffirms his fundamental contention that a subject–object (or mind–body) model deprives the existential phenomena of their true complexity. He characterizes this famous touching–touched example as follows:

> If I touch with my left hand my right hand while it touches an object, the right hand object is not the right hand touching: the first is an intertwining of bones, muscles and flesh bearing down on a point in space, the second traverses space as a rocket in order to discover the exterior object in its place.   (PP: 92)

Merleau-Ponty's initial, and I think permissible, presumption here is that we can never simultaneously touch our right hand while it is also touching an object of the world. In his final book, *The Visible and the Invisible*, he suggests that, "either my right hand really passes over into the rank of the touched, but then its hold on the world is interrupted, or it retains its hold on the world, but then I do not really touch it" (VI: 148). There is, then, a gap between ourselves as touching and ourselves as touched, a divergence between the sentient and sensible aspects of our existence, but this gap is importantly distinct from merely reinstating another dualism, and it does more than represent the body's capacity to be both perceiving object and subject of perception in a constant oscillation (as is arguably the case in Sartre's looked-at–looked-upon, dichotomy, as well as the master–slave oscillations that such a conception induces).

Rather, this example of the hand touching itself represents the body's capacity to occupy the position of both perceiving object and subject of perception, and the way in which each of these capacities depends on the other. As Merleau-Ponty puts it, "when I press my two hands together, it is not a matter of two sensations felt together as one perceives two objects placed side by side, but an ambiguous set-up in which both hands can alternate the role of 'touching' and being 'touched'" (PP: 93). This double touching and encroachment of the touching on to the touched (and vice versa), where subject and object cannot be unequivocally discerned, is considered to be representative of perception and sensibility generally. Merleau-Ponty hence tacitly argues for what he will later call the "reversibility" of the body: that the experience of touching cannot be understood without reference to the tacit potential for this situation to be reversed. As Merleau-Ponty suggests:

> I can identify the hand touched as the same one which will in a moment be touching … In this bundle of bones and muscles which my right hand presents to my left, I can anticipate for an instant the incarnation of that other right hand, alive and mobile, which I thrust towards things in order to explore them. The body tries … to touch itself while being touched and initiates a kind of reversible reflection. (PP: 93)

This suggests that the hand that we touch, while it is touching an inanimate object, is hence not merely another such "object", but another fleshy substance that is capable of reversing the present situation. Given that we cannot touch ourselves, or even somebody else, without this recognition of our own tangibility and capacity to be touched by others, the awareness of what it feels like to be touched encroaches, or even supervenes on the experience of touching (VI: 147). Any absolute distinction between being in the world as touching and being in the world as touched, such as that proposed by Sartre, does not accurately capture the experience of embodied subjectivity, which is never located purely in either our tangibility or in our touching, but in the intertwining of these two aspects, or where the two lines of a "chiasm" intersect with one another. The chiasm (a metaphor that Merleau-Ponty regularly employs in his later work) is simply an image to describe how this overlapping and encroachment can take place between a pair that nevertheless retains a divergence, in that touching and touched are obviously never exactly the same thing. In his later work he brings out the ontological consequences of this position. Unfortunately, Merleau-Ponty died before he had the opportunity to complete *The Visible and the Invisible*, which was intended to be a text of considerable proportions, but it is the earlier work that is more existential so for the time being we will set aside discussion of Merleau-Ponty's later work and focus on his criticisms of Sartre as they are expressed in *Phenomenology of Perception*.

Merleau-Ponty's critique of Sartre's conception of freedom

Do not be fooled by the first couple of pages of Merleau-Ponty's final chapter in *Phenomenology of Perception* entitled "Freedom". Some important differences between his conception of freedom and Sartre's are apparent in this chapter, despite the sympathetic tone that he adopts at the outset in explaining the Sartrean position. Although there is considerable debate in the secondary literature about whether or not Merleau-Ponty criticizes a caricature of Sartre in this chapter – a "pseudo-Sartre" as de Beauvoir claims in an essay of the same name – I will suggest that two main themes separate their respective conceptions of freedom: (i) our embodied habituality and the significance of the past (PP: 434–56); and (ii) the issue of relations with others (PP: 346–65; VI: 71–90).

Habituality

Merleau-Ponty's first critical response to the Sartrean account of our absolute freedom in regard to a situation is to argue that if it is the case that our freedom is the same in all actions, then it cannot be coherently held that there is such thing as free action (PP: 436–7). After all, freedom cannot be measured in relation to particular modes of conduct, since for Sartre the slave is equally free whether they are breaking their chains or not. This may seem to be a largely semantic point, but Merleau-Ponty also mentions the problem of motivation in this context and his fundamental criticism of the Sartrean account is that if we are always equally free, then why would freedom commit itself in projects, as in the very next instant it will find itself just as free and indeterminate? What reason would we have for adopting a course of action at all, let alone sustaining one?

Now Sartre does deal with this issue, at least to some extent. In his treatment of the phenomenon of anguish he discusses why once we are committed to projects there is some kind of inclination to go on and to complete that project. When immersed in activity we tend to non-reflectively pursue that particular activity and to finish writing the 700 pages of *Being and Nothingness*, for example, rather than simply abandoning that project half-way through. Towards the concluding stages of this book, in the chapter entitled "Existential Psychoanalysis", he also develops the idea of a fundamental or original project that underpins our behaviour. Sartre takes it that these two ideas are sufficient to refute the caricatures of his position on freedom as amounting to nothing more than a series of gratuitous and capricious "jerks" (BN: 452). However, Merleau-Ponty argues that Sartre does not accord enough attention to this issue of why we generally persist in particular activities and in responding to this problem he suggests that our bodies sustain intentions around us that we do not choose, but that we can nevertheless resist, albeit sometimes with considerable effort.

We have already seen that, for Merleau-Ponty, our bodies seek to attain equilibrium with the environment we are in. We attain this equilibrium with our environment by forming habits, or "intentional arcs" (which are the link that the body establishes between action and perception), and by acquiring embodied skills that can be easily and consistently deployed. If something has proved successful in the past, for example if we have found a parking space near the university in one area, then we are likely to continue to look for a parking space in that same area at least until it fails us. For Merleau-Ponty, our bodies inevitably adjust to the circumstances they are in, and the more they are trained to do this, the better they become at adjusting.

Now, Sartre, we must remember, posits a radical discontinuity in consciousness. The past in no way supervenes upon the present, and if, for example, we intend to remain faithful to our decision to give up gambling some weeks ago, we must call up our reasons for so doing and reinvent that decision as if it had not occurred previously. Merleau-Ponty argues that this position of Sartre's is "haunted by the spectre of the instant" and he instead asserts that for freedom to be an "active doing" it cannot immediately be undone by a new freedom (PP: 438). In other words, we cannot coherently try to negotiate the cliff-face safely and yet keep having a radical discontinuity from each moment to the next where we are always free to turn back. While Merleau-Ponty argues that we retain this possibility of changing our minds, he suggests that it is necessary that we develop habitual and embodied relations to the world that ensure that we have some kind of impetus (PP: 437), and are usually inclined to carry on, once we have begun to negotiate the precipice, for example.

For Merleau-Ponty, freedom hence needs to be projected over durations. If it is to be freedom, it must have constraints, and constraints beyond mere facticity. In the Sartrean account, facticity provides the condition for us to exercise our freedom, but does not actually play a role in consciousness, which functions through negation and is literally nothingness. According to Merleau-Ponty, however, this embodied acclimatization to our environment also influences what Sartre calls being-for-itself (consciousness) and influences our ability to project different courses of action. This will become more apparent as we go on, but the main point is that Merleau-Ponty argues that our bodies sustain around us general intentions that we are not always aware of, and do not choose, and that these can actually ramify upon the for-itself.

At the moment his conception of this embodied habituality is rather theoretical, but we have seen Merleau-Ponty's claim that movements of the body are developed almost without conscious effort in most cases. For Merleau-Ponty, there is a sort of intelligence of the body in the way that it adjusts to its environment. Many sporting activities seem to testify to this habitual being with our bodies. Merleau-Ponty mentions soccer in this regard but the basketball player who says that he or she is "in the zone" also exhibits this type of practical, embodied habituality. While the basketball player perceives the court in accordance with some general intentions, these intentions are modified by the situation in which they find themselves. Rather than involving reflective decision-making processes, the experienced basketball player simply "knows" what to do in certain circumstances on account of their past experiences. For instance, passing the ball to a team-mate, despite the opposing players, appears to the basketball player, after a lot of practice, to demand the use of a certain type of pass to avoid it being intercepted. In other words, *situations choose us, as much as we choose them*, when we are playing sport, particularly if we are well trained in a particular sport. Merleau-Ponty's point is that as we refine our skills for coping with existence (based on past experiences), scenarios show up as soliciting those acquired skilful responses. This type of habitual behaviour is far from being merely a deterministic propensity to pursue a certain line of action, or a robotic repetition of past behaviour. Although habit is built on a past-learned skill, it must also allow us to adjust to slightly different and unanticipated scenarios. Our habitual mode of being is hence constantly being slightly altered, and is more akin to a skill (PP: 143).

Another good example of this practical and embodied intelligence that Merleau-Ponty's work points us towards is the fact that when we drive a car we are intimately aware of how a particular car's gearshift needs to be treated, as well as its ability to turn, accelerate, brake and so on, and also of the dimensions of the vehicle. When we reflect on our own parking experiences, it is remarkable that there are so few minor collisions considering how many times we are forced to come very close. When reversing, many drivers need not even really monitor the progress of their car because they "know" what result the various movements of the steering wheel are likely to induce. The car is absorbed into our body image with almost the same precision that we have regarding our own spatiality. This activity is not reflective or interpretive, as we do not have to perceive the distance to a car park and then reflect on the fact that we are in a car of such and such proportions before the manoeuvre can be attempted. Rather, it is a practical mastery of a technique that ensures that the given rules can be followed blindly (or at least without reflective thought) and yet nevertheless with an embodied intelligence.

Our skilful embodiment makes it possible for us to encounter more and more differentiated solicitations to act, and this enables us to react to situations in ways that have previously proved successful and that do not require purposive thought. These examples suggest that the body itself has an intentionality of some kind, and this is not something that Sartre recognizes. Although it remains to be seen how this embodied intentionality might inhibit or have an influence on our freedom, for the moment it is important to emphasize that Merleau-Ponty also envisages this embodied habituality as applying to more intellectual endeavours and professions and in this respect it is worth briefly considering one of Hubert Dreyfus and Stuart Dreyfus's studies regarding skill acquisition in chess.

Dreyfus and Dreyfus on expertise in chess

Dreyfus and Dreyfus's studies establish that a master chess player can easily beat an exceptionally good chess player, even if they respond to their opponent's every move in less than five seconds and while they are also simultaneously counting or doing something else which preoccupies their cognitive capacity. The degree to which the master player's ability is lessened is scarcely discernible, suggesting that their reactions are predominantly habitual reactions to certain configurations on the chess board, with conscious reflection and detailed cognitive preparations not necessarily a major aspect of what is involved in deciding, even in those types of activities that seem to require the most extensive and sustained "thinking" (Dreyfus & Dreyfus 1989: 103–4).

In Merleau-Ponty's vocabulary, the master chess player accords a priority to the "I can" rather than the "I think" (PP: 137), and they need not rigorously attempt to figure out the consequences of what a certain move might be, or be absorbed by thoughts such as "Should I place my knight here or there, use my knight or my bishop for this particular move?" Although this type of thought is undoubtedly sometimes also involved, it is a far more common experience for the beginner and for the competent, who are both confounded by the enormous number of possibilities.

Again, the point of this example is that the body inclines us towards an expertise of those environments in which we consistently partake. It sustains intentions around us, such that we can react in an apparently unthinking way, and choose modes of conduct through habitual activity; that is, we choose our various moves largely through the weight of our past choices and this is not simply something that we might choose not to do.

To put the difference between these two philosophers as simply as possible, Merleau-Ponty's claim is that the radical discontinuity on which the Sartrean postulation of freedom relies (i.e. a separation between *past–present* and *present–future*) is undermined by the recognition of the ways in which the body cultivates skills and habits.

If we have mastered a technique, such as chess, basketball or even writing philosophy papers, then our past experiences of those activities actually play an increasingly significant role in our consciousness, such that there is not a radical discontinuity from the *past–present*. Even if there is still a discontinuity of some kind between past and present, for somebody well trained in their area of expertise it is not the kind of radical discontinuity that Sartre describes. On mastering a technique, an individual can become accustomed to a situation in such a way that they "understand" how best to decide and without the need for this understanding to be accompanied by any prior mental representation, or consciously determined goal. As their adjustment towards the world becomes more sophisticated, these embodied "solicitations to act" become more and more extensive and play an increasingly influential role in our consciousness and our decision-making. If this analysis is correct, our actions are hence often partly solicited by the situation and by our past experiences in similar situations, and we have an embodied intentionality toward the world that we do not choose in our decisions and certainly not in each instant.

Rocky crag

This embodied intentionality explains the differing perspective that Merleau-Ponty and Sartre have in regard to their discussions of the mountain, or "rocky crag", as Sartre calls it. Although Sartre acknowledges the facticity of the mountain – the fact that Mt Everest may simply not be scalable for a particular individual if they do not have the required strength, endurance and agility – he does not acknowledge that this facticity might actually have a *determinate* character in motivating whether or not they might decide to try to climb that rock. For Sartre, facticity and the for-itself are separate (albeit inconceivable without the other), and whatever height the mountain may be it remains the possibility of the for-itself to project the mountain as climbable. Of course, reality soon intervenes if a person is too inexperienced or weak to attempt such a climb.

For Merleau-Ponty, however, that facticity of the rocky crag actually intervenes on consciousness and makes it inordinately difficult, perhaps impossible, to perceive a certain mountain as climbable (PP: 440). For him, our bodies have their own mode of interacting with the world and this ramifies upon consciousness. In adjusting to the particularities of its environment, my body sustains around me intentions that are not dependent on my choices and decisions, and Merleau-Ponty argues that we cannot contrive it such that the mountains are small for us. He suggests that even if we imagine that we are viewing the mountains from the perspective of a much larger mountain, our hands and feet are still our reference point for making that imaginative leap (PP: 440).

Hikers
You will also recall that Sartre discusses a pair of hikers who have been walking all day. According to him, they choose when to confer meaning on their pain such that they will stop walking, and it is, of course, apparent to all of us that one of the two walkers will stop before the other. Sartre then goes on to offer an analysis of this decision as being based in their differing fundamental projects: the hiker who persists is embracing their embodied facticity, whereas the hiker who gives in seeks to escape their facticity. Given the latter's background, perhaps of cafés and inner-city urban living, which is itself part of their fundamental project, they find the pain and fatigue intolerable rather than something for them to attempt to overcome, or a privileged way in which the adversity and extremities of the mountain are revealed.

In "Freedom", Merleau-Ponty also considers this example and responds that while Sartre's account is true in one sense, what occurs when we decide to keep going, or to give in to fatigue, is not only a matter of a sudden choice made in that instant, nor even of a sudden confirmation of our fundamental project. He suggests that "here we must recognise a sedimentation to our lives, an attitude towards the world which, when it has received frequent confirmations, acquires favoured status for us" (PP: 441). In other words, one of the hikers may have spent twenty years not walking, with a certain attitude regarding their own ability to endure pain, and this is the case regardless of their fundamental project. For Merleau-Ponty, this actually impacts on their consciousness in such a way that while it is possible to persist in the hike, it is far from probable, and would take a greater negation, to use Sartre's term, than for somebody who has had a more active embodied relation to the world, pursuing gym activities and so on. *For Sartre, there are not greater and lesser degrees of freedom, but for Merleau-Ponty there are*, as our embodied adjustment to the world delimits our range of possibilities even if it never completely determines them.

Oppression: the past is the atmosphere of the present

Thus far, you will have noticed that we have looked at some of the more positive aspects of Merleau-Ponty's account of our embodied habituality; it reminds us of how we react quickly to situations that are closely related to those that we have previously encountered and without encountering something tantamount to Sartrean anguish. At the same time, this embodied habit also has a negative component since the intentions that our bodies sustain around us also make oppression possible. As Merleau-Ponty points out, this embodied habituality means that we are highly unlikely to overcome an inferiority complex that has been operative for twenty years. If we have been oppressed for a considerable period of time, our consciousness can be habituated to such an extent that certain modes of conduct become manifestly improbable. Our body assumes this denigration, lives in it, and this is not something that we can simply shed by a nihilating act of consciousness that leaves this denigration behind. For Merleau-Ponty, in situations of oppression it becomes difficult to envisage other possibilities and projects in the world. Change is still possible, but not probable, because persecution works on our entire embodied relation to the world.

In "Freedom", Merleau-Ponty suggests that this embodied intentionality is the phenomenological basis that explains statistical thought and probability (PP: 442). Probability is not something that Sartre admits into his conception of freedom. We are equally free in all situations, but Merleau-Ponty's account is able to admit of degrees. For Merleau-Ponty, the situation is far more complicated than suggesting that we are always free to adopt multiple perspectives on, say, the colonial exploitation with which many countries have been confronted. Whereas Sartre might suggest that any endorsement of that status quo, such as a black person assuming the colonialist discrimination to be justified and tacitly wanting to be white, would be in bad faith, for Merleau-Ponty this is not necessarily the case. Persistent persecution ramifies upon the for-itself and we also learn this persecution at an embodied level when we are very young and arguably unable to conceive of alternative possibilities, as Sartre presumes we can. To change this situation would require not only the radical discontinuity implied in reflection, which Sartre also takes to characterize the pre-reflective life, but also the creation of new habits over a prolonged period of time. This emphasis on the possibility of oppression that need not be assented to, because it works at an embodied level, explains why many feminist philosophers have shown interest in Merleau-Ponty's work. Although feminists have also raised some important questions regarding Merleau-Ponty's presumptions about what normal sexuality consists in – i.e. male heterosexuality – they have nevertheless found his work a useful resource for clarifying the ways in which oppression can function.

The important thing to note, in Merleau-Ponty's words, is that "the past is the atmosphere of my present" (PP: 442). It is not a set of events at a distance from me. For Sartre, our past is one aspect of our facticity, but for Merleau-Ponty our facticity actually intervenes upon the for-itself. Rather than any absolute distinction between facticity and freedom, our embodied subjectivity is located between these two polarities. This means that we are both free and determined and we will return to this idea below.

Otherness/alterity

We might remember that Sartre's solution to the "problem of other minds" – that is, his answer to the question of how we can know that other people exist – is to suggest that we have an experience (that being shame) that is only comprehensible if other people exist. Certain experiences reveal my consciousness (which is for-itself) as also being-for-others. However, Sartre nevertheless insists that this non-reflective apprehension of myself as being the object of the look of another is only momentary; this experience of being-for-others only impedes on our consciousness in that instant where we are suddenly aware that we are caught looking through a keyhole. According to him, we can immediately regain control by glaring at those who are staring at us, or by pretending that the fact that they have caught us peering through the keyhole is of no consequence. In *Being and Nothingness*, Sartre argues that this inevitably results in conflictual relations with others because each of us try to control the impact of the Other's look upon us.

For Merleau-Ponty, however, our being-for-others (that is, the feelings of shame, pride, etc.) is always in consciousness and at least partially intertwined with the for-itself. Just as for Merleau-Ponty there is encroachment between being-for-itself and being-in-itself, in that the past always overlaps with and supervenes on the present, this also applies between our being-for-itself and our being-for-others. Merleau-Ponty asks: how is it, if there are two fundamentally different categories called being-for-others and being-for-itself (and Sartre does contend that being-for-others is irreducible to the other two modes), that I could actually have an experience of an other, an alter-ego? In less obtuse terms, Merleau-Ponty is asking whether Sartre's philosophy is theoretically committed to solipsism. Elsewhere Merleau-Ponty does explicitly accuse Sartre of solipsism, despite Sartre's sustained attempts to avoid it, but the main point to ascertain is that Merleau-Ponty argues that in order for it to be possible that we recognize others (and again this is a transcendental argument) we must have being-for-others actually inside our consciousness/for-itself.

In a sense, for Merleau-Ponty, *we internalize the look of the Other at all stages rather than just in occasional experiences.* This means that oppression is again rendered possible, because our being-for-others ramifies upon our for-itself; that is, it influences our capacity to negate or nihilate given structures and to propose others. Again, this happens over a period of time and while Sartre might argue that at some level we have consented to this oppression and willingly accepted our status as the object of the Other's look, for Merleau-Ponty the body retains these meanings. Our body image, for example, is not simply chosen as Sartre's account sometimes implies. For Merleau-Ponty, as an embodied subject we accept ourselves as being constituted in certain ways, and after years of oppression our bodies tacitly accept this oppression and reflection cannot simply ignore this. Even in the most radical reflection (such as Descartes' *cogito ergo sum* or Husserl's *epoché*), Merleau-Ponty contends that we have this atmosphere of sociality and these horizons of significance that cannot be completely bracketed away.

In this respect, explanations of our behaviour in terms of the past and even our infant sociality are tenable for Merleau-Ponty. Merleau-Ponty was Head of Child Psychology at the Sorbonne for some years and his work is hence nowhere near as aggressive towards the psychological tradition as Sartre is. He examined the Gestalt tradition in detail and throughout his career liaised with his famous psychoanalyst friend, Jacques Lacan. Moreover, as we have seen, one of Merleau-Ponty's most regularly employed methods in *Phenomenology of Perception* is to examine cases where our normal relation to the world breaks down. Diplopia, aphasia and the phenomenon of phantom limbs all get a workout in this text, and it is the malfunctions of people like the war-veteran Schneider that serve to highlight and make manifest the ways of relating to the world that are presupposed by "normal" action.

Merleau-Ponty even offers this kind of psychological explanation about why a man who is being tortured might not give in to the demands of his persecutors. It might be partly on account of the fact that his war comrades expected such behaviour from him, or that for twenty years he had envisaged himself as mentally tough. These factors do not completely cancel out freedom, but it does have an influence on it, and Merleau-Ponty hence advocates a position that is neither determinism nor indeterminism. Whereas Sartre has freedom and constraint occupying separate realms (facticity is the condition for freedom but does not otherwise influence it), for Merleau-Ponty freedom and constraint are intertwined together. We are both constituted by the world and also serve to constitute it, and consciousness retains both of these aspects. Whereas Sartre says that subjectivity is defined by negation (and by a freedom that cannot be qualified), Merleau-Ponty suggests that, "I am both a general refusal to be limited to anything, but also a continual acceptance of such and such a qualified form of being" (PP: 452). In other words, we must not simply say that we continually choose ourselves, but also that the world chooses us. We are never simply a thing and never simply a consciousness that can, through negation, divorce itself from its embodied significance. The obvious question in response to this is: can Merleau-Ponty have it both ways? I think that he can, but it has consequences. If embodied subjectivity is located at the juncture of both the for-itself and the in-itself, to use Sartre's terms, this means that the generality of the situation and the world always has an impact on our decisions and choices; in fact, it becomes impossible to determine precisely what role the situation has in determining our decisions and precisely what role is contributed by our own freedom. As a consequence, there is pervasive ambiguity and this is something that de Beauvoir also argues, as we will shortly see.

Ambiguity, not authenticity

It is worth pointing out that while habit and the tendency to seek an equilibrium might help us adjust to the circumstances of our world, they do not simply make things easy. For Merleau-Ponty, "what enables us to centre our existence is also what prevents us from centering it completely, and the anonymity of our body is inseparably both freedom and servitude" (PP: 85). Moreover, Merleau-Ponty does not intend to suggest that the complicity of body and mind that we see in the mastery of a technique implies an absolute awareness of our own "subjectivity".

According to him, "there is the absolute certitude of the world in general, but not of anything in particular" (PP: 344). Knowing an individual person in a particular manifestation may presuppose an understanding of humanity in its totality, but certainly not any singular motivation for a particular act. Lived relations cannot be grasped perfectly by consciousness, since the body-subject is never entirely present-to-itself. Meaningful behaviour is lived through rather than reflected on by a distanced observer (e.g. Descartes peering down on those automatons below him in the street), and this ensures that the actions of particular individuals may be meaningful without them being fully aware of this meaning. There is ambiguity, then, precisely because we are not capable of disembodied reflection on our activities, but are involved in an intentional arc that absorbs both our body and our mind (PP: 136). For Merleau-Ponty, both intellectualism and empiricism presuppose "a universe perfectly explicit in itself" (PP: 41), but residing between these two positions, his body-subject actually requires ambiguity.

> **KEY POINT**
> Ambiguity is a condition of being a perspective on the world and yet being blind to that perspective. As the body is an amalgam of both subject and object, it is always ambiguous whether a decision, or a perception, can be traced back to the subject or to the world.

In his chapter "Temporality", Merleau-Ponty argues that ambiguity prevails both in my perception of things and in the knowledge I have of myself, primarily because of our temporal situation, which he insists cannot but be ambiguous (PP: 345–6). For our purposes it is enough to understand what Merleau-Ponty describes elsewhere as "the paradox of transcendence in immanence" (PrP: 16): that is, to understand that objects are given over to us, influenced by us, just as we are influenced by the objects that surround us. For Merleau-Ponty, this interdependence and mutual encroachment is evident in all aspects of perception and subjectivity. As he makes clear, "whenever I try to understand myself, the whole fabric of the perceptible world comes too, and with it comes the others who are caught in it" (S: 15). In the concluding words of *Phenomenology of Perception* (borrowed from Antoine de Saint-Exupéry), he insists that "man is a network of relations" (PP: 456), or "man is a knot of relations" depending on the translation, and the strong implication of Merleau-Ponty's philosophy is that this is not a knot (or network) of the Gordian variety, and that these relations are not something that we can, or even should, want to unravel. The interdependence of the knot is what gives humanity its very qualities and by dissecting it we risk losing the very thing that establishes us as human.

Again, this necessitates a certain ambiguity at the heart of our experience. Trying to discern what is a legitimate authentic project of the self, which is not induced by the demands of society, is infinitely difficult. Indeed, it is not a possibility for Merleau-Ponty and because of its overtones of an unattainable individualism he refused to use the existential concept of authenticity for his entire career. But he would not want to say that something like, but slightly different from authenticity (i.e. an individual coming to terms with his or her own situation in an empowering way), is an impossibility. In many ways, this is a primary ethical demand of his. Finally, however, this ambiguity at the heart of our experience will always be there and an authentic path is not one that we consciously choose by attempting to ensure that we are the only origin of our projects, somehow attempting what he contends is impossible: that is, the transcending of our environment. Rather, Merleau-Ponty's suggestion is that circumstances point us to, and in fact allow us to, find a way (PP: 456). The human situation is both a product of the "mind" and our sociohistorical situation, and moral achievement is a tenuous embrace of these facts. In his later work, this position will become more explicitly ontological as he spends a lot of time working out the related notions of the intertwining, the chiasm and reversibility.

Merleau-Ponty's rejection of Sartre's version of the master–slave dialectic

For Merleau-Ponty, even if one holds that Sartre managed to avoid the "reef of solipsism", his equation of consciousness with the capacity for negation has other problematic consequences. Typified by Hegel's master–slave dialectic and made famous via Sartre's interpretation of it in *Being and Nothingness*, it is a portrait of human relationships that remains entangled in a subject–object dialectic. Although Sartre sought to break away from the failures of phenomenology to adequately treat the problem of the Other, according to Merleau-Ponty his efforts were betrayed by a flawed ontology and a dualistic split between mind and body.

This claim will be considered shortly, but first it needs to be recognized that Merleau-Ponty admits of a similar phenomenon to the alienating, "internal haemorrhage" in our perspective that Sartre describes as the look. Speaking of the appearance of another in our immediate surroundings, Merleau-Ponty suggests, "round about the perceived body a vortex forms, towards which my world is drawn and so to speak, sucked in: to this extent, it is no longer merely mine" (PP: 353). Someone is appropriating my world and this description would seem to demand a philosophical position similar to Sartre's; the Other can transform me into an object, as I can transform the Other, by a process of continual looking.

However, Merleau-Ponty makes a pertinent point that, if true, does not make such a position and the resultant suggestion that "hell is other people" the necessary outcome of all human relations. He argues that the other's gaze can only induce this tumultuous ontological change from subject to object (or object to subject) if we withdraw into an abstract thinking disposition that he characterizes as an "inhuman gaze" in which we merely observe. For Merleau-Ponty, this objectification by the other's gaze may indeed be unbearable, but the situation persists only while the improbability of communication is conceded. However, for Merleau-Ponty:

> the body of others, insofar as it is a bearer of symbolic behaviour … breaks away from the condition of one of my phenomena, presents to me the task of true communication and bestows on my objects the new dimension of intersubjective being.
>
> (PrP: 125)

The body of another person is hence not just an object that has the capacity to constrain my freedom, but an object (for want of a better word) that *compels* us to attempt what is admittedly the ongoing task of communication.

Even if relations with the other are often conflictual in the manner that Sartre suggests (and who could deny that?), for Merleau-Ponty the situation can be redeemed simply "by establishing relations with him, by bringing about his clear recognition of me" (PP: 357). Embroiled in a Sartrean perspective, this recognition may seem difficult to attain, but for him it is something that the very presence of another compels us to seek (if not in every other, at least in *an* other). Moreover, for Merleau-Ponty, it is certainly not as difficult as Sartre suggests; he comments, "let him utter a word, or even make a gesture of impatience, and already he ceases to transcend me" (PP: 361). Merleau-Ponty's implication seems to be that by immersing ourselves in embodied action the subject can at least minimize the anxiety and anguish of Sartrean human relations. Perhaps even the experience of joy can be accommodated in this conception of the acting body-subject. At the very least, it seems that individual existences are far more likely to be construed as transcending each other when we remain, in an important sense, disembodied.

Even if Sartre is analysing what appears, almost incontrovertibly, to be embodied aspects of existence (such as desire, sadism, masochism, etc.), according to Merleau-Ponty this is ultimately not the case. For him, the Sartrean analysis of embodiment construes the Other as a being who cannot be reached, and interaction hence consists in limiting and controlling their effect on the for-itself. But the Other's for-itself cannot be known on this view and there is no possibility of engaging with the Other immediately and through their embodiment. Bodies can nullify each other's progress, but there is not any embodied *engagement* with the Other that merits the name.

Against this Sartrean understanding, Merleau-Ponty emphasizes that the body cannot be conceived of as simply an objectified in-itself or a subjectivized for-itself (cf. BN: 304). Although it is in some sense an object for others and a lived reality for the subject, as Sartre suggests, it is never *simply* an object or a subject. Merleau-Ponty's understanding of the "body-subject" resides between such dualities, rather than oscillating from one term of the duality to the other. As he makes explicit, this means that, "if another's body is not an object for me, nor mine an object for him, if both are manifestations of behaviour, the positing of the other does not reduce me to the status of an object" (PP: 352). This acknowledgment of the possibility of reciprocal recognition between individuals challenges Sartre's position.

Of course, Merleau-Ponty is not suggesting that Sartrean conflict is an impossible mode of human interaction, even apart from the difficulties inherent in objective thought (PP: 356) or what his later work calls "high-altitude thinking" (VI: 69), which is a kind of thinking that surveys proceedings from above, ignorant of the questioner's involvement and co-implication in that which is being questioned. There is a lived experience of solipsism that is insurmountable (PP: 357–8); relationships with other people can calcify into competing entities, and understanding the expressions on another's face can be problematic. But by paying attention to the aspects of our embodied situation that he delineates, and not falsely imposing subject–object or consciousness–thing relations ubiquitously, Merleau-Ponty thinks that these phenomena are lessened and take on a less damaging form. Moreover, his analysis serves to deny Sartre's conclusion that such relationships are phenomenologically primitive. For Merleau-Ponty, the other can look at me, penetrate me to the very fibre of my being, "only because we belong to the same system of being-for-itself and being-for-another; we are moments of the same syntax, we count in the same world, we belong to the same being" (VI: 83). In other words, for him the conflict of Sartre's being-for-others is dependent on the more fundamental experience of communication, or the fact that in Merleau-Ponty's words, "we are collaborators for each other in consummate reciprocity" (PP: 354).

KEY POINT
Although Sartre asserts that the alienating experience of being-for-others (e.g. the look) precedes and founds our experience of being-with-others as a collective group (BN: 413), and adds that the experience of a "we" is a psychological rather than ontological phenomenon, Merleau-Ponty (along with de Beauvoir) argues that *being-with-others, not being-for-others, is the more primordial mode.*

Even if we do not want to concede that our relationships with the other are as unmanipulative as Merleau-Ponty implies, in every one of our experiences, presumably, there are occasions that attest to the possibility of interaction beyond the subject–object dichotomy and its perennial role-playing. If so, this is a position that Sartre must struggle to accommodate and, on Merleau-Ponty's view, this is largely because of his dualistic conception of existence that, despite his protestations to the contrary, requires reflective consciousness (or being-for-itself) to assert a priority over the things of the world (including the body), which are being-in-itself and which it can transcend.

Ontology and alterity

In *The Visible and the Invisible*, Merleau-Ponty provides a more detailed analysis of what he considers to be Sartre's dualistic ontology and he again devotes particular attention to Sartre's treatment of the other, particularly in the chapter titled "Interrogation and Dialectic". According to Merleau-Ponty, Sartre's philosophy is a version of "high-altitude thinking", since the concepts he employs (Being and Nothingness) are not basic and necessary, but are established via dialectical argument, which comes after our primary inherence in Being (VI: 76). The important question then becomes one regarding whether or not Being and Nothingness are useful categories, and Merleau-Ponty answers with a resounding "No". By basing his entire ontology on the concepts pure Being and pure Nothingness, which for Merleau-Ponty come after all possible experience (VI: 89), Sartre does not describe experience, or the pre-reflective faith, but instead constructs a metaphysics. Phenomenology, we must remember, is supposed to be about description (PP: xi), and yet all of Sartre's analyses are guided by this rather abstract distinction between Being and Nothingness, the for-itself and the in-itself, regardless of how concrete the situation being analysed may actually appear to be (e.g. smoking cigarettes).

To Sartre's philosophy of negativity (the for-itself that is *nothingness* is responsible for meaning, and we are hence *not* just our past, *nor* our circumstances, etc.), Merleau-Ponty opposes a philosophy of inherence. In *Phenomenology of Perception*, this idea is contained in all of the ramifications of the body-subject, but in *The Visible and the Invisible* he clarifies the ontology of this inherence: Being is possible only through reversibility, the intertwining and the chiasm. Although I cannot go into detail about these aspects of Merleau-Ponty's later work here, his fundamental claim is that Sartre's emphasis on defining the mind as a pure negative that creates meaning in fact renders impossible the "openness upon being" that he characterizes as the perceptual faith (VI: 88).

The manner in which Sartre annuls our primordial inherence in Being, for Merleau-Ponty, also has analogous consequences for our relations with the other. Most important among these is that it means that on Sartre's view I cannot discover another person, or ascertain some "truth" (in a loose sense) about them, but only realize a dimension of myself that is fixed through the other's look. This implies that the other's presence adds nothing and only freezes me into what I have made of myself, and Le Doeuff has also argued that Sartre's position amounts to a "defacto solipsism" (1991: 62). The following remark of Merleau-Ponty's sums up his similarly inclined interpretation of Sartre's position: "power over me is exactly measured by the consent which I have given to my body, to my situation; he (*the other*) has alienating force only because I alienate myself. Philosophically speaking, there is no experience of the other" (VI: 71). Later on in *The Visible and the Invisible*, Merleau-Ponty repeats this characterization of Sartre's account of relations with others, suggesting that:

> If the other is really the other, that is, a for-itself in the strong sense that I am for myself, he must never be so before my eyes … it is necessary that there be no perception of an other … and that the other be my negation or my destruction. Every other interpretation, under the pretext of placing us, him and myself, in the same universe of thought, ruins the alterity of the other and hence marks the triumph of an undisguised solipsism.

> Conversely, it is in making the other not only inaccessible but invisible for me that I guarantee his alterity and quit solipsism. (VI: 79)

Sartrean philosophy hence ignores what, for Merleau-Ponty, is an essential fact of our inherence in Being: we are always involved in a world, with other people, and if we confront the other this background is nevertheless already there. Moreover, if the moral equivalent to solipsism, which Sartre was clearly trying to avoid (cf. BN: 223–33), is a blindness to the other as genuinely other, Merleau-Ponty argues that it is not surprising that Sartre would approach the moral opposite to solipsism, that being the master–slave dialectic and a rather absolute conception of the other as "inaccessible" and "invisible". However, given the faceless and anonymous conception of the other that is induced by this master–slave dialectic, these two extremes paradoxically seem to result in some rather similar consequences.

Indeed, Merleau-Ponty goes on to ask the obvious question regarding whether the Sartrean "solution" really does justice to the alterity or "otherness" of the other: he suggests that "this agnosticism in regard to the other's being for himself, which appeared to guarantee his alterity, suddenly appears as the worst of infringements upon it" (VI: 79). In other words, Sartre is accused of an agnosticism in regard to the other because he ignores our inherence in Being and because he ignores the way in which otherness is always intertwined with subjectivity. Sartre posits a radical singularity, a void of nothingness that can have no content, and he argues that given this situation the Other should not be theorized except in relation to its effects on the self. In his own way then, Sartre very much wants to preserve the alterity of the Other, despite what theorists such as Levinas have suggested about him. But Merleau-Ponty insists that speaking only of oneself, just like speaking for everybody, also misses an aspect of our experience and he insists that the respect shown for the other's alterity is only apparent. In the end, Sartre "makes of the other an anonymous, faceless obsession, an other in general" (VI: 72). And Sartre does seem to have no notion of a specific Other, but only this faceless, untouchable Other, who is absolutely transcendent. Indeed, the Other for Sartre is almost a God, which might explain his consistent capitalizing of the term. For Merleau-Ponty, this positing of a faceless, anonymous other is far from the best way to respect the other and nor is it necessary. In what represents a fitting conclusion to the main part of this chapter, Merleau-Ponty argues that:

For the other to be truly the other, it does not suffice and it is not necessary that he be a scourge, the continued threat of an absolute reversal of pro and con, a judge himself elevated above all contestation, without place, without relativities, faceless like an obsession and capable of crushing me with a glance into the dust of my world. It is necessary and it suffices that he have the power to decenter me, to oppose his centering to my own, and he can do so only because we are not two nihilations installed in two universes of the in-itself, incomparable, but two entries to the same Being, each accessible to but one of us.   (VI: 82)

Summary of key points

The body and habits
For Merleau-Ponty, the body cannot be adequately understood as either an empirical object or a constituting subject. Unlike other objects of the world, it is always with us and is not something we can possibly do without. It is also that which makes possible our apprehension of other objects in the world.

Ambiguity
The condition of being an embodied perspective on the world and yet being blind to that perspective. As the body is an amalgam of both subject and object, it is always ambiguous whether a decision, or a perception, can be traced back to the subject or to the world.

Equilibrium
The body seeks to attain equilibrium with its environment by developing skills and creating habits.

Freedom
Merleau-Ponty claims that the radical discontinuity upon which the Sartrean arguments for freedom rely (i.e. a separation between *past–present* and *present–future*) is undermined by the recognition of the embodied inevitability of creating habits, and developing skills.

This is because our bodies sustain around us general intentions that we are not always aware of, and do not choose, and which solicit us to respond to circumstances in particular ways that cannot simply be negated, as Sartre's analysis implies.

Rather, for Merleau-Ponty "the past is the atmosphere of the present" and facticity intrudes upon the for-itself. If this is so, we are not as free as Sartre thinks. There are not greater and lesser degrees of freedom for Sartre, but for Merleau-Ponty there are.

Merleau-Ponty's rejection of Sartre's version of the master–slave dialectic
For Merleau-Ponty, we internalize the look of the Other at all stages rather than just in occasional experiences. This means that oppression is possible and we are not always free to return the look, as Sartre argues.

Conflict
While conflict is inevitable, it is not the original and fundamental way of relating to others. Seeing it thus depends on withdrawing into an abstract thinking disposition, an "inhuman gaze" that belies our necessary connection with others.

Being-with-others is the primordial mode
Whereas Sartre asserts that the alienating experience of being-for-others (e.g. the look) precedes and founds our experience of being-with-others as a collective group, and adds that the experience of a "we" is a psychological rather than ontological phenomena (BN: 413), Merleau-Ponty argues that *being-with-others, not being-for-others, is the more primordial mode.*

six

De Beauvoir: feminism and an existential ethics

Simone de Beauvoir (1908–86) was Sartre's lifelong partner, but she was obviously far more than simply that. Not only was she a philosopher of great ability (at the time, she was the youngest ever student to pass the agrégation at the École Normale Superieure and hence be qualified to teach the subject), but she is also a philosopher of enduring significance. According to some sources, *The Second Sex* (1949) is one of the best-selling non-fiction books published in the twentieth century, and it has been enormously influential on generations of feminists. Moreover, like Sartre, she wrote many novels and fought against oppression in many of its various guises, most notably against imperialism, racism and sexism. Her philosophical project was almost always couched in terms of existentialism and, more particularly, in terms of Sartrean existentialism. The philosophical vernacular of existentialism is all there in her work (for-itself and in-itself, transcendence and immanence, etc.), and she thought of her work as extending Sartre's, or supplementing his, rather than as directly challenging it. However, she in fact poses many challenges to Sartrean existentialism. In different ways she challenges his account of love, oppression, otherness, bad faith and death, and her early and enduring interest in Marxism foreshadowed Sartre's own eventual modifications to his philosophy of freedom, which he presented in his later work *Critique of Dialectical Reason*. The two main texts by de Beauvoir that we will consider in this chapter are *The Second Sex* and *The Ethics of Ambiguity*.

Feminism and de Beauvoir

Before delving into an analysis of *The Second Sex* it is worth pointing out that, problematic as these categorizations may be, there are often thought to be three main paradigms of feminism:

- *Egalitarian feminism* is typified by the conviction that bodies, and particularly the reproductive aspects of bodies, need to be overcome for genuine equality. To put it simply, bodies and nature need to be overcome in favour of minds and culture.
- *Social constructionist feminism* holds that it is not biology *per se* that is oppressive for women, but the ways in which the varying social systems give meaning to biology. Hence the famous sex–gender distinction, which points out that even if there is some kind of originary sexual difference between men and women, it is nevertheless the case that this difference can be interpreted in many different ways, and the ways in which particular societies construe this sex difference is termed gender. Social constructionists try to change the way this brute sexed body is interpreted in particular societies.
- *Difference feminism* is concerned more with the lived body, which is not an ahistorical brute fact, and this is why the work of Merleau-Ponty has been important to many of them. The lived body is thought of as transgressing any mind–body dualism, and the body itself is considered to be political, cultural and so on, rather than a neutral given. Difference feminists hold that there are irreducible differences between the sexes, and also *in* sexes. Although difference feminism emphasizes difference, it is hence not a binary essentialism of difference (for more detail on these main paradigms of feminism, see Grosz (1994: 13–18)).

The Second Sex, written in 1949, has been an important text for all of these "schools" of feminism and this reflects the fact that it is a rich and perhaps also fundamentally ambiguous book. Indeed, for some theorists, de Beauvoir holds positions that appear mutually contradictory, especially in regard to key concepts such as reciprocity and autonomy, which are given a multiplicity of competing definitions. Moreover, at times she holds that many women have contributed to their situation of oppression over the years and have consented to their subjugation and she suggests that this is because the temptation to forgo liberty and to become a thing is difficult to resist. On other occasions, however, she argues that most women have not been able to envisage an alternative because their situation has been "naturalized" on account of power imbalances that have become legitimized over generations in various social institutions. In such cases, women are clearly not complicit in their oppression. No doubt this ambiguity reflects the complicated nature of both history and people, and her reluctance to countenance one simple line on this should be counted as a strength of her work and not a weakness. Perhaps more problematically, her work also suggests simultaneously that the body is something of an obstacle, as through pregnancy and the like it ties women to nature, and, on the other hand, that any reductionist biological account of what it is to be a woman is spurious and, furthermore, that the body and mind cannot be divorced from one another. Many apparently competing ideas play a role in her philosophy in this way, probably reflecting her unease with Sartrean existentialism and her indirect attempts to reformulate it. This also means that there are aspects of de Beauvoir's work that seem to endorse the social constructionist feminist project by instantiating a difference between nature and culture, and, on the other hand, difference feminists still find her work enormously valuable in problematizing this very distinction. It is perhaps apt that this self-proclaimed philosopher of ambiguity should occupy an ambiguous position in regard to feminism and its history.

The Second Sex

Not all of *The Second Sex* (and perhaps not even much of it) is, strictly speaking, philosophy. Of course, that is not de Beauvoir's main intent in this text, which is often more sociological than philosophical, and she has written many other more explicitly philosophical texts including *The Ethics of Ambiguity*. It will be taken for granted that women have been oppressed, and still currently are, in many respects, but the main philosophical aspect of this text lies in the reasons de Beauvoir gives for why this is the case, and for what makes it possible for this oppression to persist over such a long historical period. We will also focus on how her analysis impacts on her existentialism, or modifies it, and generally one of the guiding questions in this chapter will be whether it is possible to adequately thematize oppression from within an existential framework. You will remember from previous chapters that Merleau-Ponty implied that Sartre could not talk about oppression, as the for-itself always posits an abrupt break from or radical discontinuity with that which has preceded it, such that the past cannot impact on our ability to project new situations or envisage alternative possibilities, and we will continually return to this issue.

Woman as Other

The first main point to come out of *The Second Sex* is the notion of woman as Other or, as the title of her book suggests, as second. For de Beauvoir, men have historically assumed the position of subject and women have been designated as that which is other than the subject; in other words, man is the norm and woman is outside the norm. Now this kind of categorization might not even necessarily be expressed in an avowedly negative way. Indeed, women might be valorized as mysterious, or privileged in their intangible femininity, but even if this is the case the point remains that women are still defined by reference to the norm, which is presumed to be man. Adhering to the existential maxim that existence precedes essence (as both Sartre and de Beauvoir argue is ontologically the case for human existence), de Beauvoir's book contests the assumption that there is some essence that constitutes being a woman. In particular, she is concerned to undermine essentialism as it operates in social institutions, and this is because references to women being naturally "delicate", or inherently "emotional" and so on function to legitimate the confinement of women to certain roles.

> **KEY POINT**
> De Beauvoir famously proclaims at the start of Book 2 of *The Second Sex*, that *one is not born a woman, but rather becomes one* (SS: 295).

She contests both biological and metaphysical arguments that attempt to establish a feminine essence, and it is interesting to note that de Beauvoir mentions and criticizes the work of Emmanuel Levinas in this respect in a footnote. In more recent times, Levinas has become famous for his exaltation of alterity – that is, for his privileging of the aspects of the other person that can never be integrated within the expectations of a subject – but de Beauvoir points out that when Levinas exalts the feminine as otherness, when he writes that woman is mystery, he ignores the fact that she is precisely a mystery for men (SS: 16). In other words, Levinas presumes that he is saying something universal but, for de Beauvoir, he is really just arguing from the male perspective. His partial and arguably gender-based observation that women are mysterious is made into a universal ontological category.

One good way of understanding this problem of woman as Other, according to de Beauvoir, is that only a woman would write a book about the status of being a woman (SS: 15). For men, or at least for heterosexual men, de Beauvoir's claim is that their sexuality is never called into question in the same way. Now to some extent this has changed since de Beauvoir wrote *The Second Sex*. We do see many more books on what it is to be male, but it is still not on the same rate of proliferation as there are books on women. Probably many men now also occasionally question what it means to be a man, and even in something like the way that de Beauvoir questioned what it was to be a woman. However, her point is that for women the question "What does it mean to be a woman?" is a necessary question that needs to be answered before they can understand themselves and that this is not the case for men.

Now de Beauvoir thinks that, at least to some extent, otherness is fundamental and unavoidable. She argues that no group ever sets itself up as the one, or as a unity, without targeting the others, who it excludes from this oneness: foreigners, outsiders, the mad and so on (SS: 16–18). Her tacit implication is that the self (or community) needs to distinguish itself against such "otherness" in order to define itself as a unitary subject (or group). She also argues that we cannot fully understand this "one–other" dynamic unless we posit some kind of master–slave dialectic along the lines of that which Hegel, and then Sartre, have argued for, that is, unless we admit that there are mutual antagonisms between people, and some kind of hostility towards other consciousnesses. However, as well as posing such questions on the communal and political level, in contradistinction to Sartre who largely focuses on one consciousness in conflict with another singular consciousness and only briefly considers the social dynamics of group formation (BN: 413–30), de Beauvoir differs from Sartre in at least one other important respect. She suggests that when the one and the other are forced to come into contact, such as through wars, trading and so on, this absolute notion of otherness is lessened and its relativity is made manifest (SS: 17). She argues, for example, that when the foreigner comes into a culture that they have previously designated as other, the first thing they realize is that this culture has also designated them as other. In other words, they realize that this is the attitude of both parties and that there is some kind of reciprocity involved. Moreover, after some experience with this so-called other, they also realize that they share something with these people. They realize that they are people who can actually be communicated with, who laugh and so on, and hence on a communal and political level this absolute otherness breaks down.

Arguably this essentialism about the process of "othering", as well as the further claim that realizing the reciprocity of this antagonistic "othering" can furnish us with the basis for an ethics, is problematic, but given this suggestion that otherness tends to break down through contact, de Beauvoir is faced with an obvious question. Why is it that one sex has been made the norm and the other sex so consistently rendered the Other, when there are social relations all the time that show that women have some kind of reciprocity and can be communicated with? Why has the reciprocity not been recognized between the sexes? Women are not a minority, as are many groups of people who are similarly persecuted, and yet female otherness almost seems to be an absolute on account of its universality. It seems to lack the contingency, or the accidental nature, of most historical facts. Now remember that de Beauvoir cannot resort to biology to explain this oppression. Existentialism will not allow it because of the formula that existence precedes essence, which in this context means that there is no biological essence that can adequately explain human behaviour. For the moment though, de Beauvoir concludes that if woman seems to be the inessential that never becomes the essential, it is partly because she herself fails to bring about this change (SS: 21). The responsibility for female oppression lies *partially* with women.

Women and bad faith

De Beauvoir envisages the temptation to forgo liberty and to become a thing as inordinately difficult to resist for all human beings, whether they be male or female (SS: 21). She thinks of this as a terrible thing, but she points out that it is an easy road to travel down because we thereby avoid the strain and anguish involved in undertaking an authentic existence (SS: 21). In this context, it is worth remembering what Sartre says about bad faith, which is the flight from the recognition of our own freedom. Realizing that we alone bear entire responsibility for our existence can be intimidating and anguish-inducing, and as a result on his view we often pretend that we are a thing, or pretend that we are compelled to behave in a certain way, because it is easier than confronting the prospect of permanent choice without any external guarantor of value. Although de Beauvoir problematizes any simple understanding of bad faith and does not employ the notion in the cavalier and omniscient way that Sartre does, her work implies that some women, although certainly not all, have been in bad faith, and she points out that sometimes women are very comfortable with their passive role as Other. In fact, at a later stage in *The Second Sex* (SS: 641–89), de Beauvoir details three main ways in which women are complicit in their subjugation and in which they might adopt inauthentic attitudes and flee from their freedom.

KEY POINT *The three main ways in which women are complicit in their subjugation*
- *Narcissist* – the woman's freedom is denied by investing it in herself as a beautiful object and construing this as her sole source of value.
- *Woman in love* – the woman's freedom is denied on account of her identity being invested in a privileged male object.
- *Mystic* – the woman's freedom is denied by being invested in the absolute or God.

As we see in more detail in *The Ethics of Ambiguity*, de Beauvoir argues that action loses its meaning if it is not willed from freedom (and with freedom as it goal). Action that uses external objects as the guarantors of meaning and value is condemned to fall back in upon itself, to "immanence", in the term that she often employs.

However, as well as arguing that women can be in bad faith in these ways, de Beauvoir also wants to hold that after long periods of oppression it is possible for women to no longer be able to envisage other possibilities. They can no longer see an alternative situation and when this is the case they are not in bad faith. We will explore her argument for this position below, but for the moment it is sufficient to point out that this position at least appears to conflict with Sartrean existentialism. Existentialism takes as its premise the freedom of the individual and, for Sartre, somebody who could no longer project alternative possibilities and who could no longer negate their facticity would not be human. So the obvious question is: can de Beauvoir thematize her position within an existentialist framework, as she repeatedly claims she can? De Beauvoir seems to be caught between two positions. On one level, women are complicit and must be complicit in any subjugation, because she wants to maintain, as an existentialist, that human beings are always free. On another level, she also argues that many women are not necessarily complicit in their subjugation, because it is possible to be so oppressed that one literally cannot even imagine living in another world, including a world where women did not fulfil the role as other. Does de Beauvoir miss Sartre's point? Does she improve upon Sartre within the tradition of existentialism? Or does she tacitly abandon existentialism and show that it is unworkable?

There are no easy answers to such questions, but in order to address this issue some contemporary philosophers argue that de Beauvoir deploys two (or more) different notions of freedom here: ontological or absolute freedom on the one hand, but also a more practical freedom, that is freedom to *do* something or to effect concrete changes in the world. So according to this account, she holds that women are absolutely free in something tantamount to the Sartrean sense, but nevertheless there is also this issue of practical freedom to change things in the world. Arguably this does not solve the problem, however, as it seems that this distinction ultimately conflates into one as de Beauvoir maintains that if the slave lacks practical freedom for long enough, if the slave is in jail for so long that they cannot conceive of being outside jail, then this can actually impinge on their ontological freedom. In other words, if some people are oppressed for long enough ontological freedom can actually be modified and reduced. She thinks that this is the case for some women and therefore they are not in bad faith when they do not revolt against sexual inequality. This suggestion tacitly calls Sartre's philosophy of freedom into question, although her own adherence to the terms of existential philosophy often makes this difficult to comprehend. Some scholars have argued that she was consistently challenging Sartre's position but did not publicly state it because of their relationship and other such factors (see Kruks 1990; Le Doeuff 1991).

Mitsein *and the "we"*

De Beauvoir also goes on to explain that one reason for women not themselves bringing about a change or revolution is that women have historically lacked the concrete means for organizing themselves into a unit that can stand face to face with the correlative unit or group: that is, men. She suggests that women have had no past, no history, no religion of their own, and no solidarity of work and interest as, for example, the proletariat has always had (SS: 18–19). The working class share being exploited by landowners, and they also share a history, and hence have the unity to say "we" and unite together. De Beauvoir argues that women historically have not been able to say "we" in the same way. While women do share in common the fact that they have been exploited by men, she points out that this has occurred in many different ways. Moreover, she suggests that women have never been herded together in the way that there have historically been ghettoes of black people, of Jewish people and of poor people. De Beauvoir's implication is that when grouped together people can begin to conceive of a common project and discontent can thereby develop into a revolution. She suggests that because women live dispersed among men, this counts against their chances of engaging in a communal and sustained protest.

De Beauvoir makes the further claim that because women are spread out and dispersed among men they also tend to associate with race and class before they associate with other women. In other words, she thinks that a white rich woman, even if she is oppressed and cast in a servile role, will feel more of a bond with white rich men, for example, than with poor black women (SS: 19). De Beauvoir's point is simply that female identity, because of the ways in which society has been organized, is very much bound up with the identity of the men around them, be they fathers, husbands or sons.

In *Situation and Human Existence*, Sonia Kruks (1990) concisely explains what de Beauvoir thinks is required for oppressed people to attain something akin to liberation. Kruks argues that a transition from oppression to free transcendence can take place only when "my" situation is not, strictly speaking, mine, but is also part of a more general situation which transcends my immediate experiences. Kruks hence reaffirms the importance of the realization of a collectivity, of a "we", for any emancipatory process, and it is this that de Beauvoir argues that women have generally not had. The affirmation of "sisterhood" in 1970s feminism was an attempt to change this situation and to enable women to conceive of themselves as united with each other. After all, an individual woman might disagree with a patriarchal social situation, but their personal liberty will not result in an action without others feeling similarly. For their personal disagreement with particular aspects of their lives to ferment and become a revolution, it is necessary that the people around them are also free and transcendent. This suggestion has an ethical significance that de Beauvoir examines in detail in her earlier work, *The Ethics of Ambiguity*.

The Ethics of Ambiguity: an ethics of reciprocal transcendence

Contrary to the objection that existentialism's descriptions of ontological freedom are really meaningless to us if we are not free to change things in the world and to exercise our freedom to *do* – a position that is best exemplified by the Frankfurt School theorist Herbert Marcuse in his essay entitled "Existentialism" (1948) – *The Ethics of Ambiguity* attempts to show that existentialism's talk of freedom does have a concrete content. In other words, de Beauvoir wants to show that existentialism is not purely about saying that we are as free in the cage as if we are not in the cage (EA: 79). Such a characterization may be partially true of Sartre's ontology, but de Beauvoir's philosophy was always more concerned than Sartre's with the political, even if they were both heavily involved in political *practices*. There are some obvious potential reasons for this difference, not least because as a woman de Beauvoir felt the effects of political oppression in a way in which a white, wealthy, middle-class man such as Sartre did not. De Beauvoir's analysis also emphasizes that oppression works against particular social groups, more than on the level of individuals, whereas Sartre simply suggests that *Mitsein*, or being-with-others, follows essentially the same conflictual structure as that which occurs between individuals (BN: 413–30). In the process, her work offers the best and perhaps the only sustained example of an existentialist ethics, although it retains the existential insistence on avoiding any kind of moral prescriptivism.

The Ethics of Ambiguity asserts the tragic condition of the human situation with its spontaneous urge for freedom always being counterposed against the external weight of the world. Unlike Camus's ostensibly similar descriptions of the absurd, for de Beauvoir human existence is an ambiguous mixture of these two aspects and this explains why in this text she wrestles both with the historical materialism of Marx and Engels, as well as with the critical idealism of Kant and others. Extending Merleau-Ponty's analysis, she argues that we are simultaneously both a subject and an object and, to put her fundamental claim bluntly, she holds that *to live ethically we must assume the ambiguity, rather than flee from it by pretending that we are biologically determined, or a subject who is wholly outside of their situation and can survey it*. As she puts it, "coming to recognise and accept oneself in one's ambiguity is the necessary pre-condition of the moral life" (EA: 81).

Theoretically, Sartre's notion of bad faith should also involve a similar injunction, in that it seeks an ambiguous reconciliation of transcendence and facticity, but in practice this is supplanted by his rather exclusive emphasis on only one of the two terms: transcendent freedom. Of course, we have also seen that Sartre recognized that freedom required a situation and that by freedom he does not mean freedom to do anything, to click your fingers and be a millionaire, but freedom to construe things differently and to always have aspirations for the future and for that which is not part of your immediate facticity. Unlike de Beauvoir, however, Sartre never insisted that our transcendence required the transcendence of others. For Sartre, it was almost the contrary situation in that he argued that the freedom of another person is the only thing that can inhibit my freedom; recall the shame felt by the person peering through the keyhole and the way in which their project of peering through the keyhole (or of watching the rock concert) is suddenly made impossible, or at least altered, by the perspective of another person.

In both *The Second Sex* and *The Ethics of Ambiguity*, de Beauvoir, on the other hand, argues that an individual's transcendence (or freedom) actually requires the freedom and transcendence of other people. She quite unequivocally suggests that, "it is not true that the recognition of the freedom of others limits my own freedom: to be free is not to have the power to do anything you like; it is to be able to surpass the given towards an open future" (EA: 91). And she suggests that it is other people who can help give us an open future. We have seen how this is so in relation to oppressed people needing to be able to conceive of a common project, but we can also think about de Beauvoir's point in a way that is relevant to all of us, whether we are oppressed or not. Discoveries, inventions, industries, culture, painting and books are all examples of transcendence by individual people. However, these ideas and discoveries also open up new concrete possibilities to other people and new opportunities for transcendence. For example, the fact that Sartre and de Beauvoir wrote their books makes it possible for us to engage with their thoughts and then transcend them in different directions. If they had not written their books, then this opportunity would not be there. Similarly, the projects of our friends open up new spaces for us to transcend.

But if we are not equal with these others, if those other people are not also free, de Beauvoir argues that this does not happen. For example, if you experience yourself as superior to another person, you will not be open to the new possibilities that their thoughts and behaviour open up; instead, they would be dismissed as mediocre. On the other hand, if you experience yourself as lesser than another person, you will not consider their thoughts and work to relate to you; it would be treated as from a higher and incomprehensible domain. This means that in a phenomenological and existential sense, the world is a smaller place for either of these two hypothetical kinds of people, and it follows from this that we need relationships of equality if we are going to have the full opportunity to deploy our own transcendent freedom. In this context, de Beauvoir argues that oppression is self-defeating even for the oppressor. The oppressor undermines his or her individual freedom by creating a world in which not all are free and they thereby limit their own capacity for transcendence if they are not engaging with other people's projects.

Now de Beauvoir wants to hold that all human beings still transcend their facticity. Like Sartre, she still wants to argue that, "what happens to me by means of others depends upon me as regard its meaning" (EA: 82). If I have been picked on all my life, I still retain the capacity to determine whether this fact will motivate me to prove these people wrong, or whether it will "cause" me to develop a complex of some kind or another. Generally, individuals confer meaning on such facts of their past. However, for oppressed people de Beauvoir argues that transcendence is condemned to fall back uselessly into itself because it is so completely cut off from its goals. If people can *never* attain what their transcendent dimension aspires to, then this capacity to transcend may also be at least partly obliterated. She argues that, "my freedom, in order to fulfil itself, requires that it emerge into an open future" (EA: 82), and if that future is not open then over time the capacity to actually project into the future, to imagine alternative lives, becomes obscured. When women are not allowed in the public realm, or to occupy positions as an intellectual, for example, then their space for transcendence is limited. There needs to be social equality for reciprocal transcendence to be possible. De Beauvoir states that if a dominant group keeps "me below the level which they have conquered and on the basis of which new conquests will have been achieved, then they are cutting me off from the future, they are changing me into a thing" (EA: 82). For de Beauvoir, over time oppressed people can be unable to even envisage other possibilities and are hence unable to even recognize that they are oppressed.

For de Beauvoir, human life involves two things: perpetuation and transcendence. It is the transcendence aspect that is uniquely human and unlike Sartre's account she suggests that it does admit of degrees (as Merleau-Ponty suggests in his own criticisms of Sartre's account of freedom), and it is this transcendence that needs to be emphasized by any morally just arrangement of society. She suggests that, "if all it does is maintain itself, then living is only not dying" (EA: 82–3). For de Beauvoir, "a life justifies itself only if its effort to perpetuate itself is integrated into its surpassing and if this surpassing has no other limits than those which the subject assigns himself" (EA 83).

In this regard, there seem to be some similarities between de Beauvoir's position and liberalism, which also emphasizes freedom of choice (even if it does not take seriously enough the anguish such permanent choice can induce), but she is clearly not a conservative liberal. She suggests that, "we have to respect freedom only when it is intended for freedom" and "a freedom which is interested only in denying freedom must be denied" (EA: 91). The libertarian insistence on property, possessions, capital, comfort and so on is not something that we need to respect. Instead, there are elements of Marxism in her work and she consistently cites Marx in *The Ethics of Ambiguity*. She represents the conservative liberal as asking: "But what right does one have to want something for others?": in other words, why should we care about the oppression of others if our own liberty is being respected? De Beauvoir's point is that our own liberty is not being respected if others are oppressed. She offers two reasons why we should be concerned (EA: 86):

1. In order to not be a tyrant myself (any abstention is complicity)
2. In order that new possibilities be opened to the liberated slave and through them to all humanity.

She also rails against what she evocatively calls "the curators of the given world", who "side with what has been over what has not yet been" (EA: 91). Clearly Sartre would agree with this admonishment; the curators of the given world are perhaps the primary example of bad faith in his work. But for de Beauvoir we also cannot simply discard the past, which Sartre might be accused of doing in the radical discontinuity that he repeatedly insists on between the past and the present. Rather, as she suggests, "to abandon the past to the night of facticity is a way of depopulating the world. I would distrust a humanism which was too indifferent to the efforts of the men of former times" (EA: 92). She goes on to suggest that "a genuine ethics does not teach us either to sacrifice it or deny it (the past): we must assume it" (EA: 95). Both a rejection of the past and a valorization of the past are wrong: she, like Merleau-Ponty, seeks a middle way that does not presuppose a radical disjunction between past, present and future, and this is something that Sartre's philosophy of freedom arguably relies on.

In her book, de Beauvoir also distances herself from the universalizing aspirations of Kant and Hegel, and from much of the tradition of moral philosophy. For her, any philosophical rejection of the particular, of the individual, cannot be genuinely ethical. Instead, she affirms the sanctity of individual freedom, first and foremost, and then points out that each individual also needs a community of free people in order to best transcend their circumstances, and you will recall that for her individual projects fall in upon themselves and lose meaning if they do not intersect with the projects and plans of others. De Beauvoir describes various examples of this kind of inauthentic attitude in *The Ethics of Ambiguity* – the adventurer, the passionate man, the demonic man – the most important of which she calls "the attitude of seriousness" (this term also occurs in Sartre's *Being and Nothingness*; BN: xiv, 580, 626), in which values are considered to be *a priori* given and not chosen. The "serious man" is closely related to Kierkegaard's conception of the second life-stage, misleadingly called the "ethical stage": it desires an objective and external moral standard with unconditioned values and subordinates freedom to this cause – it might be religious fanaticism, or the military or even a revolutionary cause, but in Western countries it is perhaps more likely to be fame, money and power. De Beauvoir thinks that this type of attitude can give rise to the tyranny that she had just witnessed in the Second World War, in which some cause is privileged as more important than the people who adopt it. For her though, the ends rarely justify the means (cf. EA: 124–5), and this makes it all the more surprising that she and Sartre (with their colleague Francis Jeanson) so unrelentingly criticized Camus's *The Rebel* (first published in French in 1951) in *Les Temps modernes*.

Transcendence

As should be apparent, de Beauvoir's criteria for suggesting that women are oppressed is not their happiness or their lack of it (SS: 28–9). In *The Second Sex*, she argues that happiness is too insubstantial a notion to serve her purpose and this is clearly intended to be a rejection of one of the dominant moral philosophies of her time and ours: utilitarianism. Utilitarianism holds that whichever social situation leads to the greatest happiness for the greatest number (or maximizes welfare, or informed preference satisfaction, etc.), is the most just policy, or state of affairs. "Act utilitarianism" requires that we make a calculative judgement about what will lead to the greatest utility, defined in any of the above ways, for the greatest number and that is the course of action that we should take. If we want to figure out whether euthanasia should be legal, we simply need to figure out whether it being legal would lead to greater overall happiness than it being illegal. Of course, these things are difficult and perhaps impossible to figure out, but for utilitarians this is the kind of ideal that should motivate our decision-making processes.

Now de Beauvoir argues that happiness is a misleading criterion. First, she thinks that some women may think that they are happy when they are simply not aware of the alternatives, and here the Marxian notion of false consciousness seems to make an appearance. Secondly, she also thinks of this idea of weighing up happiness as clumsy and impossible (SS: 28). At one stage she rhetorically asks, "Who can really adjudicate on whether or not another is happy?" (*ibid.*). Instead, her criteria for saying that women are oppressed is the notion of transcendence, which she sometimes takes as synonymous with the notion of liberty, and she criticizes anything that she construes as passivity. As she comments in *The Ethics of Ambiguity*:

> The trick of tyrants is to enclose man in the immanence of his facticity and to try to forget that he is always, as Heidegger puts it, "infinitely more than he would be if he were reduced to being what he is" … man is a being of the distances, a movement toward the future, a project.   (EA: 102)

An existential outlook is always projecting into the future and never resting content with what has gone before: one achieves liberty only through reaching out towards other liberties and de Beauvoir even argues that there is no justification for existence other than its expansion into an indefinitely open future (SS: 29). As a consequence, her criteria for saying that women are oppressed is that they do not have the same opportunities as men to expand into the future and to project future possibilities: that is, they lack the same opportunities for transcending the facticity of their situation. In fact, de Beauvoir argues that the liberation of women may not even lead to the happiness that utilitarians are after, particularly in the short term. Life may well be difficult for a liberated woman, but her fundamental claim is that: "Every time transcendence falls back into immanence there is degradation. If the subject consents to this, it is a moral fault. If inflicted upon the subject, it is an oppression. In both cases it is evil" (SS: 29). Here we again see that de Beauvoir thinks that women can be in bad faith if they consent to this degradation and passivity, but it can also be imposed on women and it is also worth noting that de Beauvoir clearly privileges activity as opposed to passivity.

Now some feminists argue that these are faulty notions. Indeed, philosophers such as Le Doeuff in *Hipparchia's Choice* (1991), and Genevieve Lloyd in *Man of Reason* (1992), argue that existentialism is a doctrine that cannot support feminism and this is particularly because of its valorization of "activity" and transcendence. They suggest that we need to deconstruct, or undermine, what it is that de Beauvoir means by activity and transcendence, which are gendered concepts that presuppose forms of social life and action that tacitly restrict women to the domestic sphere. They also claim that de Beauvoir at times simply takes over traditionally masculine values and makes them the goals of women. That is, de Beauvoir sometimes appears to assume that certain kinds of projects in the world are the most valuable kind of activity, without thinking that perhaps this is a masculine conception of value that itself needs to be called into question. And it cannot be denied that de Beauvoir is particularly keen on public life, whether it be writing philosophy, or writing books of literature, or being business leaders, or being leaders of political parties. She tacitly implies that these are the kinds of projects that women should aim for, as they are the most transcendent, and as we will shortly see there is also a consequent devaluation of pregnancy, motherhood, home-management and so on in her work.

Again, however, de Beauvoir insists that some situations cannot be transcended as they are structured so as to inhibit people acting otherwise. This most often happens when their situation is envisaged as "natural", and this is a theme that concerns her at length in *The Ethics of Ambiguity*, where she highlights that one of the ruses of oppression is to camouflage itself behind a so-called "natural" situation. Colonialist rhetoric, for example, often argues that the indigenous group needs to be enslaved because they are naturally promiscuous, violent and so on. A paternalistic attitude towards them is required because the colonialists know (or think they know) their interests better than the indigenous people themselves and without it there would be social chaos. Oppression hence tends to justify itself by reference to its use-value, by the suggestion that society will be happier and more harmonious overall, and this is precisely the kind of rhetoric that de Beauvoir is against (EA: 95). She contends that, "*nothing is useful to man if the latter is not in a position to define his own ends and values, if he is not free*" (EA: 95). She admits that we can never respect all freedoms at once, but argues that we have to authentically face this tension and to emphasize freedom rather than happiness.

But the point remains that in certain social situations individual choice becomes radically circumscribed and cloaked in references to nature. This can sometimes mean that oppressed circumstances cannot be transcended because their situation is not apprehended as one among other possibilities – it is instead the natural order of the world. When this happens, no choice is possible and women have not created this situation and hence are not responsible for it, and de Beauvoir points out that many social institutions also tend to erode the development of autonomy in women, causing them to perceive their capacities and deficiencies as both natural and immutable. For her, marriage and the sex-based division of labour are particularly problematic in contributing to this conception of naturalness that ultimately necessitates that men and women do not encounter each other as equals. As we will see, this makes the prospect of genuine love between them eminently unlikely.

Love and relations with others

In the chapter entitled "The Woman in Love" (SS: 652–78), de Beauvoir suggests that because of the influence of gender stereotypes, men and women have historically had very different attitudes towards love. Moreover she argues that this difference has made genuine love between the sexes improbable, although her heterosexism seems to preclude her from considering homosexuality as a genuine alternative. To put her point crudely, women are envisaged as devoting themselves completely to their lover and engaging in a project that she calls "love-religion" (SS: 653), but men are not thought of as committing with the same degree of openness and abandon: for them, love is treated more like a property. Men often want to possess their beloved as if she were a trophy, or quite literally a prized possession, and even where men do not treat their beloved as mere objects in such an obvious way, she asserts that there are still important differences in the way they love compared to women. Men want to be loved and perhaps even to love a little bit in return, but they also have all of the other aspects of their lives. The beloved woman is one value among other values, and men wish to integrate love within their lives, not to abandon their lives to love, as she suggests women are forced to do for various social and economic reasons.

De Beauvoir repeatedly insists that these different ways in which men and women love has nothing to do with laws of nature. It is their different social situations that reflect the different values that they place on love. Destined to the male from childhood, habituated to think and comport herself in certain ways, many women will dream only of transcending herself to one of those purportedly superior beings. Because the social and economic structure of society doomed women to dependence, the only way out of this situation for women is through valorizing one man as God-like, as the absolute and the essential, who by association confers value on their own life. In this case, we might alter Marx's famous phrase and say that love, rather than religion, is the opium of the masses. At least, love is the opium that allows women not to face their own oppression and to avoid the truths of patriarchy, just as Marx says that religion ensured that the working class was peaceful and docile and did not rebel against its oppression at the hands of the owners of the means of production.

Of course, de Beauvoir also asserts that women do not often succeed in deifying any of the men they attempt to valorize (SS: 654). According to her account, women dream of this absolute soul-searing love, but familiarity will often destroy the man's prestige. Men, after all, are human and fallible and they clearly are not the God-like people that society has taught women that they should be. De Beauvoir goes on to argue that even if briefly successful, this project of love-religion almost inevitably ends in catastrophe. The abandoned woman no longer has a career to fall back on and she also points out that older abandoned women have little opportunity of finding another *grand amour*. Moreover, she suggests that such an existence is almost inevitably problematic for the woman in love: she lives a life of trepidation, worried that her source of value will leave for someone else. As de Beauvoir evocatively says, the woman in love:

> lives in fear and trembling before this man who holds her destiny in his hands without quite knowing it, without quite wishing to ... The innumerable martyrs to love bear witness against the injustice of a fate that offers a sterile hell as ultimate salvation. (SS: 678)

The lack of reciprocity in the way that men and women love inevitably causes resentment and it also robs the woman of her transcendence, of engaging in projects in the world. Identifying herself with the man and his pursuits in the world, women are doomed to immanence and cannot find self-realization in their own acts: they are passive (SS: 653).

Disregarding the various binary oppositions at work in de Beauvoir's text and the value hierarchy that she ascribes to them – transcendent–immanent, active–passive – we can better understand her point by recalling Sartre's characterizations of the look. According to his ontology, which does not discriminate between the sexes, all of us find the experience of the look troubling and hence seek to minimize its impact and, on his account, we are always free to return the look. However, de Beauvoir's analysis suggests that women have gradually come to conceive of themselves as the looked-upon (as the object of society's looks) in contrast to the man who permanently envisages himself as the looker, or as the judging gaze. According to de Beauvoir, women experience themselves as objects and as passive things, whereas men experience themselves as subjects, and relationships between the sexes hence becomes even more unequal owing to this opposition between looker and looked-upon being so static. It means that women are not "*pour soi*" (for-themselves) in the same way as men. Instead, their social existence is predominantly for-others, as they are permanently ensnared in a look from which there may be no opportunity to turn the tables.

Clearly this is not real love, which de Beauvoir thinks can only be redeemed in a situation of equality. She suggests that only on the day when women can love in their strength, not in their weakness, will real love be possible, and this requires the cultural and economic independence of women. For de Beauvoir, "genuine love ought to be founded on the mutual recognition of two liberties" (SS: 677) in which the lovers experience themselves as both self and other. Neither would give up transcendence and she insists that this kind of reciprocity is possible, contrary to Sartre. For Sartre, to experience ourselves as an object in the eyes of another is to momentarily be denied our transcendence. On de Beauvoir's analysis, however, others do not just threaten my world but they also potentially enrich it through the opening up of future projects for me. Moreover, for her all projects are implicitly collaborative, and as such they can be both violent and generous to the other but they are not necessarily either. She supplements this analysis in *The Ethics of Ambiguity*, arguing that both men and women need to develop a consciousness of themselves as inevitably and simultaneously both subject and object (EA: 81). Towards the end of this book she suggests that if both would assume the consequent ambiguity with a "lucid modesty, correlative to an authentic pride, they would meet each other as fellows and would live the erotic drama in friendship" (EA: 232). On this view, love is not inevitably problematic and de Beauvoir's account hence raises the question whether Sartre's ontology, which suggests that love is merely a "ruse", is a genuine ontological description of the human–world relation or just a partial description of human beings in a patriarchal and capitalist society.

Death

De Beauvoir has a complicated position on death, which sits somewhere between the extremes of Heidegger's and Sartre's characterizations of it. In the untranslated *Pyrrhus et Cinéas* (1943), de Beauvoir adopts a position that seems closely related to Sartre's conviction that death cannot be my possibility. She states that:

My death interrupts my life only when I die, and that only from the point of view of others. Death does not exist for me while I am alive; my project goes right through it without meeting any obstacles. The full impetus of my transcendence runs into no barriers; it alone determines when it shall run down, like the sea which strikes against a smooth shore and stops at a certain point, to go no further. (PC: 61)

It is interesting to note, however, that in her later book, *Old Age*, published in 1970 and with her own death much closer, de Beauvoir insists that we are all inhabited by what she calls a "generalized ageing" and she also offers an account of temporality not dissimilar to that of Heidegger in *Being and Time*. Moreover, in *The Ethics of Ambiguity*, written only a few years after *Pyrrhus et Cineas*, de Beauvoir writes of the ambiguity that is most fundamental of all and declares that: "every living moment is a sliding toward death. But if they are willing to look it in the face, they also discover that every movement toward death is life" (EA: 127). On account not only of acknowledging that every living moment is a sliding towards death but also in looking for the redemptive and life-giving aspects of this movement, de Beauvoir's position here seems much closer to the Heideggerian conception of being-towards-death than to its Sartrean renunciation.

The body

De Beauvoir's account of embodiment is a complicated one. She clearly emphasizes the importance of the body, as Marcel and Merleau-Ponty also did. At times, she also controversially uses the specifically female experience of embodiment to explain the origins of women's oppression: to put the problem crudely, the child-bearing capacity of women places them more in the grip of nature than it does men. In her discussion of biology and history in Book 1 of *The Second Sex*, de Beauvoir notes that women experience certain phenomena that men do not – pregnancy, menstruation, lactation and so on – and that these differences constitute an important difference in women's situation and provide some kind of explanation about why women have been so persistently associated with nature. These aspects of female embodiment necessitate that women spend large amounts of time in "natural functions" associated with their reproductive capacities, and this in turn ensures that managing things like a career are, at the very least, difficult.

In other words, there is a conflict in women's lives between their role as a mother and their aspirations towards civic and political involvement. De Beauvoir sees these two aspects of life (civic and maternal) as being mutually exclusive, and the ambiguity of women's embodiment is at least partly the source of this conflict in that it makes a full transcendent subjectivity more difficult to attain (SS: 587).

At the same time, de Beauvoir does not want to hold that this is an inevitable ontological condition: these "biological facts" that differentiate the sexes do not directly cause (or legitimate) the situation of oppression. On the contrary, elsewhere in this text she also states that there are no merely neutral facts of an unbiased observer; facts are always interpreted from a certain situation with certain ends in mind. To return to the problem at hand, de Beauvoir employs a sex–gender distinction and suggests that it is completely conceivable that a society might interpret the "fact" of pregnancy differently. There is also a suggestion in her work that technological changes mean that even if the association of the female body with nature were understandable in an agrarian society, for example, that is not the case in the throes of industrialization and capitalism. In this respect, she bemoans the lack of crèches, which means that women are forced to choose between the civic and the personal when this need not be the case. De Beauvoir also suggests that ideally technological developments will mean that women do not have to give up their careers for pregnancy and motherhood. She is not always clear about what kind of reproductive technologies she is thinking about, but she insists that we need to relieve women of their confinement to maternal roles.

Although this is not so apparent in the "Introduction" to *The Second Sex*, elsewhere in this text there is something of an anti-family line of thinking, and she clearly thinks of pregnancy and parenthood as an obstacle to freedom, which she construes as limiting the mother to a reproductive and domestic role. Neither parenthood nor pregnancy is what de Beauvoir considers to be a "creative project". Creative projects are those that give best expression to the transcendent side of human existence. Admittedly, de Beauvoir talks a little about what she terms "free motherhood". That is, motherhood outside marriage, and without women being the main (or sole) carer, and this seems to be her ideal. As she comments:

Economic evolution in woman's situation is in the process of upsetting the institution of marriage: it is becoming a union freely entered into upon the consent of two independent persons; the obligations of the two contracting parties are personal and reciprocal … Woman is no longer limited to the reproductive function which has lost in part its character as natural servitude and has come to be regarded as a function to be voluntarily assumed. (SS: 425)

The main issue that comes out of this, however, is whether women should just take over male goals and aspirations, or rather should redefine them such that this active–passive binary opposition is called into question and such that some of these projects such as child-bearing might be thought of as valuable. This practical issue of whether or not child-bearing is a constraint on freedom, or a creative project in itself, has been an ongoing issue in feminist literature, but I raise this issue of reproduction because of what it signifies about de Beauvoir's attitude towards the body more generally, which is complicated. In many of her comments she places bodily existence on the same footing as consciousness and insists that an important reciprocity obtains between body and consciousness. Experiences of the body are informed by our concepts, and concepts are also informed by our experiences of the body. But her attitude towards parenting, and her tacit suggestion that the female body offers a reason (although not a necessary one) why women have been viewed as close to nature over the centuries, runs the risk of implying that the female body is thought of as a constraint on women's liberation, and as legitimating a nature–culture hierarchy with culture and the mind privileged over the passive body, which is considered to be a burden: a raw-datum that cannot be altered. That said, within her own work there are also resources to undermine this account as we have seen.

Sexual difference and existentialism

Although the amount of contemporary secondary literature on de Beauvoir is enormous and hence cannot be summed up here, her work has raised some particular questions about the relationship between existentialism and the problem of sexual difference. Indeed, what becomes clear from her work is that the problem of sexual difference was largely ignored by her contemporaries, Sartre, Merleau-Ponty and Heidegger.

This omission has been analysed by many contemporary feminists and one of the early texts to pursue this, Le Doeuff's *Hipparchia's Choice*, engages at great length with both Sartre and de Beauvoir, and criticizes Sartre for sexism. Le Doeuff points out that Sartre has many strange sexual metaphors in the later stages of *Being and Nothingness*: apparently his sexist descriptions of holes motivated Courtney Love to adopt that name for her rock band Hole. More relevantly for our purposes, Le Doeuff also claims that Sartre's various examples of concrete situations only include women when they have something to do with sex. They never have a history or even a workplace. Women are only a sexed body in Sartre's work and Le Doeuff also claims that when Sartre talks about actual sexual encounters there is no acknowledgment of the difference between sexes. There is only "my flesh" and "the other's flesh".

While Merleau-Ponty is not accused of sexism to the same degree as Sartre, it remains the case that his project of analysing embodiment, and of analysing sexuality, does not take into account the difference between men and women's experiences of embodiment and sexuality. As feminists such as Judith Butler have pointed out, he presupposes that what he says about the body applies to both men and women equally, and many feminists want to dispute that this is the case. Theorists such as Butler argue that we cannot talk coherently about neutral and abstract bodies, but only about specific contextualized bodies: that is about male and female bodies, about sick and well bodies, or about old and young bodies and so on. This raises an interesting question: do men and women experience the world and their bodies differently? De Beauvoir illustrated the tension between species and the personal that women feel, as well as the way in which women are persistently the object of the look in patriarchal culture. Much of the richness of *The Second Sex* derives from her analysis of the ways in which women experience the look in any manner of different ways. If we grant that these experiences are different to those of men, the further questions is: are these differences existentially and ontologically significant? Following in de Beauvoir's footsteps, most feminists these days will argue that they are.

"Throwing like a Girl"

For further reading on this issue, Iris Marion Young's famous 1970s essay, "Throwing like a Girl", is a useful resource, even if Young has since adjusted her position. Drawing on the work of both Merleau-Ponty and de Beauvoir, Young discusses the different styles of bodily motility and movement between the sexes and, more specifically, why women throw differently to men. For her, no physical fact about women's bodies, including muscular differences, necessitates that they throw differently to men. If the difference between the way in which men and women throw were simply about muscles, then women would be expected to compensate for this supposed muscular weakness by throwing with a style more like men; that is, by putting more of their bodies into their action and by maximizing the capacities of their bodies by putting their entire bodies into the throwing. Instead, Young suggests that virtually all women's physical activities fail to make use of the body's spatial and lateral possibilities, arguing that there is also a typical style of running like a girl, climbing like a girl, swinging like a girl, hitting like a girl and so on. What unites these different kinds of activity is that the whole body is not put into fluid and directed motion; women concentrate their efforts on the parts immediately required for the task and, for example, do not use their legs when lifting as much as men do. As for throwing, they only use the parts of the body immediately required for the task.

Young's explanation of this difference is to suggest that the tension between woman as a free subject, and woman as culturally oppressed, is expressed on an embodied level. In simpler terms, she thinks that women are inhibited at the levels of their bodies. Rather than being with their bodies, women are at an ambivalent distance from their bodies; there are wary and hesitant about their bodies, which they take to be the object of movement and not the movement's originator. In order to explain this, Young contends that in movement women posit themselves as the object being looked at, as the object of society's gaze, and this omnipresent awareness that they might be being watched means that women are more self-reflexive in action than men. But to sum up, Young's main point is that women experience the ambiguity of their bodies in a different way to men, and her implication is that there is a bigger divide between mind and body for women than there is for men.

Now there are various possible explanations for this kind of difference. Of course, girls have historically spent less time using their bodies in sporting activities than do boys; they have less practice in an embodied context. As Young points out, women are also taught to behave like a girl: taught not to get hurt, not to get dirty and so on, and to conduct themselves in a certain manner. Now, even if we want to hold that this difference between men's and women's bodily movements is no longer as obvious as Young's essay would have us believe, her analysis does seem to show that men and women can and do experience their bodies very differently.

We could supplement this analysis by pointing out the apparently obvious; that the significance of breasts is manifestly different for men and women. As Grosz points out, breasts are a bodily attribute that is subjectively lived (that is phenomenally experienced) and they also function as an object within a particular society, but both the way that breasts are subjectively experienced and the way that they function as objects in our society is obviously very different for men and women (1994: 108). We might conclude from this that the relation between inner and outer, between being a body and having a body, are also importantly different for men and women. If so, this means that Sartre and Merleau-Ponty's descriptions, which both presume gender neutrality, are only a partial description of what it is to be embodied. This again raises questions about whether existentialism is simply a thematization of the kind of consciousness produced by patriarchal capitalism, or whether it really gets at something universal about the human condition. Can it account for sexual difference, or for that matter, racial difference (see Franz Fanon's *Black Skins, White Masks* (1991)), such as the experience of ethnic minorities?

Summary of key points

Woman as Other
- There is no essence that constitutes being a woman; *one is not born a woman, but rather becomes one* (SS: 295).
- Women have unjustifiably been designated as second, and as other than men (SS: 16).

Bad faith and inauthenticity
De Beauvoir envisages the temptation to forgo liberty and to become a thing as very difficult to resist for all human beings, whether they be male or female, but she thinks of it as a terrible thing (SS: 21). In *The Second Sex* she describes three main roles in which women might inauthentically be complicit in their subjugation: the *narcissist*, the *woman in love*, and the *mystic* (SS: 641–89). In *The Ethics of Ambiguity*, she describes four general examples of bad faith: the *adventurer*, the *passionate man*, the *demonic man*, and the *attitude of seriousness*, the last of which subordinates freedom to an overarching cause (religion, revolution, fame, money, power, etc.)

Freedom
- De Beauvoir argues that action loses its meaning if it is not willed from freedom, and with freedom as it goal. Freedom and transcendence are more important than happiness, or usefulness, or any other possible criteria for the "good life".

- Unlike Sartre, however, she insists that after a long period of oppression women may no longer be able to conceive of other possibilities. Rather than oppose bad faith to authenticity and true freedom, in this case oppressed women occupy a middle ground between these two extremes.

An Ethics of Ambiguity
- To live ethically and authentically, we must assume the ambiguity of the human condition, rather than flee from it by pretending that we are biologically determined, or a rational subject who is wholly outside of their situation and can survey it.
- Rather than an individual's freedom being threatened and (momentarily) inhibited by the appearance of others, as Sartre analysis of the look suggests, for de Beauvoir it is other people who open up new possibilities in the future for us. Full individual freedom (or transcendence) requires that it emerge on to an "open future", which depends on the freedom of others.
- Social change (including in regard to the overturning of patriarchy) requires recognition of a "we": only then can individual discontent develop into a common project and a revolution.

Love
Historically, de Beauvoir argues that women have devoted themselves completely to their lovers in a project of "love-religion" (SS: 653), but men have not committed with the same degree of openness and abandon; for them, love is treated more like a property. This, however, is because of patriarchal social and economic inequalities, and the possibility of reciprocal and meaningful love depends on the establishment of genuine equality between the sexes.

The body
Women generally experience the conflict between species and individual, between perpetuation of the species and their own personal freedom, in a more immediate and pressing way than men.

seven

The legacy of existentialism: deconstruction, responsibility and the time of the decision

It is hard to think of many contemporary European philosophers who have not endorsed the denunciation of existentialism for being a humanism that was initiated by Heidegger and has been perpetuated in the anti-humanism of structuralists such as Louis Althusser and Roland Barthes. Concerned with the way in which both languages and systems produce individuals as subjects, structuralism took over from existentialism both academically and perhaps even in terms of public attention. Structuralism sought to arrive at a stable and secure knowledge of a system or a structure by charting differences within that structure and, significantly, it sought to do so without any references to subjectivity and consciousness, which were, as we have seen, a significant part of existential phenomenology.

However, it was not long before structuralism was itself being challenged by poststructuralism in the late 1960s. Philosophers such as Michel Foucault (at least in his middle and later work), Jean-François Lyotard, Gilles Deleuze and Jacques Derrida were all important in this regard, challenging the "centrist" assumption of structuralism that an understanding of one key or central element of the structure – whether it be kinship laws, the workings of language, the educational system, or the devices employed in a literary text – allows for an explanation of the entire system. Poststructuralism also cast into question structuralism's rather strict determinism, instead insisting on the role of unpredictable and random forces in the genesis of any structure, law or norm. Opposing structuralism's quasi-scientific claims to objectivity, rationality and intelligibility, poststructuralism instead pointed to certain moments, or "events", that disrupt any stable and secure sense of meaning and identity.

Despite this problematization of structuralism's simple determinism, and despite their concern to show the way in which the event resists and exceeds all of our attempted reconstructions of it, it has generally been assumed that poststructuralist concerns have remained at a distance from the existentialist's wartime preoccupations with freedom, death, responsibility and anguish. This is largely because poststructuralists have continued to endorse the structuralist idea of "the death of the subject", and have continued to highlight problems with, and the limits to, humanism. In less provocative terms, this means that it is spurious to begin from the assumption that consciousness and subjectivity are fundamental when they are in fact socioculturally produced, albeit not in as overdetermined a way as the structuralists might have thought. In that respect, it is unsurprising that theorists such as Jean-Luc Nancy, Foucault, Derrida and many others have continued to directly associate existentialism with humanism.

Although there are some valid reasons for this reception of existentialism that structuralism and poststructuralism arguably share in common, notably some of Sartre's own hasty comments in *Existentialism is a Humanism*, this way of thinking nevertheless obscures two key points:

KEY POINT
- It obscures the resources within existentialism that do not admit of humanism in any traditional sense, even if it is the case that consciousness is prioritized (and this later clause is called into question by major aspects of the work of Merleau-Ponty and Heidegger).
- It obscures the significant similarities between aspects of existentialism and some contemporary poststructuralist thinkers, particularly their shared concern with: questions about responsibility and their rejection of moralistic "knights of good conscience"; their critique of determinism (including scientific determinism); their search for the conditions and limits of rationality (including the way in which events and existence exceed our rational reconstructions of them); and, finally, their interest in the body.

To some extent, this book has already shown the diversity within existentialism that problematizes any too quick association with humanism. For example, while Derrida's later interest in the question of animality can be seen to undermine aspects of Sartre's work, animals were an ongoing concern of Merleau-Ponty's from the 1930s on (see

The Structure of Behaviour), and his work always resisted the claim that meaning is exclusively attributable to consciousness (a position that is implied by the phenomenological reduction as Husserl formulated it). Rather than pursue these kind of claims further, however, this chapter will address the second point above by highlighting some of the often overlooked similarities between existentialism and poststructuralism, particularly the poststructuralism of Derrida, which has come to be termed deconstruction.

Sartre and Derrida: deconstruction and responsibility

Although intimately associated with the name of Jacques Derrida (1930–2004), it needs to be stated from the outset that deconstruction is not an external method that is applied to particular *books*. Rather, deconstruction is an ongoing process that is always already at work in *texts*, and texts is to be understood in the broadest possible sense, including contexts (see *Limited Inc.*). To summarize the strategy, at least as it was initially formulated and practised, deconstruction sought both to reverse the dominant oppositions that sustain a text (or concept) before also showing how these oppositions are themselves always already displaced in the text (and context) in question. Because of Derrida's early focus on particular books, however, deconstruction is frequently associated with Barthes's famous statements regarding "the death of the author", and it is clear that for Derrida the process of reading is allocated a place of considerable importance and the significance of authorial intentions is diminished. Is that enough to distinguish Derrida's position from that of the existentialists? Although it is true that a deconstructive and close reading of both fictional and philosophical texts was not part of Sartre's philosophical *modus operandi*, we have already seen that Heidegger's engagement in a process of "destructive retrieval" in relation to the history of philosophy was an important and formative influence on the strategy of deconstruction. Moreover, other scholars have suggested that the strategy of deconstruction was both influenced and pre-empted by Merleau-Ponty's conception of a "hyper-dialectic" in his final, unfinished book, *The Visible and the Invisible* (see Gasché 1994: 29–30; and Reynolds 2004: 55–66). Although these points cannot be considered in detail here, it seems that the focus on texts is not enough, on its own, to install any substantive barrier between deconstruction and existentialism.

That said, it remains the case that in the introduction to his doctoral thesis on Husserl Derrida began by stridently distancing himself from

Sartre, Merleau-Ponty and existentialism. In the process he posited a gap between his deconstructive position and existentialism that arguably was not breached for over twenty years. This understanding of deconstruction as completely post-existentialist, as well as the associated reductive dismissal of Sartre's work, is somewhat hasty, however, and it is worth pointing out that Derrida's characterization of existential thinkers significantly changes in his post-1990 work. For example, Derrida observes in the interview published in *A Taste for the Secret* that although he did distance himself from the "philosophy of existence", as well as a certain existentialist interpretation of Husserl, his:

> intention was certainly not to draw away from the concern for existence itself, for concrete personal commitment, or from the existential pathos that, in a sense, I have never lost … In some ways, a philosopher without the ethico-existential pathos does not interest me very much.   (Derrida 2001a: 40)

He then goes to on to affirm the importance of the proto-existentialist Kierkegaard to his own work, adding that "the resistance of existence to the concept or system – this is something I attach great importance to and feel very deeply, something I am always ready to stand up for" (*ibid.*: 40). Derrida's "quasi-existential" affirmation of the resistance of existence to conceptual system-building is very important here, as it links to a broader tendency of virtually all poststructuralist thought. After all, it is not only Derrida, but also Deleuze, Lyotard and, more recently, Alain Badiou, who exalt the importance of the event and the way in which it is irreducible to, and exceeds, particular rational representations of it. Although these poststructuralist characterizations of the event are not univocal in their meaning, their use of the concept of the event is closely related to that of existence (or *existenz*), as it is employed by Sartre, de Beauvoir, Jaspers and Heidegger. Both the poststructuralists and the existentialists are keen to point to certain limits to knowledge (e.g. the way in which it can never fully grasp the event, or existence) and we will return to this point towards the end of this chapter, when we consider the affirmation of the future that is also an integral part of contemporary poststructuralist thought.

Along with this endorsement of Kierkegaard, however, it is important to note that Derrida's view of his immediate existential predecessors in France has also gradually become more positive. For example in *Memoirs of the Blind* (1993) and *On Touching: Jean-Luc Nancy* (2005) he discusses Merleau-Ponty in a largely positive manner, and his essay

"Salut, Salut: Dead Man Running" (2002a) talks about Sartre, again in a positive light. That said, it is a pity that this essay on Sartre does not involve much explicit philosophical negotiation with Sartre's key ideas. After all, existential thinkers, and Sartre in particular, have focused on issues concerned with decision-making, responsibility and the like, and such themes have also become a sustained and explicit focus of Derrida's later writings. In fact, it can be coherently argued that the issue of responsibility is an important one for poststructuralism generally; in different ways, a concern with responsibility to otherness is evident in the work of Derrida, Levinas, Lyotard and Foucault. Perhaps a rapprochement of existentialism and poststructuralism can be effected around the locus of responsibility, which is clearly also a major area of concern for the existentialists, even if it might be argued that their emphasis is more clearly concerned with responsibility to the self, rather than with responsibility to other(s). It is to this theme that I will now turn, first by consideration of the related notion of decision-making.

Drawing on the work of Kierkegaard, in multiple different texts Derrida argues that the instant of the decision must be mad, provocatively telling us that a decision requires an undecidable leap beyond all prior preparations and rational calculations for that decision (Derrida 1995: 77). According to him, this applies to all decisions and not just those regarding the conversion to religious faith that preoccupies Kierkegaard. A decision is never simply about weighing up pros and cons, and figuring out a solution as in mathematics. We may ask ourselves questions such as "Should I leave my partner?" or "Should I use my knight or my bishop for this particular chess move?" We may even work out that it is definitely in our best interests to leave our current lover, or to use the knight in order to best facilitate a checkmate. However, the decision itself does not automatically follow from this. It still needs to be taken and that requires a leap beyond any prior preparations for that decision. This is the place that his work meets up with Sartre's, for whom, as we have seen, any decision must be equally unjustifiable and equally mad. This is dramatically evinced in Antoine Roquentin's existential struggles in *Nausea*, but also throughout the entirety of *Being and Nothingness*. Derrida and Sartre come together in their rejection of any Kantian categorical imperative that claims that all decisions can and should be based on reason. This understanding of the decision also has clear consequences for issues to do with responsibility and it is on such a theme that this surprising proximity between Sartre and Derrida is reaffirmed.

Notwithstanding his complicated account of fundamental projects, Sartre disavows the possibility of providing any rational justification for our choices. The most famous example of this is recounted in both *Being and Nothingness* and *Existentialism is a Humanism*. Sartre recalls a student of his who came to see him with an ethical dilemma, basically to seek guidance about whether he should look after his sick and dying mother on her deathbed, or join the resistance movement to fight his country's Nazi oppressors. Sartre not only refused to give an answer but he also intimated that this kind of conflict is involved in all attempts to be responsible. Significantly, we have also seen in earlier chapters that responsibility is never easy on Sartre's understanding; there is no risk of being self-satisfied, with a good conscience (Heidegger's analysis of conscience also avoids this risk), and complacent with the choices that we have made. On the contrary, assuming responsibility is very intimidating and liable to induce the experience of anguish, because all such decisions are ultimately unjustifiable. In this regard Sartre is against any form of prescriptive morality that tells us what to do, much as Derrida also is in, to cite merely one example, *The Gift of Death* (1995).

Although questions remain regarding whether or not Derrida thinks that responsibility can ever be assumed, as Sartre's analysis implies, Derrida nevertheless (re)stages an analogous dilemma in his reading of Abraham's biblical sacrifice of his son, Isaac, on Mt Moriah. In *The Gift of Death*, Derrida points to a fundamental tension between responsibility for all others (e.g. freeing the world from the Nazi party, in Sartre's example) and responsibility for a singular loved one (e.g. the sick mother). Responsibility involves enduring this trial of the "undecidable decision", where attending to the call of a particular other (such as God in Abraham's case) will inevitably demand an estrangement from the "other others" and the more general ethical demands of a community, who in this case would obviously be horrified by Abraham's willingness to sacrifice his son. Whatever decision one may take, whether it is to prefer a singular other or to prefer all others, it can never be wholly justified (Derrida 1995: 70). For both Derrida and Sartre, to have a good conscience, to assume that one's hands are clean and that one is acting on the side of the good and the just, is to inevitably presage a greater violence.

Whereas it is true that Sartre is rightly famous in the history of philosophy for his many and varied arguments for freedom, and it is also true that Derrida has rarely discussed freedom (but see one of his last books, *Rogues* (2005), where it is given sustained attention), any simple opposition between them on this issue of freedom would also, I think, be misleading. After all, Sartre's concept of "the situation" refers to the necessary intermingling of facticity and freedom, and he insists that there is freedom only in a situation and there is a situation only through freedom. He also goes on to claim that situation and motivation for pursuing certain projects are indistinguishable, suggesting that: "the situation, the common product of the contingency of the in-itself and of freedom, is an ambiguous phenomenon in which it is impossible for the for-itself to distinguish the contribution of freedom from that of the brute existent" (BN: 487). Taking this ambiguity of the "situation" into account, Sartre does not seem to be as committed to a conception of the free and sovereign subject who decides as might be suspected, even if he is nevertheless closer to such a conception than Derrida. Indeed, for Derrida, any theory of the subject is incapable of accounting for the slightest decision, because such a view would necessarily involve "the unfolding of an egological immanence, the autonomic and automatic deployment of predicates or possibilities proper to a subject, without the tearing rupture that should occur in every decision we call free" (1999b: 24). In other words, if a decision is envisaged as simply following from certain character traits, then it would not genuinely be a decision. Clearly, however, a decision, for Sartre, does not flow from any egological immanence – recall that there is no character trait of "cowardice" that dictates that the hiker will give in to his fatigue – and his philosophy does not constitute a theory of the subject in that sense. Rather, the subject is literally no-thing, except in reflection, and this ensures that, for Sartre, decisions are always characterized by a radical rupture with immanence and the past. We have seen that Merleau-Ponty criticized him for this by pointing to the omnipresence of habitual skill acquisition, but Derrida is now suggesting that the kind of rupture that Sartre spoke about is, in fact, absolutely necessary if there is to be such a thing as a decision.

Of course, it would be difficult to deny that there are some significant points of difference between Sartre and Derrida's conception of the decision. In *Politics of Friendship* (1997), for example, Derrida argues that far from returning us to any sovereign conception of free will, what needs to be considered is the fundamentally "passive" aspect of a decision that is always made for the other, and he insists that there is no freedom without the other. He eventually concludes: "*in sum, the decision is unconscious* – insane as that may seem, it involves the unconscious but is nevertheless responsible" (1997: 69). This suggestion that the decision is always passive, partially unconscious, and for the other, highlights that Derrida is not returning us to a Sartrean paradigm of the activity and projects of the for-itself. Indeed, from Sartre's perspective the above invocation of the unconscious would be a flight from freedom, a "game of excuses", and therefore in bad faith. Moreover, we also do well to remember that Sartre's rejection of Heidegger's understanding of being-towards-death was precisely on the grounds that such a view amounted to living for the Other's perspective and Sartre insisted that this was impossible; on his view we cannot live and decide for the other. Speculatively extending this dialogue between these two French philosophers, there are good reasons to suspect that Derrida would respond to Sartre by trying to show that first and foremost one must always be responding to the other and living for the other. Although Sartre might denigrate this as an impossible ambition, for Derrida the impossibility of this ambition would be that which impels and motivates us. Derrida would also undoubtedly seek to problematize the ease of Sartre's distinction between good faith and bad faith, particularly as the latter is associated with any use of the concept of the unconscious. Indeed, one could easily argue, from a deconstructive point of view, that so-called bad faith is in fact constitutive of all faith. This seems to be Derrida's implication in "Salut, Salut" (2002a), his final piece of writing on Sartre's work and *Les Temps modernes*. So although there are some important connections between these two philosophers, they seem to part company when in comes to Sartre's analysis of concepts such as bad faith, which tacitly reinstate a moral vision of the self who decides, as opposed to Derrida's concern with the other.

A similar difference between Derrida and existentialism is apparent on the issue of death. Existentialism, as we have seen, tends to involve some interest in the issue of death, and any number of Derrida's books have been concerned with death: see *Memoires: For Paul de Man* (1989), *Aporias* (1993a), *Spectres of Marx* (1994), *The Gift of Death* (1995), *Demeure: Fiction and Testimony* (2000) and *The Work of Mourning* (2001b). Derrida has also written on Heidegger's conception of being-towards-death in numerous texts, but one significant aspect of his analyses is that there is no clear valorization of any "authentic" attitude towards death. The different ethical injunctions that Sartre and Heidegger derive from death are not so forcefully apparent in Derrida's work and this is significant. Perhaps the most that could be said is that Derrida's position, at least in some of his recent writings on responsibility and decision-making, amounts to a "quasi-existentialism". We have seen his insistence that existence (and the event) always partly resists our knowledge and representations of it, and his further comment that a philosopher without the recognition of this existential pathos is of no interest to him. We have also seen his emphasis on the difficulty of assuming responsibility and the transcendental necessity of the decision involving a leap beyond prior preparations for it. These are all themes deeply indebted to existential thought, but if Derrida's recent work can be coherently, albeit provocatively, described as a quasi-existentialism, it is clearly one without the ethics of authenticity betrothed to it. In that respect, his philosophical position might be more closely related to the work of Merleau-Ponty than is commonly assumed. After all, Merleau-Ponty's work could also be summed up as advocating a milder form of existentialism, precisely because it lacks the ethics of authenticity that Sartre, Heidegger and de Beauvoir all hitched to their philosophical systems, albeit in very different ways. I argue for this relationship between Merleau-Ponty and Derrida in greater detail in my monograph *Merleau-Ponty and Derrida* (2004), but for the moment I hope only to have begun to destabilize any stark opposition between deconstruction and existentialism.

Camus and Derrida: the question of politics

There is also an important and underestimated link between the works of Camus and Derrida, both born in French-colonized Algeria, which is worth drawing attention to. Camus famously stated that he belonged to the "party of those without a party". Likewise Derrida always resisted co-option to any particular political party, even in the middle of the student revolutions in Paris in May 1968. In his theoretical work, Derrida also proposes paradoxical concepts such as "religion without religion", "faith without faith" and so on. Although Derrida is borrowing these concepts from the work of Maurice Blanchot, they also echo Camus's phraseology above, and in some quarters (predominantly Marxist) Derrida has also been criticized in much the same way as Camus was by Sartre and others for not taking a political stand. In a sense, both Camus and Derrida provide us with the grounds for critiquing either political extreme, but do not fill in their respective middle way with any normative content.

The line of reasoning that Camus and Derrida employ to argue against totalitarian political extremes is also curiously similar. In *The Rebel*, for example, Camus famously advocated rebellion rather than revolution, because he thought the latter had been responsible for an enormous amount of bloodshed in the twentieth century. Instead of admitting the revolutionary doctrine that "the end justifies the means", he advocated perpetual rebellion and described the state of mind that accompanies this as an "agonized serenity"; that is, as both an urgent and agonized demand for the moment, and simultaneously serene in such a way as to preclude this demand becoming a self-enclosed moment in which the revolution is enacted (Camus 1953: 266).

Now it almost goes without saying that Derrida is not as naive as Camus. Unlike Camus, Derrida sees a degree of violence as necessary and inevitable, and he is perhaps even prepared to sanction a violent act of revolutionary founding (of a state, a constitution, etc.) in a way that Camus would not. In that respect, Derrida is not so quick to relieve himself of the necessity of "dirty hands". For him, politics is about negotiation and not simply moral principles. However, it remains the case that this distinction between revolution and rebellion that Camus draws, is closely related to the distinction that Derrida's later work frequently makes between the *messianic* structure of existence, which is open to an *unknown* ungraspable other who might come, and the historical *messianisms* (i.e. the Islamic, Jewish and Christian religions), who are open to the coming of a specific other of *known* characteristics. Both Derrida's conception of the messianic, and Camus's understanding of rebellion, proceed without a grand goal or intent that the messiah or revolution should arrive. A conviction that the messiah has arrived, or that the time of the revolution has come, is often a prelude to violence in which one kills in the name of the messiah, or of a future just state. As Camus and Derrida have shown us, when the future is thought of as known, this tends to lead to either fascism or communism in which that future state of affairs can justify the violent means needed to get there. Instead of repeating this mistake, their respective notions of the messianic and rebellion advocate a perpetual openness towards the future and to that which *might* come; they do not treat the future as preordained or known, as the historical messianisms and revolutions have done.

This emphasis on the future in Derrida's work will be returned to below, but it is also interesting to note that in his recent essay, "The University Without Condition" (2002c), Derrida argues that the university should be a privileged site from which to contest claims to sovereignty. There are other sites that resist the phantasm of sovereignty, such as psychoanalysis, but Derrida suggests that what is needed in the humanities is questioning and deconstruction, rather than some kind of sovereign mastery that answers and thereby presumes to preclude further questions. What is needed, Derrida repeats, is a principle of "resistance", a term that could perhaps be exchanged for Camus's favoured word, rebellion. Indeed, Derrida describes the new humanities, or the humanities to come, as the "place of irredentist resistance … a sort of principal of civil disobedience, even of dissidence in the name of a superior law and a justice of thought" (2002b: 208).

Of course, for deconstruction that superior kind of justice cannot be named, as in Marxism. Marxism described and thereby circumscribed the future, rather than remaining open to the future that is "to come". Deconstruction consistently insists that this is not the way to go, because the resistance thereby threatens to become a form of orthodoxy that is no longer critical and hence itself legitimates institutional violence. Rejecting the teleological understanding of the future of the Marxists, Derrida's strategy of deconstruction can never be finally completed or successful, but must instead maintain an ongoing critical vigilance about all claims to accomplish any such radical success, whether in regard to the overcoming of capitalism, or a rupture with traditional metaphysical ways of thinking. Again, it is for similar reasons that Camus advocated a state of perpetual rebellion rather than revolution, seeing the violence of the twentieth century as an inevitable consequence of all absolutist thinking.

Although it has only briefly been explored here, this relationship between Camus and Derrida should not surprise us unduly. If post-structuralist thinkers these days can be crudely, although perhaps aptly, characterized as "the left minus Marxism", then we can see why Derrida might be politically closer to Camus than to the more militant Sartre and de Beauvoir, who were yet to be "minus Marxism". He would also be closer to the politics of Merleau-Ponty in the *Adventures of the Dialectic*, where Merleau-Ponty rejected his prior Marxist leanings, disagreed with Sartre's uncritical support of the Soviet Union in the Korean War, and accused him of perpetuating a renewed Leninism, an "ultrabolshevism".

A future politics?

As has been suggested, Derrida invokes the future and the "to come" in many of his recent writings, pointing to the way in which all laws, or norms, need to be open to revision and open to that which might come (but not to that which *must* come), rather than closing themselves off from change. In the process, he emphasizes a conception of the future that cannot be imbued with any determinate content, just as "justice" cannot be imbued with any determinate content; instead, appeals to such concepts disrupt any and every empirical determination (or law) of a just cause, or state of affairs. Derrida's politics as a result rejects any teleological understanding of the future as goal-directed, because the "to come" must remain entirely undetermined and this emphasis on the radical difference of the future serves as a guardrail against absolutisms of all sorts. While Derrida repeatedly acknowledges the necessity of normative and calculative politics, he eschews any substantive theorization of it in favour of emphasizing a politics of the future, and of a radical difference that is incalculable.

Although Derrida might be said to take this position to its extreme, to differing extents all of the philosophers considered in this book are concerned with describing and enumerating transcendental conditions for ethics and politics, rather than any normative ethics itself. Even de Beauvoir, the most explicit proponent of an existentialist ethics, was not prescribing any kind of universal recipe for action or a single monistic theory of what is valuable (recall that transcendence cannot be reduced to happiness). As she comments:

> It will be said that these considerations remain quite abstract. What must be done, practically? Which action is good? Which action is bad? To ask such a question is also to fall into a naive abstraction … Ethics does not furnish recipes any more than do science and art. One can merely propose methods.
>
> (EA: 134)

In other words, de Beauvoir's work offers, among other things, a method for questioning that is said to be a necessary precondition for ethical action. In this respect, de Beauvoir's ongoing insistence on the importance of an "open future" bears some significant similarities to the transcendental import that Derrida accords to that which is "to come".

Whereas this chapter has focused on an analysis of deconstruction, most of the major poststructuralist thinkers have also exalted the importance of the future in related ways. Although this cannot be rigorously justified here, Deleuze, for instance, also makes many similar points to Derrida at various stages throughout his career, according an ethico-political impetus to interruptions to the temporal order that open on the future (and the future must be understood as pure difference that does not have the identity and unity of a subject affixed to it, and undermining it). Subjectivity habitually anticipates the future, projects towards the future, and thereby deprives the future of its genuine futurity; it makes of the future a "future-present", and this is not a genuine exposure to difference. In fact, it is not misleading to suggest that the entirety of Deleuze's work can be understood as a sustained attempt to disrupt that kind of "domestication" of difference and the future. Consider *What is Philosophy?*, where he and Guattari write against any privilege accorded to communication and consensus. They comment that what we lack most is "*resistance* to the present" (Deleuze & Guattari 1994: 108), and we have already seen the importance that Camus and Derrida accord to resistance, and the way in which the thought of an open future can contribute to that resistance. Moreover, like de Beauvoir and Sartre, Deleuze also rejects transcendent and other-wordly determinants of success or value (such as wealth and religion, but also philosophical systems) and instead famously argues that life should be understood according to immanent criteria (good–bad, rather than good–evil, and Deleuze hence extends Nietzsche's point).

In a different way, a transcendental commitment to the future, and to the different, is also the impetus behind Foucault's various archae-ologies and genealogies. Foucault's work shows us that far from vari-ous developments in Western culture being immutable or inevitable, they are in fact highly contingent and his analysis of myriad different ways of structuring power, subjectivity and the like indirectly works to enhance what he famously calls "the undefined work of freedom". While Foucault's understanding of freedom is not explicitly thematized until the very final stages of his career, his genealogies both presuppose some semblance of freedom and also derive much of their persuasive efficacy from the future possibilities that are opened up by them. Again, it is important to note that Foucault deliberately left the future open-ended and refused any notion of history as directed toward any particular end. Although philosophers such as Lyotard, Deleuze and Foucault all had Marxist incarnations in the early stages of their careers, they were, to differing extents, cast aside and this is important. My argument here is not the reductive and untenable one that all positions that disavow Marxism are equivalent. Rather, it is simply that there are some under-acknowledged connections between these poststructuralist thinkers, who do reject Marxist understandings of the future and instead exalt the indeterminate aspect of the future, and their existential predeces-sors, and this is at least partly because of certain shared assumptions in their conceptions of time, identity and the future.

Indeed, it seems to me that existential thinkers such as Sartre, Heidegger and de Beauvoir in particular were vital influences on this aspect of contemporary thought. In this respect, it is worth briefly recalling Sartre and de Beauvoir's extreme philosophies of freedom and engagement in "projects", and their more general insistence on the importance of our futural orientation. At the same time, we are perhaps even better served recalling Heidegger's transcendental insistence on the importance of time in *Being and Time*, as well as the priority that he suggested must be accorded to the "not yet", the "to come", the possible and the future. On the other side of the spectrum, although we have seen that Merleau-Ponty thinks that habits and skilful coping with our environment are very important, for ontological reasons he also critiques any reliance on intuition in *The Visible and the Invisible*, with the political implication that attempting to fit judgements to our intuitions is akin to preserving that status quo and therefore a conservatism. His rejection of this promises a more radical politics.

Although we have explored many important differences between these existential thinkers throughout this book, one of their shared movements is an attempt to show that things could always have been otherwise, and that there is something about human existence that cannot be contained within the immanence of a subject and certainly not a rational subject. There is always something excessive, or mad, that is part of existence and which, to borrow Derrida's understanding, we might say is made possible by an unknown future that haunts the time of what we take to be the present. From a certain perspective this may seem like an obvious point for these European philosophers to make, but this insistence on the importance of the futural dimension of time is, in fact, frequently undermined by various other philosophers and theorists. To cite merely a few examples, consider psychoanalysis and its methodological reliance on the past (e.g. the way in which certain childhood events, such as the "primal scene", are fundamental to any symptoms of adult life), traditional Husserlian phenomenology and the privilege that it accords to a "now" moment or the present, as well as large parts of Anglo-American moral and political philosophy, which tend to oscillate between postulations of atemporality or an overt dependence on notions like intuition. Although it might be argued that the existentialists' conceptions of the future remain domesticated by the subject and their horizons of significance, and hence not radically different and "monstrous" as some of the poststructuralists might prefer, I am not convinced that this is the case, and I hope that the main expositional chapters of this book have borne this out. On the other hand, even if there is an element of truth to such a charge against the existentialists, it might still be argued that the ghost of subjectivity is a necessary and inevitable evil, and in this respect, a non-caricatured and respectful dialogue between poststructuralism and existentialism on this issue is well and truly overdue.

Questions for discussion and revision

two Heidegger and the existential analytic

1. What is the ontico-ontological difference? Why have Western philosophers forgotten it?
2. Explain the distinction between the ready-to-hand and the present-at-hand. Why is it important?
3. What does Heidegger mean by *das Man*, or "the they"?
4. Do Heidegger's descriptions of *Mitsein* overcome the problem of other minds? Why?
5. Explain the significance of the three key existentialia – moods, understanding and fallenness/discourse – that Heidegger describes.
6. Why does the analysis of moods (state of mind) occupy such a large part of *Being and Time*?
7. How does anxiety (*Angst*) reveal our thrownness? Why is this important?
8. On what basis does Heidegger distinguish authenticity and inauthenticity? Is Adorno's critique of this distinction convincing?
9. Explain Heidegger's conception of interpretation as the making explicit of the "forestructures of our understanding". Evaluate whether or not he is committed to a form of relativism.
10. Why does authenticity necessarily involve recognition of our being-towards-death?
11. On what basis does Heidegger argue that the experiences of conscience and guilt are the conditions of possibility for morality, rather than simply the experiences of us feeling bad when we transgress an already existing moral order?
12. For what reasons does Heidegger denounce humanism in his "Letter on Humanism"? Is his own *Being and Time* still a humanism?

three Condemned to freedom: Sartre's phenomenological ontology

1. What does Sartre mean by arguing that existence precedes essence for human beings?
2. What are the two main ontological components of *human* existence for Sartre, remembering that we will introduce a third in Chapter 4?
3. What is bad faith? Can it be avoided?
4. Why does Sartre think psychoanalysis is in bad faith and constitutes a "permanent game of excuses"? Is he right?
5. How is anguish different from fear?
6. Explain the difference between anguish in the face of the future, and anguish in the face of the past.
7. What is the relationship between facticity and freedom?
8. What are Sartre's three fundamental arguments for negation and nothingness that he poses in the "The Problem of Nothingness"? Why does he think that they establish human freedom?
9. What are Sartre's three ontological aspects of embodiment? Explain the differences between them.
10. If consciousness is irremediably embodied, as Sartre suggests, does this undermine the freedom of the for-itself?
11. Why does Sartre disagree with Heidegger's position on death? What are the differences between suggesting that we must recognize our finitude (Sartre) and that we must recognize our mortality (Heidegger)?
12. Is Sartre's suggestion that we are in bad faith to allow our life to be dominated by the horizon of death consistent with his position that good faith should reconcile and coordinate our transcendence *and* our facticity? Could death not be considered to be part of our facticity?
13. Why does Sartre hold that being dead leaves us as "defenceless prey" to the Other?

four Sartre: hell is other people

1. What are the three kinds of relations with other people that Sartre describes?
2. Explain Sartre's phenomenological proof of the Other through an analysis of the phenomenon of the look. Is it convincing?
3. Why does Sartre think that relations with other people are necessarily conflictual?
4. Why does Sartre argue that love is a ruse, and is "triply destructible" (BN: 377)?
5. What are the two main attitudes towards others that Sartre describes?
6. What is the relation of the caress to desire?
7. What is the distinction between the desirous attempt to reveal the other's body-as-flesh, and the instrumental use of another's body as an object?

8. Why does Sartre think that sexuality (but not intercourse) is a necessary component of being-for-others that is ontologically prior to biological considerations? Is he right?

five Merleau-Ponty and the body

1. Explain Merleau-Ponty's notion of the body-subject. Does it avoid a dualistic account of the mind–body relation? Is it true to our experience? Why?
2. What does Merleau-Ponty mean by insisting on ambiguity? Is he correct?
3. What is the significance of Schneider's injuries? Why do they highlight problems with the intellectualist and empiricist accounts of learning and behaviour? What is the significance of the distinction that Merleau-Ponty draws between the "I can" and the "I think"?
4. Explain Merleau-Ponty's disagreement with Sartre on the phenomenon of the "touching–touched"? Why does he challenge Sartre's suggestion that touching and being touched are separate and irreconcilable phenomena?
5. Describe Merleau-Ponty's critique of Sartre's understanding of freedom. Is it successful? De Beauvoir suggests that Merleau-Ponty attacks "pseudo-Sartreanism" in an essay of the same name. Is she right?
6. Compare and contrast Merleau-Ponty's analysis of the hiker who gives in to his fatigue with Sartre's understanding. Who is right?
7. What are the main aspects of Merleau-Ponty's disagreement with Sartre in regard to relations with other people? Does Sartre's position amount to a "de facto solipsism" as Le Doeuff explicitly argues, and Merleau-Ponty implies, when he calls Sartre's position an "agnosticism about the other"?
8. What does Merleau-Ponty mean by using concepts such as chiasm and reversibility?
9. Merleau-Ponty criticizes Sartre's "master–slave" account of our relations with others. Who is right? Why?
10. Critically assess the extent to which Merleau-Ponty remains an existentialist despite his criticisms of Sartre's philosophy.
11. Why does Merleau-Ponty distance himself from the existentialist emphasis on being authentic? Do you think authenticity is an important and helpful idea?
12. In *The Visible and the Invisible*, Merleau-Ponty criticizes Sartre's key ontological categories of Being and Nothingness and the "philosophy of negativity" that supports them. Explain and evaluate Merleau-Ponty's argument.

six de Beauvoir: feminism and existential ethics

1. Explain de Beauvoir's critique of traditional man–woman relations, especially as it is exemplified in her notion of woman as Other.
2. Why does de Beauvoir think that women need to affirm a collectivity, or a "we", in order for social change to be possible?

3. Does de Beauvoir view the female body as an obstacle or a hindrance to engaging in "creative projects"? If so, is she right about this?
4. Does her analysis of female oppression sit comfortably with her existential insistence on radical freedom? Do you think we are completely free, or do you think oppression can change the way that we think without our consent?
5. Why does de Beauvoir disagree with Sartre's argument that our relations with others are necessarily conflictual? Is she right? Why?
6. De Beauvoir discusses the differences between "love-religion" and "love as a property", and associates these with women and men respectively. Explain this view and also what she thinks is required for reciprocal love to be possible.
7. Explain de Beauvoir's position on death and where she sits in relation to the debate between Heidegger's emphasis on being-towards-death and Sartre's insistence on its impossibility.

Further reading and references

There are many general texts on existentialism that are worthy of consideration, but relatively few that have been released in recent times. David Cooper's *Existentialism* (London: Routledge, 2001) is a good thematic study that is unusual in emphasizing the closeness between Heidegger and Sartre's philosophies. Sonia Kruks's *Situation and Human Existence: Freedom, Subjectivity and Society* (London: Unwin Hyman, 1990) pays more attention to the work of de Beauvoir and has some interesting reflections on Sartre's later work, most notably his *Critique of Dialectical Reason*. Also worth considering are introductory books on phenomenology, which often offer very helpful elucidations of the work of Heidegger, Sartre and Merleau-Ponty, in particular. In this respect, I recommend three: C. Macann, *Four Phenomenological Philosophers: Husserl, Heidegger, Sartre, Merleau-Ponty* (London: Routledge, 1993); D. Moran, *Introduction to Phenomenology* (London: Routledge, 2000); and D. Cerbone, *Understanding Phenomenology* (Chesham: Acumen, 2006). If one is looking for more detail on the link between some early existential thinkers, such as Nietzsche and Kierkegaard, and their twentieth-century developments, books on existentialism released in the 1960s and early 1970s are the best bet.

Heidegger

Given that my focus in this book has been on Heidegger's *Being and Time*, it is worth pointing out that there are three main commentaries on this notoriously difficult text: H. Dreyfus, *Being-in-the-world: A Commentary on Heidegger's Being and Time, Division 1* (Cambridge, MA: MIT Press, 1991), S. Mulhall, *Routledge Philosophy Guidebook to Heidegger and Being and Time* (London: Routledge, 1996), and M. Gelven, *A Commentary on Heidegger's Being and Time* (DeKalb, IL: Northern Illinois University Press, 1989). All are very useful, although it is Dreyfus's that has been the more influential despite his reluctance to consider Division 2 of *Being and Time* (and the material on death) in much detail. While free web resources are not always to be trusted, there is a good introduction to Heidegger (and in fact to all of the thinkers considered in this book) available in the *Internet Encyclopedia of Philosophy* (www. iep.utm.edu/h/heidegge.htm). In terms of critical contributions and collections of essays on Heidegger, there are again several worthy of consideration, including H. Dreyfus and H. Hall (eds), *Heidegger: A Critical Reader* (Oxford: Blackwell, 1992) and C. Guignon (ed.), *The Cambridge Companion to Heidegger*, (Cambridge: Cambridge University Press, 1993). Also worth examining because of its focus on the existential significance of Heidegger's thought is J. Richardson's *Existential Phenomenology: A Heideggerian Critique of the Cartesian Project* (Oxford: Oxford University Press, 1986), and John Haugeland's essay "Truth and Finitude: Heidegger's Transcendental Existentialism", in *Heidegger, Authenticity and Modernity*, M. Wrathall and J. Malpas (eds), 43–77 (Cambridge, MA: MIT Press, 2000).

Sartre

Although there are innumerable introductory books on Sartre, to my knowledge none take the reader through each section of *Being and Nothingness* in the way that Dreyfus, Mulhall and others do with Heidegger's *Being and Time*. That said, some of the first English-language books on Sartre can be helpful, such as Mary Warnock's *The Philosophy of Sartre* (London: Hutchinson, 1965) and Hazel Barnes's *Sartre* (Philadelphia, PA: Lippincott, 1973). There are also more systematic expositions of his ontology available, including Peter Caws's *Sartre* (London: Routledge, 1979), and Klaus Hartmann's *Sartre's Ontology* (Evanston, IL: Northwestern University Press, 1966). Christina Howells's "Sartre", in the *Routledge Encyclopedia of Philosophy* (London: Routledge, 1998) is a good place to begin further research, and Christian Onof's entry on Sartre for the *Internet Encyclopedia of Philosophy* (www.utm.iep. edu/s/sartre.htm) is admirably clear. On a more difficult and critical level, C. Howells (ed.), *The Cambridge Companion to Sartre* (Cambridge: Cambridge University Press, 1992) is useful, as is Maurice Natanson's rejection of Sartre's ontology in his *A Critique of Jean-Paul Sartre's Ontology* (The Hague: Martinus Nijhoff, 1973). Some interesting work has also been done recently by Thomas Busch, who explores some of the nuances of Sartre's conception of freedom in *The Power of Consciousness and the Force of Circumstances in Sartre's Philosophy* (Bloomington, IN: Indiana University Press, 1990). In a related vein, although one that focuses upon Sartre's later work, Thomas Flynn has also written an important book examining Sartre's relation to Marxism: *Sartre and Marxist Existentialism* (Chicago, IL: University of Chicago Press, 1990).

Merleau-Ponty

There are many good books on Merleau-Ponty, among them Martin Dillon's *Merleau-Ponty's Ontology* (Bloomington, IN: Indiana University Press, 1988), Stephen Priest's *Merleau-Ponty* (London: Routledge, 1998), Monica Langer's *Merleau-Pon-*

ty's Phenomenology of Perception (Basingstoke: Macmillan, 1989), and the recently released *Cambridge Companion to Merleau-Ponty*, T. Carman and M. Hansen (eds) (Cambridge: Cambridge University Press, 2004). Not all of these are overly attentive to Merleau-Ponty's significance for existentialism, however, and in this respect probably the best text to look at is Jon Stewart (ed.), *The Debate Between Sartre and Merleau-Ponty* (Evanston, IL: Northwestern University Press, 1998). It contains all of the key texts in the debate between Sartre and Merleau-Ponty, including some of those written by de Beauvoir, and it is also complemented by some of the most perceptive secondary commentaries on their interrelation.

Although my book has focused on Merleau-Ponty's interactions with Sartre in his two main philosophical texts – *Phenomenology of Perception* and *The Visible and the Invisible* – there are also several other texts by Merleau-Ponty whose existence it is important to be aware of. What follows is a brief summary of these.

In "Hegel as Existentialist", in *Sense and Nonsense*, H. Dreyfus and S. Dreyfus (trans.) (Evanston, IL: Northwestern University Press, 1964), Merleau-Ponty suggests that Hegel can be redeemed as an important existentialist figure, and he points out that it was Hegel who first emphasized that "man is a place of unrest" (SNS: 66), a theme that is common from Kierkegaard to Sartre. Merleau-Ponty also endorses the young Hegel's focus on death, and in this text there are also some comments on Heidegger. In particular, Merleau-Ponty suggests that Heidegger "lacks not historicity but, on the contrary, an affirmation of the individual: he does not mention that struggle of consciousnesses and that opposition of freedoms without which co-existence sinks into anonymity and everyday banality" (SNS: 69). This repeats Sartre's criticism of Heidegger's notion of *Mitsein* in *Being and Nothingness*.

In "Battle over Existentialism", in *Sense and Nonsense*, Merleau-Ponty discusses his relationship with Sartre in more positive terms, and defends Sartre against certain caricatures of his work, although he nevertheless argues that he remains too dualist, "too exclusively antithetic" (SNS: 72).

In "The Philosophy of Existence", in *Texts and Dialogues: Merleau-Ponty*, H. Silverman and J. Barry (eds) (Atlantic Highlands, NJ: Humanities Press, 1992), Merleau-Ponty retrospectively presents a historical overview of the milieu and development of French existentialism, considering the contribution that the idealism of Léon Brunschvicg and Henri Bergson had on Sartre and himself.

In "The Child's Relations with Others", in *The Primacy of Perception*, J. Edie (ed. and trans.), 96–155 (Evanston, IL: Northwestern University Press, 1964), Merleau-Ponty uses both psychoanalytic and ontological arguments to suggest that there is something missing with Sartre's argument that conflict is the primary mode of relating to others. In particular, he argues that this mode of conflict is dependent on, and presupposes, a more primordial self–other union – a "transitivism" – of the infant with their mother, as well as the external world, more generally.

In the long essay "Sartre and Ultra-Bolshevism", in *Adventures of the Dialectic*, J. Bien (trans.) (Evanston, IL: Northwestern University Press, 1973), Merleau-Ponty contends that Sartre's consciousness–thing distinction gives him political troubles, particularly in regard to his attempted rapprochement of existentialism with Marxism, the latter of which ultimately seeks to overcome any kind of subject–object mode of relation. According to Merleau-Ponty, Sartre effectively posits the Communist party as the subject, while the workers assume a position equivalent to the object, and the result is that the party is envisaged as holding the proletariat in existence; Sartre's position hence constitutes a renewed Leninism, or an ultra-Bolshevism. For Merleau-Ponty, the deterministic versions of Marxism constitute a philosophy of objectivity, and Sartre's position remains a philosophy of subjectivity. Both are envisaged as ultimately terroristic.

De Beauvoir

There are, to my eyes, more recent secondary texts on de Beauvoir than any of the other figures with which this book has been concerned, and that is partly because her work remains a significant site of contestation within the various different "schools" of feminism. Some of the most useful recent texts on her work are: K. Arp, *The Bonds of Freedom* (Chicago, IL: Open Court, 2001); N. Bauer, *Simone de Beauvoir, Philosophy and Feminism* (New York: Columbia University Press, 2001); D. Bergoffen, *The Philosophy of Simone de Beauvoir: Gendered Phenomenologies, Erotic Generosities* (Albany, NY: SUNY Press, 1997); and M. Simons, *Beauvoir and The Second Sex: Feminism, Race and the Origins of Existentialism* (Lanham, MD: Rowman and Littlefield, 1999). Of course, unlike Heidegger, Sartre and Merleau-Ponty, de Beauvoir's own writings are admirably clear and *The Ethics of Ambiguity*, B. Frechtman (trans.) (New York: Kensington Publishing, 1976) should itself be read from beginning to end. Although there are many books that focus on, and perhaps overdetermine, the significance of the romantic relation between Sartre and de Beauvoir, the most influential and interesting of these is Michele Le Doeuff's *Hipparchia's Choice: An Essay Concerning Women, Philosophy etc.*, T. Celous (trans.) (Oxford: Blackwell, 1991).

Key texts

Camus, A. 1942. *The Myth of Sisyphus*, J. O'Brien (trans.). Harmondsworth: Penguin.
Camus, A. 1951. *The Rebel*, A. Bower (trans.). Harmondsworth: Penguin.
de Beauvoir, S. 1972. *The Second Sex*, H. Parshley (trans.). Harmondsworth: Penguin. [First published in French in 1949]
de Beauvoir, S. 1976. *The Ethics of Ambiguity*, B. Frechtman (trans.). New York: Kensington Publishing. [First published in French in 1947]
de Beauvoir, S. 2005. *Pyrrhus et Cinéas*. Reprinted as "Pyrrhus and Cineas", in *Simone de Beauvoir: Philosophical Writings*, M. A. Simons (ed.). Champaign, IL: University of Illinois Press. [First published in French in 1943]
Heidegger M. 1996. *Basic Writings*, D. Krell (ed.). London: Routledge.
Heidegger, M. 2004. *Being and Time*, J. Macquarrie & E. Robinson (trans.). Oxford: Blackwell. [First published in German in 1927]
Merleau-Ponty, M. 1964. *The Primacy of Perception: And Other Essays on Phenomenology, Psychology, the Philosophy of Art, History and Politics*, J. Edie (ed.). Evanston, IL: Northwestern University Press.
Merleau-Ponty, M. 1964. *Sense and Non-Sense*, H. Dreyfus & S. Dreyfus (trans.). Evanston, IL: Northwestern University Press.

Merleau-Ponty, M. 1964. *Signs*, R. McCleary (trans.). Evanston, IL: Northwestern University Press.

Merleau-Ponty, M. 1965. *The Structure of Behaviour*, A. Fischer (trans.). London: Methuen. [First published in French in 1938]

Merleau-Ponty, M. 1968. *The Visible and the Invisible*, A. Lingis (trans.). Evanston, IL: Northwestern University Press. [First published in French in 1964]

Merleau-Ponty, M. 1996. *Phenomenology of Perception*, C. Smith (trans.). London: Routledge. [First published in French in 1945]

Sartre, J.-P. 1956. *"No Exit", and Three Other Plays*, S. Gilbert & L. Abel (trans.). New York: Vintage.

Sartre, J.-P. 1965. *Situations*, B. Eisler (trans.). London: Hamish Hamilton.

Sartre, J.-P. 1991. *Transcendence of the Ego*, H. Barnes (trans.). New York: Hill and Wang. [First published in French in 1938]

Sartre, J.-P. 1992. *Notebooks for an Ethics*, D. Pellauer (trans.). Chicago, IL: University of Chicago Press.

Sartre, J.-P. 1994. *Being and Nothingness: An Essay in Phenomenological Ontology*, H. Barnes (trans.). London: Routledge. [First published in French in 1943]

Sartre, J.-P. 2000. *Nausea*, R. Baldick (trans.) Harmondsworth: Penguin. [First published in French in 1938]

Sartre, J.-P. 2001. *Existentialism is a Humanism*. Reprinted in *Existentialism: Basic Writings*, C. Guignon & D. Pereboom (eds). Indianapolis, IN: Hackett. [First published in French in 1946]

References

Adorno, T. 2002. *The Jargon of Authenticity*. London: Routledge.

Deleuze, G. 1994. *Difference and Repetition*, P. Patton (trans.). New York: Columbia University Press.

Deleuze, G. & F. Guattari 1994. *What is Philosophy?*, H. Tomlinson *et al.* (trans.). New York: Columbia University Press.

Derrida, J. 1982. "The Ends of Man", in *Margins of Philosophy*. Chicago, IL: University of Chicago Press.

Derrida, J. 1989. *Memoires: For Paul de Man*, P. Kamuf *et al.* (trans.). New York: Columbia University Press.

Derrida, J. 1993a. *Aporias*, T. Dutoit (trans.). Stanford, CA: Stanford University Press.

Derrida, J. 1993b. *Memoirs of the Blind: The Self-Portrait and Other Ruins*, P. Brault & M. Naas (trans.). Chicago, IL: University of Chicago Press.

Derrida, J. 1994. *Spectres of Marx: The State of the Debt, the Work of Mourning and the New International*, P. Kamuf (trans.). New York: Routledge.

Derrida, J. 1995. *The Gift of Death*, D. Wills (trans.). Chicago, IL: University of Chicago Press.

Derrida, J. 1997. *Politics of Friendship*, G. Collins (trans.). London: Verso.

Derrida, J. 1999a. "'Eating Well', or The Calculation of the Subject: An Interview with Jacques Derrida", in *Who Comes After the Subject?*, J. Nancy *et al.* (eds and trans.). New York: Routledge.

Derrida, J. 1999b. *Adieu to Emmanuel Levinas*, P. Prault & M. Naas (trans.). Stanford,

CA: Stanford University Press.

Derrida, J. 2000. *Demeure: Fiction and Testimony*, E. Rottenberg (trans.). Stanford, CA: Stanford University Press.

Derrida, J. 2001a. *A Taste for the Secret*. Cambridge: Polity.

Derrida, J. 2001b. *The Work of Mourning*, P. Brault & M. Naas (ed. and trans.). Chicago, IL: University of Chicago Press.

Derrida, J. 2002a. "Salut, Salut: Dead Man Running", in *Negotiations*, E. Rottenberg (trans.). Stanford, CA: Stanford University Press.

Derrida, J. 2002b. *Negotiations*, E. Rottenberg (trans.). Stanford, CA: Stanford University Press.

Derrida, J. 2002c. "The University Without Condition", in *Without Alibi*, P. Kamuf (trans.). Stanford, CA: Stanford University Press.

Derrida, J. 2005a. *Rogues: Two Essays on Reason*, P. Brault & M. Naas (trans.). Stanford, CA: Stanford University Press.

Derrida, J. 2005b. *On Touching: Jean-Luc Nancy*, P. Kamuf (trans.). Stanford, CA: Stanford University Press.

Descartes, R. 1986. *Meditations on First Philosophy*, J. Cottingham (trans.). Cambridge: Cambridge University Press.

Dillon, M. 1988. *Merleau-Ponty's Ontology*. Bloomington, IN: Indiana University Press,.

Dreyfus, H. & S. Dreyfus 1999. "The Challenge of Merleau-Ponty's Phenomenology of Embodiment for Cognitive Science". In *Perspectives on Embodiment: The Intersections of Nature and Culture*, H. Haber & G. Weiss (eds). London: Routledge.

Fanon, F. 1991. *Black Skin, White Masks*. New York: Grove Press.

Foucault, M. 1970. *The Order of Things: An Archaeology of the Human Sciences*. New York: Vintage.

Gasché, R. 1994. *Inventions of Difference: On Jacques Derrida*. Cambridge, MA: Harvard University Press.

Grosz, E. 1994. *Volatile Bodies: Towards a Corporeal Feminism*. Sydney: Allen & Unwin.

Howells, C. 1999. *Derrida: Deconstruction from Phenomenology to Ethics*. Cambridge: Polity.

Kruks, S. 1990. *Situation and Human Existence: Freedom, Subjectivity and Society*. London: Unwin Hyman.

Lloyd, G. 1992. *Man of Reason*. Minneapolis, MN: University of Minnesota Press.

Le Doeuff, M. 1991. *Hipparchia's Choice: An Essay Concerning Women, Philosophy etc.*, T. Selous (trans.). Oxford: Blackwell.

Lyotard, J. F. 1984. *The Postmodern Condition*. Minneapolis, MN: University of Minnesota Press.

Marcuse, H. 1948. "Existentialism: Remarks on Jean-Paul Sartre's L'Etre et Le Neant". *Philosophy and Phenomenological Research* **VIII**, 317–30.

Reynolds, J. 2004. *Merleau-Ponty and Derrida: Intertwining Embodiment and Alterity*. Athens, OH: Ohio University Press.

Young, I. 1990. "Throwing Like a Girl". In *Throwing Like a Girl and Other Essays in Feminist Philosophy and Social Theory*. Bloomington, IN: Indiana University Press.

Chronology of key events, texts and thinkers

1843–55   In various texts, the Danish philosopher Søren Kierkegaard (1813–55) challenged the religious orthodoxy of his time, as well as the enlightenment emphasis on rationality. He instead called for a lived commitment and a "leap of faith" that he insisted involved facing up to the prospect of "dread".

1879–90   In *The Birth of Tragedy* (1879), German philosopher Friedrich Nietzsche (1844–1900) argued for a more Dionysian and excessive relation to the world, in opposition to the Apollonian rationality that he thought unduly dominant. In his later books, he diagnosed the ressentiment and slave morality afflicting his times, and tried to encourage a more life-affirming relation to the world through provocative ideas such as the "will to power", the eternal return of the same, and the *Ubermensch*.

1900–   Edmund Husserl (1859–1938) was the founder of phenomenology, a
1920   way of thinking that focused on our experiences and tried to discern the essences of such experiences. Husserl's work, and particularly his *Logical Investigations* (1900) and *Ideas* (1913), were taken up in very different ways by Heidegger (who was his student and assistant for a time), Sartre, Merleau-Ponty and many others.

1913–32   Writing his early works just after the First World War, German philosopher Karl Jaspers (1883–1969) developed the notion of *Existenz*, arguing that we have no fixed or essential self; the self is instead only its possibilities and what it might become. Jaspers suggested that the revelation of the lack of any essential self is best revealed in "limit situations", which include death, suffering and guilt (*Philosophy*, 1932), and this was directly influential upon the work of his compatriot Heidegger.

1927	Martin Heidegger (1889–1976) published his famous existential work, *Being and Time*, which immediately attracted great interest in Germany, concerned as it was with moods, facing up to the prospect of one's own death, and with how these phenomena shed light on a question that he thought Western philosophy had forgotten: the question of Being.
1933	Heidegger was made Rector of the University of Freiburg. At the time he was a supporter of Nazism and made several controversial comments (and introduced policies) that seem to many to have been anti-Semitic.
Early 1930s	Emmanuel Levinas's translations of Husserl's work were published in France, making the methods of phenomenology available to philosophers such as Sartre and Merleau-Ponty.
1938	Jean-Paul Sartre's (1905–80) remarkably evocative novel *Nausea* was published to widespread acclaim, along with his philosophical monograph *Transcendence of the Ego*.
1939	Start of the Second World War, and the German occupation of France. Both Maurice Merleau-Ponty (1908–61) and Sartre did military service. In 1940 Sartre was captured and imprisoned; in prison he continued to study Heidegger's *Being and Time*.
1941–49	With liberation, Sartre quickly attained a greater fame on the basis of his novels, as well as plays such as *Flies* and *No Exit*, but also because of his political engagement. He, de Beauvoir, and Merleau-Ponty were the founders and co-editors of the influential political, literary and philosophical magazine *Les Temps modernes*.
1942	Albert Camus (1913–60) published his philosophical treatise on the absurd, *The Myth of Sisyphus*, which argued, among other things, that the only truly serious philosophical question is whether or not to commit suicide. His compelling novella *The Outsider* was, however, far more significant in relation to bringing the mood of existentialism to a wider audience.
1943	Sartre completed his philosophical magnum opus, *Being and Nothingness*, and it quickly became the core text of French existentialism, preoccupied as it is with freedom, responsibility and authenticity.
1945	Merleau-Ponty published his very important book, *Phenomenology of Perception*, which both endorsed and subtly refined Sartrean existentialism by focusing on the significance of our embodiment.
1945	Sartre's public lecture, "Existentialism is a Humanism", gave existentialism a more optimistic tenor, one that Heidegger later rebuffed in his essay "Letter on Humanism".
1947	Simone de Beauvoir (1908–86) published *The Ethics of Ambiguity*, which developed the ethical significance of existentialism. She also published many existential novels both during and after this period.

1949	De Beauvoir published her enormously influential treatise on the situation of women, *The Second Sex*.
1951	The release of Camus's *The Rebel* in 1951 created a furore at *Les Temps modernes* because Camus refused to countenance any kind of Marxist revolution. This dispute resulted in Camus and Sartre (who had become more closely aligned with the Communist Party following the Korean War) acrimoniously ending their friendship. It was also a political issue regarding Marxism that was responsible for Merleau-Ponty and Sartre ending their friendship some years later.
Late 1950s, early 1960s	The structuralism of theorists such as Roland Barthes, Claude Lévi-Strauss, Louis Althusser, Michel Foucault (his early work) and others began to assume the limelight in French intellectual life.
1960	Camus died tragically in a car accident. Sartre published *Critique of Dialectical Reason*, which sought to bring together existentialism and Marxism.
1961	Merleau-Ponty died before completing his great work, *The Visible and the Invisible*. The Algerian struggles for independence from France became fiercer.
1964	Theodor Adorno (1903–69) published a scathing critique of Heidegger called *The Jargon of Authenticity*. Sartre turned down the Nobel Prize for literature.
1967	Jacques Derrida (1930–2004) published three very influential books that have been associated with poststructuralism: *Of Grammatology*, *Writing and Difference* and *Speech and Phenomena*. His work, along with that of philosophers such as Gilles Deleuze, Jean-François Lyotard, and Michel Foucault, problematizes certain structuralist assumptions and has been very influential until the present day.
May 1968	Student uprisings in Paris and around the world.
1980	Sartre died and 50,000–100,000 people flocked to his funeral in the streets of Paris,
1986	De Beauvoir died.

Index